Iōng Po-kua
Kóng Kòo-sū ê Lâng
Lū Khun-hān Phînn-ôo Po-kua Suán-tsip

Framed by the Sea:
Through a Square Window
onto the Island
Penghu Ballads: A Selection by Lu Kun-han

呂坤翰澎湖褒歌選集

用褒歌說故事的人

呂坤翰 Lū Khun-hān ╳ 吳明翰 Gôo Bîng-hān 作

陳春星 Tân Tshun-sing 繪

小野心
YETHINGS

獻給阮的牽手，阿玉
For my wife, A-gio̍k-á

目次
Contents

6	前言
10	推薦序／徐韶良
12	推薦序／徐銘謙
14	自序
18	一心想做文明人

22	一 島嶼
24	媽宮市
28	湖西鄉
32	白沙鄉
36	西嶼鄉
40	吉貝村
44	望安鄉
48	將軍村
52	東吉村
56	西吉村
60	東坪村
64	西坪村
68	花嶼村
72	七美鄉

76	二 地景
78	澎湖島嶼海產濟
82	海上漁田——箱網現流上鮮
86	珍貴海產——海膽
90	澎湖南方四島蓋神奇
94	東坪山勢第一奇
98	嶼坪好山景
102	鋪路做義工
106	小王子平台
110	澎湖縣花——天人菊
114	澎湖茗茶——風茹草
118	阮兜
122	三口井的故事

126	三 信仰
128	澎湖天后宮
132	澎湖上元節
136	東嶼坪池府王爺生日
140	東吉村中元普渡

144	㈣ 生活	216	㈥ 鄉愁
146	澎湖較早的生活情	218	讀書才會出頭天
150	以早的東嶼坪	222	菩薩老師
154	落雨天歹起火	226	西坪哥、東坪妹
158	掠魚、生囝	230	嶼坪鉸刀師
162	哪會按呢	234	衛國做兵上光榮
166	克難學校	238	食穿全靠君一人
170	快樂的澎湖人	242	思君情深深
174	澎湖人愛褒歌	246	阿公勇壯、阿媽活潑
		250	鄉愁

178	㈤ 勞動	254	後記
180	天照甲子佇咧行		
184	熱天炤小管	258	索引地圖
188	浮著塗魠好過年	258	澎湖海域箍一輾
192	大流去抾螺仔	260	西嶼坪
196	作田人的心聲	262	東嶼坪
200	台灣牛強閣勇		
204	擔肥去壅田		
208	雨水來到當著時		
212	塗豆大豐收		

掃描 QRcode，連結 Youtube 頻道 ▶ 用褒歌說故事的人，感受作者原音重現。

前言 | INTRODUCTION

褒歌：生活的詠嘆調

作者 ———— 吳明翰

Taiwanese Ballads (po-kua) : The Cantatas of Life

Wu Ming-Han

　　褒歌（po-kua）是台灣民間一種充滿活力和韻味的傳統歌謠，又稱七字仔（tshit-jī--á）、閒仔歌（îng-á-kua），在不同地區可能表現為山歌、採茶歌等。原則上它以七個字為一句、四句為一首的形式，用台語吟唱，唱詞講究押韻，但形式卻不拘一格。演唱者可以根據當下情境、情感與靈感自由發揮，增減字句數，展現出台語豐富的表現力。

　　褒歌的內容如同台灣這片土地一樣豐富多彩，從人文風土、男女情感、生活百態到個人感悟，都能成為吟詠的主題。也因為台灣各地有著不同的人文風土和生活風情，孕育出多元的褒歌主題。例如，北部茶區的褒歌多以採茶和茶農心情為主，吟唱出茶韻中的人生百味；而澎湖的褒歌則以討海生活為主，展現了討海人與大海拚搏的堅毅，以及對家鄉的眷戀。目前在新北坪林、金山，還有澎湖等地，仍有擅唱褒歌的老前輩，部分歌謠也被採集發表出版。澎湖西嶼的二崁村更將四句聯刻寫在屋牆上，成為當地觀光特色。

　　專研褒歌的洪敏聰老師在其著作《二崁褒歌》中，對澎湖褒歌做了深刻的詮釋：「澎湖的褒歌，創始於何時已無可考，但漸已式微，甚至消失也不無可能。褒歌是一種地方文化，是生活的記錄，是音樂與詩歌的結合，是時光與澎湖海島環境交融而產生的聲音，是原始的創作，是生活轉化而來的聲音。」

　　用來吟唱澎湖褒歌的台語，在發音和用字上具備獨特的地方風格，與台灣本島的台語有所不同。發音方面，澎湖人的口音通常較柔和，有些字的發音就有了差異。例如，「箸」（筷子）在台灣多半讀作「tī」，澎湖則讀作「tū」，「魚」（hî）在澎湖讀作「hû」，「汝」（你，lí）是「lú」，「去」（khì）則是「khù」；另外，「雞」（ke）在澎湖讀作「kue」，但「火」（hué）則讀作「hé」，正好相反。澎湖的褒歌因澎湖腔獨特的台語而展現出鮮明的地方特色。這種音律與用詞的差異，使得澎湖褒歌不僅深情流暢，更增添了獨有的氣韻。

　　本書的作者呂坤翰老師，本名呂通要，1944年出生於西嶼坪，屬於三級離島，為望安鄉所管轄。自幼，他便喜愛聆聽大人唱褒歌，雖然那時只覺得這是大人的娛樂，對內容意義似懂非懂。在當地的國民學校就讀後，他升入馬公中學初中部及台南師院，隨後回到家鄉嶼坪國小任教約十年。在任教期間，他曾簡單記下一些觀察，但因公務繁忙而未能持續記錄。

1974 年左右，約三十歲的他再次離開故鄉，到台中龍井和台南任教。直到 2002 年退休後返鄉，與親戚久別重逢，提起以前的人總會在這種時刻褒幾首歌，沒想到只剩下太太的大姊還會，當下唱了許多優美而有趣的歌謠。對於故鄉的居民相繼為生活搬遷離鄉，傳唱的歌謠文化也日漸凋零，心中感到無比惆悵。這促使他萌生想為故鄉嶼坪，甚至整個澎湖風土留下一些記錄的念頭。

　　對許多人而言，「褒歌」或許是一個陌生的名詞，但對呂坤翰來說，卻是抒發心聲的最佳方式。自 2002 年以來，他將生活中的所見所聞、所思所感，化作一首首真摯動人的褒歌，記錄在舊日曆紙上。題材內容包羅萬象，涵蓋人文風土、親情羈絆、討海生活、季節更迭，還有趣味軼事、勵志箴言及男女情愛等，作品的創作足跡也遍及他所遊歷過的各地，至今已累積超過一千兩百首作品。

　　本書精選其中 56 首，主要為呂坤翰在 1950 至 1970 年間的成長回憶，透過島嶼、地景、信仰、生活、勞動、鄉愁等 6 個篇章，引領讀者走進呂坤翰的褒歌世界，感受澎湖獨特的生命力與文化肌理。褒歌皆以台文呈現，並附上羅馬字，讓更多人有機會認識每個字的發音和澎湖獨特的腔調。創作背景及相關的澎湖經驗，則在褒歌後以中英文並列，希望讓更多不同語言或文化背景的讀者，能跨越語言的隔閡，體會其中的韻味與情感。

　　本書繪者陳春星先生，雖然並非科班出身，但憑藉對繪畫的熱愛，工作之餘追隨畫家雷驤學習長達 15 年，累積豐富的繪畫技巧和人文素養。他也曾在 2017 和 2018 年兩度徒步走遍澎湖群島，對澎湖有深厚的認識，更於 2022 年參與東吉嶼手作步道。春星在擔任步道志工期間，已經創作過一系列「島嶼人物」，這次為了貼近每一首褒歌的情境，他更是與呂坤翰老師一起實地走訪，而全書的水彩畫也都經由呂老師確認細節，帶來生動且有趣的閱讀體驗。

　　如果您曾經聽過澎湖褒歌，這本書一定會讓您想起很多美好往事；如果您對澎湖褒歌還不太熟悉，這本書可以帶您認識其質樸又滿滿草根的力量。每次與呂老師搭乘交通船往返南方四島時，他總是靜靜地望著窗外，透過那正方形的船窗，回味著家鄉的故事與人生。透過這本書一幅幅方框裡的水彩，您也可以沈浸於呂坤翰老師的褒歌風采。

Taiwanese Ballads (po-kua) are a traditional form of folk song that richly embody the cultural essence of Taiwan. Typically composed of seven-character lines and four lines per verse sung in Taiwanese, these ballads focus on rhyme, yet the performance style remains fluid and unrestrained. Singers are free to adapt the lyrics according to their emotions and inspirations, altering the number of words to showcase the expressive power of the Taiwanese language.

The themes within Taiwanese Ballads mirror the vibrant tapestry of life in Taiwan, encompassing human experiences, emotions, daily life and personal reflections. Because of the diverse cultural and lifestyle characteristics across different regions of Taiwan, these ballads exhibit a wide variety of themes. For instance, ballads from the northern tea-producing areas often revolve around tea picking and the feelings of tea farmers, while those from Penghu focus on life of fishing and the sea. Particularly notable are the ballads inscribed on the walls of houses in Jī-khàm (Erkan) village of Sai-sū (Xiyu) Township in Penghu, which have become a special attraction for visitors.

Professor Âng Bín-tshong, a researcher of Taiwanese Ballads, has provided deep insights into the ballads of Penghu. He notes that while the origin of these ballads is difficult to pinpoint, they are gradually fading away, with the possibility of complete disappearance looming. He describes the Penghu Ballads as a local cultural expression; they serve as records of life and represent the fusion of music and poetry.

The author of this book, Mr. Lu Kun-Han (originally named LŪ Thong-iàu (Lu Tong-Yao)), was born in 1944 on Sai-sū-pîng (Xiyuping) Island, which is governed by Bāng-uann (Wang'an) Township. From a young age, he developed a love for listening to adults singing Penghu Ballads. After graduating from the Tainan Teacher's College and returning to his hometown to teach, he made some initial observations. However, because of the demands of teaching, he was unable to continue his exploration. It was not until his retirement in 2002, during a visit back to his hometown, that he was struck by the village where only his wife's elder sister still sang Penghu Ballads. This brought a deep sense of sadness regarding the decline of this cultural heritage, prompting him to create a record of his hometown and the cultural features of Penghu.

For many, the term Penghu Ballads may seem unfamiliar but for Lu Kun-Han, it represents the best means of expressing his innermost feelings. Since 2002, drawing inspiration from his life experiences, he has transformed his observations and reflections into heartfelt compositions carefully recorded on old calendar pages. His subjects span a wide range of themes, including culture, familial bonds, fishing life, seasonal changes, amusing anecdotes, inspirational proverbs and romantic love. To date, he has penned over 1200 pieces.

This book features a curated selection of 56 songs, primarily drawn from Lu Kun-Han's reflections between 1950 and 1970. It is organised into six chapters exploring themes such as the Island, Landscapes, Faiths, Life, Labor and Nostalgia, guiding readers into the world of Lu Kun-Han. Each piece is presented in Taiwanese with accompanying Lô-má-jī (Romanization System) to enable a broader audience to

appreciate the pronunciation and unique phonetics of Penghu. The background behind his compositions and insights from his time in Penghu are provided in both Mandarin Chinese and English, making it accessible to readers from diverse linguistic and cultural backgrounds, allowing them to grasp the essence and emotions embedded within.

The illustrator of the book, Mr. Chen Chun-Xing, is not formally trained in art but through a deep love of painting, studied under the renowned artist Lay Hsiang for 15 years while working. He has gained a lot of artistic skill and cultural knowledge. He also walked across the Penghu archipelago in 2017 and 2018 to gain important insights into the region and in 2022, participated in the construction of an Eco-Friendly Trail on Tang-kiat (Dongji) Island. To understand the essence of each piece, he conducted field visits with Mr. Lu Kun-Han and I confirm details, aiming to produce vivid and realistic visual representations.

If you have ever listened to Penghu Ballads, this book will undoubtedly bring back many cherished memories; if you are unfamiliar with them, it will immerse you in the simple yet rich local flavor of these works. Each time I travel with Lu Kun-Han on the ferry to the southern islands of Penghu, he quietly gazes out the window, reminiscing about the stories and life of his homeland through the square window. Through this book, depicted in the watercolors, you can also dive into the charm of Lu Kun-Han's Ballads.

推薦序 | FOREWORD
傳唱土地與海洋的歌

海洋國家公園管理處 處長 ———— 徐韶良

Ballads of the Land and the Sea

Hsu Shao-Liang
Director of the Marine National Park Headquarters

　　本書在浩瀚的台灣海峽與遼闊的澎湖南方四島國家公園之間，記錄了一場意義深遠的相遇⋯⋯。當故鄉轉化成為國家公園之後，一位年輕的解說員與一位離鄉數十載的耆老在海島相逢的故事。這不僅是一場個人與個人的邂逅，更是文化與記憶、自然與傳承的交會。

　　呂老師是來自西嶼坪的退休教師，目前已移居台南。一次陪同師母重返娘家所在及自己曾經任教的東嶼坪，走在國家公園剛修好的手作步道上，恰巧與擔任解說員的明翰相遇。這樣與遊客間的萍水相逢，原本只是解說員的日常，但熱忱的明翰細心地體會到，這對老夫妻對於腳下的土地有著特殊情感，在他的親切招呼下，於是展開了國家公園與呂老師一系列的褒歌主題合作，包括多次手作步道志工假期活動與「褒出海島人生」紀錄片等。

　　在呂老師褒歌聲中，承載著南方四島過往的風土人情，也映照出海洋的深邃與鄉愁的悠遠。難得明翰能夠主動把握住每一次與鄉親互動的機緣，以國家公園的視角，細細聆聽，用心記錄。配合他的攝影專長，通過聲音、文字、影像與畫作的形式，展現呂老師對於澎湖這片土地的情懷，將這些褒歌的旋律與故事，化為一座座連結人與環境、時空與文史的橋樑。讓即將消逝的聲音得以存續，讓海洋的呼喚不因時間的推移而沉默。

　　這是一部關於傳承的書。它提醒我們，在快速變遷的世界裡，文化記憶與自然資產同樣珍貴，值得我們用心守護。更重要的是，它讓我們重新看見，人與自然、人與人之間的每一次相遇，都可能是一場無可取代的緣分。當您看到這本書的時候，也就是讀者與作者在創作與欣賞之間相遇的時刻，希望您也能珍惜這份情緣，仔細品味呂老師與明翰為我們帶來這份澎湖最真切的海味。願這本書能喚起更多人對故鄉的情感、對自然的責任。在時代的浪潮中，繼續傳唱出屬於我們這片土地與海洋的歌。

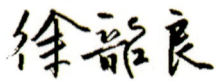

This book narrates a profound encounter between the vast Taiwan Strait and the expansive South Penghu Marine National Park: the story of a young park ranger meeting an elder who has lived away from his hometown for decades, amidst the embrace of these islands. This is not merely a meeting between two individuals; it is a confluence of culture and memory, nature and heritage.

Mr. Lu Kun-Han, a retired teacher from Sai-sū-pîng (Xiyuping) Island, now resides in Tainan City. During a visit accompanying his wife back to her hometown of Tang-sū-pîng (Dongyuping) Island, he unexpectedly crossed paths with Wu Ming-Han while walking along a newly constructed eco-friendly trail in the national park. Such serendipitous encounters between rangers and visitors are typical of a park ranger's daily routine. However, Ming-Han, filled with enthusiasm, keenly sensed the special connection this elderly couple had with the island.

In their friendly conversation, a series of collaborations emerged between the national park and Mr Lu, revolving around a theme of ballads. This included several participations in eco-friendly trail volunteer activities and the production of the documentary 'Singing Out Island Life'.

Within Mr Lu's Penghu Ballads, the rich cultural heritage of the four islands of southern Penghu is captured, reflecting the ocean's depth and the nostalgia of distant memories. It is truly remarkable how Ming-Han always seizes every opportunity to connect with local residents, listening attentively and recording their stories through the lens of the national park. Combining his photography skills, he presents Mr Lu's deep affection for the land of Penghu through sound, text, images and paintings, transforming the melodies and stories of these ballads into bridges that connect people with their environment and history with place. This preserves voices that are on the verge of fading, allowing the echoes from this small island to resonate beyond the passage of time.

This is a book about heritage. It reminds us that in a rapidly changing world, cultural memory and natural resources are equally precious, deserving our heartfelt preservation. More importantly, it prompts us to recognize that every encounter—between humans and nature and between individuals—can be an irreplaceable connection. When you hold this book, you are experiencing a moment of meeting between the readers and the authors, a moment of creation and appreciation.

I hope you cherish this bond and savor the true flavors of Penghu that Mr Lu and Ming-Han bring to us. May this book evoke a deeper emotional connection to our homeland and a sense of responsibility toward nature. As time flows, let us continue to sing the songs that belong to our land and ocean, nurturing a deeper bond with both cultural and natural heritage.

推薦序 | FOREWORD

生活成詩，鄉愁成歌

台灣千里步道協會 副執行長　——— 徐銘謙

Life Becomes Poetry, Nostalgia Becomes Song

Hsu Ming-Chien
Deputy Executive Director, Taiwan Thousand Miles Trail Association

　　有生活感的詩，帶畫面的文字，唱片封面的設計，手感十足的鄉土畫，組合成這本《用褒歌說故事的人》，令人相當驚艷的藝文作品。

　　翻開方窗的封面、打開見海中小島大景，彷彿重現每回搭船到南方四島的過程，場景歷歷在目、猶新如昨日。一頁頁翻讀下去，我跟著回顧了東嶼坪、西嶼坪、東吉島、西吉島，憶起 2020 年前後連續四年，每年暑熱上島手作步道的見聞與聲息，彷彿能聞到空氣中淡淡的鹹氣，聽見澎湖特有的口音，跟著褒歌也度過了我不曾體驗過的澎湖秋冬。

　　呂坤翰老師的褒歌就是這麼有畫面，能夠帶你穿越時空，彷彿跟著他小時候脫光上衣海泳的那個午後，眼前已是頹圮的廢墟卻能夠被他的歌產生視覺欺騙，腦海竟能重現當時聚落生活的細節。

　　記得當時手作步道活動開放報名的時候，同事告訴我，有一對出生在東嶼坪、西嶼坪、年近 80 歲的夫妻想報名參加。由於手作步道需要拿工具，有相當程度的勞動，更不要說時值炎夏酷熱的澎湖。擔心參加者對活動性質有所誤解，同事特別打電話過去婉拒，不意最終卻被對家鄉懷抱熱情的報名夫妻說服，我們決定還是破例讓他們同行，但是為了安全起見，並未讓他們參加做步道的活動。

　　在島上做步道的時候，揹著相機的明翰引導一對老夫妻到步道上來看志工們工作。那是我第一次遇見呂老師，原來他們就是那對感動我們同事的夫妻。呂老師身體健朗，在步道上看前看後，對於志工們做的成果讚不絕口，當日就為此做了一首褒歌。之前我們在淡蘭古道工作時，知道此地山區流傳褒歌，未想原來澎湖也有道地的褒歌，且社區有好多歌王歌后，信手拈來都能入詩歌。

　　後來熱血的明翰陪著呂老師到處去唱褒歌錄音、接受訪問。有一天明翰熱切地告訴我，他要幫呂老師把褒歌出版成書，當時聞訊實在很難想像，用唱的褒歌要成為一本文字書的樣子。一年後真的成書了，除了呂老師的詩歌，搭配明翰的照片，春星的畫，不厭其煩細心的美編，竟然用文字流動編排彷彿跟著曲調迴旋，讓褒歌真的名符其實地躍然紙上，像讀五線譜那樣，竟然能在閱讀時彷彿腦中有音樂，而且封面設計就像唱片規格，真的遠超出我的想像。

　　推薦朋友們把這本書帶回家，當作藝術品來收藏，去澎湖的時候帶著它同行，對著景點打開來讀唱，你會發現有如戴上 AR 隱形眼鏡，有擴增實境的效果喔！當然這也需要喚醒你與生俱來的想像力！

Poetry infused with life, vivid imagery in words, meticulously designed album covers and hand-painted artworks come together in this remarkable collection, *Framed by the Sea: Through a Square Window onto the Island - Penghu Ballads: A Selection by Lu Kun-Han.*

As I open the cover of this square window and gaze upon the small islands and magnificent vistas of the sea, I feel transported back to those enchanting journeys to the four islands of southern Penghu. Each scene comes alive, as fresh in my memory as if it were just yesterday. As I turn the pages, I am reminded of Tang-sū-pîng (Dongyuping), Sai-sū-pîng (Xiyuping), Tang-kiat (Dongji) and Sai-kiat (Xiji) Islands. These islands and their stories bring back memories of my experiences starting in 2020 when I spent four consecutive summers crafting eco-friendly trails. I can almost sense the faint brine in the air, hear the special accent of Penghu and feel the warmth of Lu Kun-Han's Penghu Ballads, which accompanied me through autumn and winter seasons in Penghu that I had never experienced before.

Mr Lu's ballads are indeed vivid; even amidst the dilapidated ruins, his ballads conjure a visual illusion, allowing my mind to recreate intricate details of community life from those times.

I recall when we opened registrations for the trail-building activities. My colleague, Lai Yan-Ju, informed me about an elderly couple in their late 70s born on Tang-sū-pîng and Sai-sū-pîng Islands who wished to participate. Given that the trail work required tools and a considerable amount of labor under the scorching summer sun of Penghu, there were concerns that they might misunderstand the nature of the work. My colleague reached out to decline their participation gently, only to find this couple with such a profound love for their hometown convincing us otherwise. We decided to make an exception for them, though for reasons of safety, they did not actively participate in the crafting.

While we were building the trail, Ming-Han, bearing a camera, guided the elderly couple to observe the volunteers at work. It was my first encounter with Mr Lu and astonishingly, they were the couple who had so moved my colleague. Mr Lu, robust and curious, admired the results of the volunteers' efforts and the very next day, he composed a ballad in tribute. Previously, while working on the Tamsui-Kavalan Trail, we had learned of the local ballads present in the mountainous regions but I was pleasantly surprised to discover that Penghu too harbored its own authentic ballads.

Later on, the impassioned Ming-Han accompanied Mr Lu on a journey to sing ballads, introducing the national park, recording audio and participating in interviews. One day, Ming-Han enthusiastically shared his intention to help Mr Lu publish Penghu Ballads in a book. At the time, it seemed challenging to envision how a poetic composition sung could transform into a written work. Yet, a year later, it truly came to fruition, featuring not only Mr Lu's ballads but also Ming-Han's extensive collection of photographs from Penghu, along with the enchanting artworks of Chun-Hsing and the meticulous and dedicated editing that made the layout of the text seem to dance along with the melodies. This brought Penghu Ballads to life on the pages—a reading experience akin to interpreting sheet music, where each word resonates like music within the mind and the cover design resembles an album cover, far exceeding my expectations.

I encourage friends to bring this book home as a piece of art to be cherished. When visiting Penghu, carry it with you and read the ballads aloud at various scenic spots. You will discover an augmented reality effect, as if putting on AR glasses! Of course, this also requires awakening the imagination that resides within you!

自序 | PREFACE
用褒歌說故事的人

作者　———　呂坤翰

A Storyteller of Penghu Ballads (Po-kua)

Lu Kun-Han

Translator ● Wu Ming-Han

　　我是出世佇咧一个澎湖南方四島的一个小島，叫做「西嶼坪」（Sai-sū-pîng）。

　　細漢（suè-hàn）的時陣，阮--遐（hiâ）猶無電火（tiān-hé），當然就無電視通看 looh。普通時的時陣，我攏坐佇阮阿母的身邊，聽伊佮厝邊頭尾的人，唱出彼款日常生活的心聲，個唱--的彼款歌，閣有押韻，真好聽。彼當時因為我當咧讀小學，我足認真的綴（tè）阮老師咧學習這（tse）國語（Kok-gú），所以我就無認真去學習這褒歌的代誌。等甲我做老師的時陣，我又閣認真教好每一個學生，所以我嘛無共（kā）庄頭的人咧褒的歌加（ke）記錄落（lueh）。

　　2002 年，有一改炁（tshuā）阮太太回鄉（hiunn）去探親，我煞發現東嶼坪（Tang-sū-pîng）、西嶼坪的人搬--走了的足濟足濟，遐--的所在，會曉唱歌的，就干焦阮太太的大姊，予我感覺足感慨的：遮爾仔好的台語（Tâi-gú）褒歌文化，有可能就斷--掉 looh。轉來台灣本島了後，我家己就按呢想：「我都已經退休 looh，我嘛有時間矣，我閣嘛足有興趣的，不如咧，家己來創作看覓，共這份台語的褒歌文化繼續加傳--落去。

　　一開始 neh，我是將東嶼坪、西嶼坪四箍圍仔的島嶼做主題（tsú-tuê），一島寫一條褒歌。形式方面，我就照古早的四句聯仔的寫法：七字一句，兩句做一對，兩對佮（kap）成一首，每句尾仔的字攏著愛有押韻。經過（king-kè）阮太太一直咧鼓勵，我就一直寫，就寫較濟的。所以我就共平時生活的記持、人文風土、男女愛情到信仰風俗攏全部來去寫。內容若較豐富的，毋是四句寫會了的，我就會加加（ke ka）幾句，予這首褒歌閣較完整，就按呢，我就共家己的作品號做「新時代的褒歌」。

　　予我想袂到，2021 年我閣轉去東嶼坪，竟然為我的創作掀開了新--的一頁。

　　我佮（kah）阮太太，佇東嶼坪手--牽手當咧散步的時陣，雄雄煞看著，有一个穿著咱海洋國家公園制服的查埔人，伊手提一个大 khà-mì-lah（相機），足認真的咧翕相（hip-siòng），阮嘛是足好奇的，就隨伊去招伊開講，才知影伊是咱海洋國家公園咧食頭路的研究員吳明翰（GÔO Bîng-hān）先生。伊真興趣翕相，嘛不時仔佇海管處的面冊（Facebook）頂分享南方四島的人文風土。有一段時間，伊的作品介紹東嶼坪、西嶼坪攏非常詳細，我就會佇相片的頂懸留話、共伊鼓勵。想袂到，阮煞佇東嶼坪相拄--著！

　　我問明翰先生：「你是按怎欲（berh）寫這號故事？」伊就講：「我發現遮倚無幾戶，序細嘛攏毋捌咧轉來。所以我就想借這相片來介紹，予嶼坪人的後一代會了解家己的故鄉。」想袂到來遮食頭路一冬外的人，竟然會遮爾仔珍惜阮的故鄉。自彼陣開始，我就感受著阮兩个人有真奇妙的緣份。

　　閣來，伊手--指（kí）東嶼坪的前山講：「遐有一陣當咧修造手工步道的人，佮今年已經是第二年矣，汝敢想欲去看覓？」我嘛真好奇，就綴伊去到現場。去到現場了後，我

才發現講，遮的山路實在是足歹行的，但是這陣攏予遮志工修理甲平平坦坦（pînn-pînn-thánn-thánn），真好行。上蓋予人（hông）感動的就是，遮志工個攏自願家己開錢來。就按呢，我按呢手捗擎擎（tshiú-ńg pih-pih），我就參加個的行列，落去做志工，為家己的家鄉出一點仔力。

彼暗，我就共這改的感受寫出一條褒歌，號做〈鋪路做義工〉。這條褒歌佮我以早對生活記持寫--出的作品無啥仝款，這改我是家己真真正正的體驗。閣較重要的是，我對現時的家鄉有閣較全新的了解矣。

做這條〈鋪路做義工〉了後，我又閣創作幾若條的作品，譬如：〈澎湖南方四島蓋神奇〉、〈東坪山勢第一奇〉、〈小王子平台〉、〈東吉村中元普渡〉佮〈東嶼坪池府王爺生日〉，配合明翰翕的相片，共逐站仔的地景佮生活故事一首一首展開。這個時陣，阮的心內有一種想法，就是用褒歌來唱澎湖的故事。

毋過，佇過去20外年創作的1200外條褒歌內底，欲揀出適合的作品，實在是較困難。因為大部份的作品攏來自我1950年佮1970年的記持，彼個時陣，生活誠艱苦，島上無一個人有相機，相片就免閣講矣。所以，欲按怎予人褒歌的時陣，會當體會我講--的故事，這又閣是一件真大的挑戰。

我嘛是真幸運，目前我身邊有一陣真優秀的少年人來咧共我鬥相共（tàu-sann-kāng）。起先，協同作者吳明翰先生佮我鬥陣來共作品揀--出來，整理做六大主題，伊嘛提供伊翕相的相片，閣寫說明的賞析，嘛閣翻譯做英文；陳春星（TÂN Tshun-sing）先生佮我做伙轉去澎湖，將一島一島的所在、景緻，攏用水彩筆共--畫起來；陳亮均（TÂN Liāng-kun）先生伊真用心，伊聽我共每一首的褒歌唱--出來，為我揣出正確的台文字，嘛共羅馬字寫--落來；王藝臻設計師為我的冊創作典雅閣足嬌的設計；古庭維館長負責編輯規本（pńg）的潤稿，嘛是提出真寶貴的意見；潘燕玉老師佮澳洲的Hugo老師為阮校對中文佮英文的內容；林佳誼總編輯予這本書一條新的性命；猶閣有蔡明孝、周志展，佮海洋國家公園管理處的好朋友，個一直攏支持我、鼓勵我，才予我佇82歲的時陣有法度完成這本冊。

雖然這56條褒歌所唱--的故事大部份攏消失--去--looh，透過這改的創作，留起一寡珍貴的記持佮風景。我就是欲將這本冊，獻予不管時攏是頭一個聽我褒歌的牽手陳渼樺（TÂN Bí-huâ），佮晟養（tshiânn-ióng）我的母親，澎湖。

I was born on a small island called Sai-sū-pîng (Xiyuping) in the four islands of Southern Penghu.

As a child, there was no electricity on the island, which meant no television sets or radios. My joy came from sitting beside my mother and listening to her sing the heartfelt melodies of everyday life with our neighbors. The rhymes were beautiful and easy to remember. At that time, I was too busy with my studies to learn these songs and later, as a teacher, I was too focused on my work to find time to learn these lovely melodies. Thus, these tunes remained in my heart, to be remembered.

In 2002, during a visit back home, I found that many villagers had moved away, leaving my wife's elder sister as the only remaining person who could sing Penghu Ballads (po-kua). Witnessing this culture's decline saddened me. I thought that I was retired and had ample time, so why not create my own works to help keep this culture alive?

Initially, I based my creations on nearby islands, writing one song for each. I followed the traditional form of four lines per song, with seven characters per line, two lines forming a couplet and two couplets creating a full song, ensuring they rhyme. Encouraged by my wife, Chen Mei-Hua, I began producing more works covering themes from life memories and cultural practices to love and faith. If a piece was rich enough, I would add more lines to complete it, referring to my work as 'New Era Ballads'.

In 2021, my return to Tang-sū-pîng (Dongyuping) Island unexpectedly opened a new chapter in my creative journey.

While my wife and I were walking, we spotted a man in a national park uniform with a big camera, concentrating on capturing the beauty around him. Out of curiosity, we spoke to him and learned he was national park researcher Wu Ming-Han, who had a passion for photography and often shared stories of the park on the official Facebook page. His works served as a bridge between my hometown and me, especially when he introduced photographs of Tang-sū-pîng and Sai-sū-pîng Islands; I couldn't help but leave encouraging comments. Little did I know we would meet on the island!

I asked Ming-Han why he wanted to write these stories. He replied, 'I've noticed there are only a few households left here and the next generation rarely returns. I hope these pictures and stories help the younger generation understand their homeland and appreciate its beauty, starting their own journey of rediscovery'. I was surprised that someone who had been working here for only a year could hold my homeland in such high regard. I sensed a special connection between us.

He then pointed towards Tang-sū-pîng Island and said, 'There is a group of volunteers building an eco-friendly trail; it's already the second year. Would you like to see it?' Curious, I decided to follow him to the site. Upon arrival, I found that the previously rugged path had been improved and made much smoother. What touched me most was that these volunteers had funded their trips to create a better pathway for visitors. I joined their ranks, becoming the oldest trail volunteer, contributing to the construction of this hometown path.

When I returned home, I wrote a piece, 'Inspiring Tales of Eco-Friendly Trail Volunteers on Tang-sū-pîng Island', for the Penghu Ballads. This work differed from my previous pieces drawn from memory; it was based on my own experience and provided me with a

攝影｜陳光照

fresh perspective on my current hometown.

Since then, I have created works such as 'Four Rare Islands in Southern Penghu', 'Special Hills of Tang-sū-pîng Island', 'The Little Prince Viewing Platform', 'Ghost Festival in Tang-kiat Village' and 'Ritual of Tî Ông-iâ Worship on Tang-sū-pîng Island'. Accompanied by Ming-Han's photographs, these pieces showcase current landscapes and life stories. Gradually, we conceived the idea of using ballads (po-kua) to tell the stories of Penghu.

Selecting suitable pieces from over 1200 ballads I had created over the past 20 years proved to be quite a challenge. Many works stemmed from my memories between 1950 and 1970, a time when life was tough; few people on the island owned a camera, let alone had photographs. Thus, helping readers deeply appreciate these stories while reading was another challenge.

Fortunately, I was surrounded by exceptional young people who patiently assisted me. Co-author Mr Wu Ming-Han helped catalog my works, summarising them into 6 major themes while providing photographs and writing appreciation notes and translations. Mr Chen Chun-Xing accompanied Ming-Han and me back to Penghu, visiting the locations of my stories and illustrating their essence. Mr Tan Liang-kun listened as I sang each ballad, proofreading the Taiwanese characters and transcribing it into Romanisation for readers. Designer Wang Yi-Jhen (Lori) created an elegant, minimalist design for my book. Mr Ku Ting-Wei proofread the manuscript and provided invaluable advice. Ms. Pan Yan-Yu and Mr. Hugo van den Berghe from Australia helped us proofread the Mandarin Chinese and English content. Chief editor Ms Lin Chia-Yi gave the book new life. Additionally, Tsai Ming-Hsiao, Zhou Zhi-Zhan and the partners from the Marine National Park Headquarters continually offered support and encouragement, enabling me to publish *Framed by the Sea: Through a Square Window onto the Island - Penghu Ballads: A Selection by Lu Kun-Han* at 82.

Many stories within these 56 ballads have long since faded, yet I have managed to capture fleeting fragments, preserving the precious memories of life through this meaningful creation. I dedicate this book to my wife, Chen Mei-Hua, who is always the first to listen to my ballads, and to my nurturing homeland, Penghu.

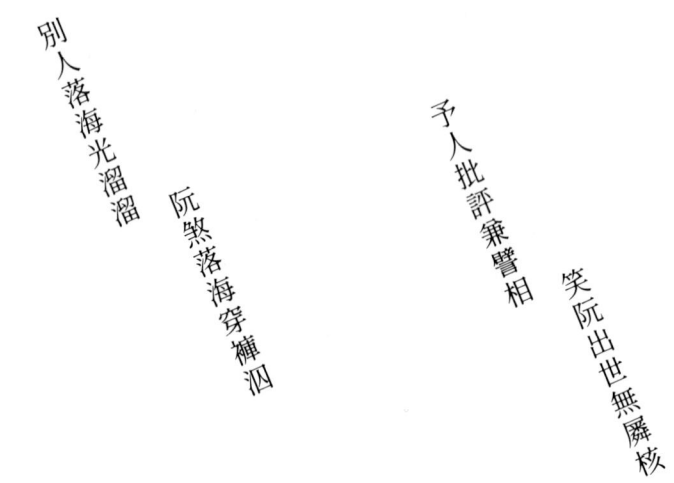

It-sim Siūnn Tsò Bûn-bîng-lâng
一心想做文明人
Determined to Become an Educated Person

Pa̍t-lâng lo̍h-hái kng-liù-liù, gún suah lo̍h-hái tshīng khòo-á siû.
Hōo lâng phue-phîng kiam phì-siùnn, tshiò gún tshut-sì bô lān-hu̍t.

九歲的呂坤翰在 1953 年步入學校大門，開始了他的求學之旅。他回憶起 1970 年以前，離島的男生到海邊戲水，每次都脫得光溜溜一絲不掛。可是在他心中，對這樣的習慣總有些羞赧。因此，每當他跟小伙伴們去海邊嬉戲時，一定堅持穿著褲子。除了其他小朋友們回去聚落後會取笑他，當他自豪地穿著那條濕漉漉的褲子返家途中，還經常聽到長輩們嘲弄他沒有「屄核」。對他來說，脫光衣服下海不僅令人尷尬，也缺少對他人的尊重，實在「誠無體面」（tsiânn bô thé-bīn）。時間荏苒，呂坤翰成為一名老師之後，便開始向學生們傳遞這份觀念——在水中玩樂，穿上褲子是重要的禮貌且較健康。他於 2002 年回鄉探親時，沒有再看到海邊的男生脫褲下水，不禁欣慰「真正大家攏愛做文明的人矣！」

• • •

At the age of nine, Lu Kun-Han started primary school in 1953. He recalls that before 1970, boys on the island would frolic in the sea completely naked. However, he always felt that such a practice was somewhat inappropriate. Therefore, whenever he played by the seaside with his friends, he insisted on wearing his shorts. Yet, on his way home, proudly wearing his damp trousers, he found himself the target of teasing not only from his peers but also from adults who mockingly pointed out that he was 'without testicles'. For him, playing in the water without clothes was not only embarrassing but also lacked respect for others—it was simply impolite. As Lu Kun-Han grew up and became a teacher, he began to pass on this belief to his students—that wearing trousers while having fun in the water is of great importance. When he retired in 2002 and returned home to visit relatives, he was delighted to notice that he no longer saw adult men or boys at the beach without their trousers. He happily remarked, "Everyone has become more cultured now!"

用褒歌說故事的人／呂坤翰 | 21

島 TÓ-SŪ 嶼

　　對於出生在西嶼坪的呂坤翰來說，那片熟悉的故鄉，就是他童年世界的全部。然而，當他十五歲考上馬公初中，在前往澎湖本島求學的那趟航行，他驚訝地發現，原來澎湖如此廣闊、豐富，處處都是驚喜。望安、將軍、虎井、桶盤與馬公，每一座島嶼都有著獨特的風貌與魅力。自那一刻起，他的視野開始航向整個澎湖。

　　在這些吟唱「島嶼」的作品中，呂坤翰用心記錄自己在澎湖群島的所見所聞。每一首島嶼褒歌不僅講述各島的故事與歷史，還深刻反映了他親自造訪後所感受到的人文風情，以及在地交流的溫暖。

　　每個島嶼都有無數故事，而每個故事更蘊涵人與土地之間深厚的聯繫。讓我們透過這些島嶼褒歌，一起探索屬於澎湖的人情旅事吧！

ISLAND

For Lu Kun-Han, who was born on Sai-sū-pîng (Xiyuping) Island, that familiar hometown was his entire childhood world. However, when he turned 12 and went to the Magong Secondary School, it was during the journey to Penghu Main Island for his studies that he was astonished to discover just how vast and full of surprises Penghu was. Bāng-uann (Wang'an), Tsiong-kun-ò (Jiangjun'ao), Hónn-tsínn (Hujing), Thàng-puânn (Tongpan) and Má-king (Magong)—each island possesses its own special character. From that moment on, the entire Penghu Archipelago became a world he longed to explore. In these works that celebrate 'islands', each piece not only narrates the stories and histories of the various islands but also documents, in a travelogue style, the cultural experiences Lu Kun-Han encountered during his visits to each island, as well as his interactions with the locals. Every island has countless stories and behind each story lies a profound relationship between people and the land. Let us explore the tales belonging to the islands of Penghu through these Island Ballads!

Má-king-tshī

媽宮市

Má-king City

澎湖一市五个鄉　　上蓋鬧熱是媽宮　/　黃昏觀音亭上媠　　散步賞景規大堆
　　欲食點心揣中正　　靑菜魚肉揣北辰

明朝媽祖上早來　　保咱平安閣發財　/　興仁地理好所在　　淸朝蔡進士逐家知

這是澎湖的光彩　　伊的名聲迵全台　/　中央老街好景致　　一井四空向上天

名產嘛是滿滿是　　鹹餅烏糖粿麻糍　/　港墘碼頭早漁市　　去買現流魚上鮮

遊艇載客四界去　　南海旅遊上省時　/　澎南風櫃上出名　　大湧拍空風櫃聲

海水浴場佇嵵裡　　展身游泳好時機　/　隔壁山水嘛袂穤　　耍水的人笑哈哈

烏崁高麗菜世界大　　鮮脆甘甜上好食　/　桶盤地像覆面桶　　海墘蓮花座蓋全

虎井山是軍事地　　塌窩地才徛民家　/　北回歸線對遮過　　地景眞正蓋特別

媽宮好耍好迌迌　　毋是咱唎家己褒　/　好空共恁鬥相報　　閒著罔來澎湖趖

Phînn-ôo tsit tshī gōo-ê hiunn, siōng-kài lāu-jiát sī Má-king.
Beh tsiah tiám-sim tshē Tiong-tsìng, Tshinn-tshài hû-bah tshē Pak-sîn. / Hông-hun Kuan-im-tîng siōng suí, sàn-pōo siúnn-kíng kui-tuā-tui.
Bîng-tiâu Má-tsóo siōng tsá lâi, pó lán pîng-an koh huat-tsâi. / Hing-jîn tē-lí hó-sóo-tsāi, Tshing-tiâu Tshuà Tsìn-sū ták-ke tsai.
Tse sī Phînn-ôo ê kong-tshái, i ê miâ-siann thàng tsuân Tâi. / Tiong-iong lāu-kue hó kíng-tì, tsit tsínn sì khang hiòng tsiūnn-thinn.
Bîng-sán mā sī muá-muá-sī, kiâm-piánn oo-thn̂g-ké muâ-tsî. / Káng-kînn-á bé-thâu tsá-hû-tshī, khù bué hiān-lâu-á hû siōng tshinn.
Iû-thíng tsài kheh sì-kuè khì, Lâm-hái lú-iû siōng síng-sî. / Phînn-lâm Hong-kuī siōng tshut-miâ, tuā íng phah khang Hong-kuī siann.
Hái-tsuí-ik-tiûnn tī Sî-lí, tián-sin iû-íng hó-sî-ki. / Keh-piah San-suí mā buē-bái, sńg-tsuí ê lâng tshiò-hai-hai.
Oo-khàm ko-le-tshài sè-kài tuā, tshinn-tshuì kam-tinn siōng hó-tsiah. / Tháng-puânn tuē tshiūnn phak bīn-tháng, hái-kînn-á liân-hue-tsō kài kâng.
Hónn-tsínn suann sī kun-sū-tuē, lap-o-tuē tsiah khiā bîn-ke. / Pak-huê-kui-suànn tuì tsia kuè, tuē-kíng tsin-tsiànn kài tik-piát.
Má-king hó-sńg hó-tshit-thô, m̄-sī lán leh kai-kī po. / Hó-khang-ê kā lín tàu-sio-pò, îng--tòh bóng lâi Phînn-ôo sô.

26 | 島嶼 TÓ-SŪ

澎湖縣有一個市、五個鄉，其中最熱鬧的非媽宮莫屬。在這裡，中正路上各式點心引人垂涎。如果想要買菜、買魚或肉，大家都會到北辰市場，因爲那裡的鮮貨最齊全。黃昏時分，居民們最愛在觀音亭散步，欣賞迷人的夕照彩霞。蔡廷蘭進士是澎湖本地第一位也是唯一的進士，是澎湖的光榮，名聲更是響徹全台。中央老街有各式的伴手禮，遊客總在這裡挑選心儀的紀念品。四眼井更是獨具特色，設計別出心裁，吸引遊客的目光。清晨時分，第三漁港熱鬧非凡，新鮮的漁獲剛剛登岸，閃閃發光的魚兒讓人食指大動想立即嘗鮮。南海遊客中心的遊艇帶著客人們走向南海，讓他們在碧海藍天下享受來自大海的樂趣。澎南的風櫃，驚人的浪花拍打著岩石，噴出的水霧中，有此起彼落著咕嚕聲，真的有趣極了！對於喜愛游泳的小朋友，嵵裡的海水浴場無疑是夏日的最佳去處。而隔壁庄的山水沙灘也別具一番風味，無需付入場費，讓人玩得不亦樂乎！在烏崁，高麗菜又大又鮮脆，帶著自然的甘甜。媽宮真是一個美好的地方，熱情善良的居民，優美的自然風光、澎湃的海鮮、土產期待著每一位朋友能在明年再度光臨，留下更多美好的回憶！

· · ·

Penghu County features a bustling city and five townships, with Má-kíng (Magong) being the most vibrant. Zhongzheng Road offers a tempting selection of snacks, while the Pak-sîn (Beichen) Market is the go-to spot for fresh produce, seafood and meat. At dusk, locals enjoy strolling at the Kuan-im-tîng (Guanyin Temple), admiring the beautiful night scenery. TSHUÀ Tîng-lân, the first and only Jinshi from Penghu, is celebrated for bringing pride to the region and earning recognition throughout Taiwan. Central Old Street is filled with souvenir shops, where tourists often find beloved keepsakes. The unique Four-Eyed Well attracts visitors with its special design. The Third Fishing Port comes alive in the mornings as fresh catches are offloaded, with glittering fish tempting buyers. The South Sea Visitor Centre offers yacht trips into the South Penghu Sea, allowing guests to enjoy the delights of the sea. At Hong-kuī (Fenggui), impressive waves crash against the rocks, creating an intriguing spectacle. In Oo-khàm (Wukan), locally grown cabbage is crisp and sweet.
Má-kíng is a beautiful place with friendly residents and stunning landscapes, eagerly awaiting visitors to return next year to create more wonderful memories!

湖西隘門沙灘闊　海上遊樂人人『誇』

　林投公園　連相倚　隨恁𨑨迌抑『溜達』

　上　蓋　出名　龍　門　港　貨船載貨有夠『夯』

　　台　灣　運回　的　物件　眞濟攏運轉來遮

　　欲　觀　日出　揣菓葉　好天觀樓看會著

　　北寮　摩西　分　海　嶼　地質誠是蓋特殊

　　水　退　用　行　過　赤嶼　水漲變佇海中浮

　　　熱　天　機　場　上無閒　日日載客幾外千

　　　　糖棗　好食　人　人　興　風茹茶草上好啉

　　　來　遮　耍水　看　風景　自然攏嘛好心情

Ôo-sai-hiunn

湖西鄉
Ôo-sai Township

Ôo-sai Ài-mn̂g sua-than khuah, Hái-siōng iû-lo̍k lâng-lâng "khua".
Nâ-tâu kong-hn̂g liân sio-uá, suî lín tshit-thô ia̍h "liu--ta".
Siōng-kài tshut-miâ Liông-mn̂g-káng, hè-tsûn tsài hè ū-kàu "hang".
Tâi-uân ūn huê ê mi̍h-kiānn, tsin tsuē lóng ūn tńg-lâi tsia.
Beh kuan ji̍t--tshut tshē Ké-hio̍h, hó-thinn kuan-lâu khuànn-ē-tio̍h.
Pak-liâu Môo-se hun-hái sū, tē-tsit tsiânn sī kài ti̍k-sû.
Tsuí--thuè iōng kiânn kuè Tshiah-sū, tsuí--tīnn piàn tī hái-tiong phû.
Jua̍h-thinn Ki-tiûnn siōng bô-îng, ji̍t-ji̍t tsài kheh kuí-guā-tshing.
Tsìnn-tsó hó-tsia̍h lâng-lâng hìng, hong-jû-tê-tsháu siōng hó-lim.
Lâi tsia sńg-tsuí khuànn hong-kíng, tsū-jiân lóng mā hó sim-tsîng.

30 | 島嶼 TÓ-SŪ

湖西隘門的沙灘寬廣美麗，吸引人們親近玩水嬉戲，大家都喜愛這片美好的海域。附近的林投公園也是適合散步的好地方。龍門港的設計完善又出色，不僅能供漁船停放，又能容納貨船來往，其中幾艘專門從布袋港到龍門港，為澎湖運送物資。想要欣賞日出的朋友，在好天氣時，絕對不能錯過菓葉的觀日樓，那裡的美景會讓所有人留連忘返。最特別的要數北寮奎壁山的摩西分海，當潮水退去時，一條小路悄然浮現，潮水湧入時，整個赤嶼會神秘地懸浮在海中央，令人驚嘆不已。湖西的糊棗可是這裡的名產，甜美可口，而風茹茶則是最受歡迎的清涼飲品。夏天時，機場滿滿是來訪的遊客，大家都迫不及待地想要探索澎湖的魅力。

• • •

Ài-mn̂g (Aimen) Village in Ôo-sai (Huxi) Township boasts an expansive beach, always crowded with people enjoying the water, making it a beloved spot in this beautiful coastal area. Nearby, Nâ-tâu (Lintou) Park is also an excellent place for a leisurely stroll. The construction of Liông-mn̂g (Longmen) Harbor is impressive, accommodating not only fishing boats but also numerous cargo vessels, including several that transport goods from Budai Harbor in Chiayi County to Longmen Harbor for Penghu. For those keen to watch the sunrise, Ké-hio̍h (Guoye)'s Sunrise Lookout is a must-visit on clear days, offering stunning views that leave everyone satisfied. Particularly special is the 'Moses Splitting the Sea' at Ku-piah-suann (Kuibishan) in Pak-liâu (Beiliao) Village. As the tide recedes, a path quietly appears and when the tide rises, the entire Tshiah-sū (Chiyu) Isle emerges in the middle of the sea, leaving onlookers in awe.

Pe̍h-sua-hiunn

白沙鄉
Pe̍h-sua Township

中屯風車倚規排　替咱生電予咱開 ／ 岐頭海域好藏沬　順看水族熱帶魚

鳥嶼福伯蓋靈聖　烏金石壁蓋出名 ／ 員貝嶼像大扇貝　石筆石硯蓋古錐

赤崁海產嘛蓋濟　欲買海產來遮提 ／ 麥芽扁魚酥閣脆　巧味丁香螺仔膆

干貝醬料芳嗲嗲　攪麵攪飯也配麋

紫菜青苔規大塊　煮魚煮卵上 OK ／ 後寮有條天堂路　有閒罔去慢慢趖

通樑出名大榕樹　廟前『納涼』心清幽 ／ 目斗嶼有倚燈樓　暝時予船做目標

大倉海域生態濟　觀賞研究無問題 ／ 白沙鄉是好所在　歡迎逐家閒就來

Tiong-tun hong-tshia khiā kui pâi, thè lán sinn tiān hōo lán khai. / Kî-thâu hái-hik hó tshàng-bī, sūn khuànn tsuí-tsòk jia̍t-tuà-hî.
Tsiáu-sū Hok-peh-á kài lîng-siànn, oo-kim tsio̍h-piah kài tshut-miâ. / Uân-puè-sū tshiūnn tuā-sìnn-puè, tsio̍h-pit tsio̍h-hīnn kài kóo-tsui.
Tshiah-khàm hái-sán mā kài tsuē, beh bué hái-sán lâi tsia the̍h. / Be̍h-gê pínn-hû soo koh tshè, khá-bī ting-hiunn lê-á-kuê.
Kan-puè tsiùnn-liāu phang-teh-teh, kiáu-mī kiáu-pn̄g iā phè buê.
Tsí-tshài tshinn-thî kui tuā-tè, tsú hû tsú nn̄g siōng "oo--khe". / Āu-liâu ū tiâu Thian-tông-lōo, ū-îng bóng khù bān-bān-á sô.
Thong-niû tshut-miâ tuā tshîng-tshiū, biō-tsîng "nà-liâng" sim tshing-iu. / Ba̍k-táu-sū ū khiā ting-lâu, mî--sî sái-tsûn tsò bo̍k-piau.
Tuā-tshng hái-hik sing-thài tsuē, kuan-sióng gián-kiù bô-būn-tuê. / Pe̍h-sua-hiunn sī hó-sóo-tsāi, huan-gîng ta̍k-ke îng tō lâi.

中屯海邊一景：矗立整排的高大發電風車。岐頭則是玩水和潛水的好地方，附近還有一座神奇的水族館，可以觀賞到五彩斑斕的海洋生物。赤崁的海產豐富多樣，像麥芽扁魚干、丁香膎、螺仔膎、紫菜干、青苔干和小卷干等。後寮有一條名為「天堂路」的海中小徑，值得大家走去探險。在通樑，有一片巨大的榕樹，樹棚（tshiū-pînn）繁茂，特別適合夏天來參觀時，在樹下納涼。白沙鄉是個充滿樂趣的地方，玩沙、戲水，讓人陶醉不已。

・ ・ ・

On Tiong-tun (Zhongtun) Island, there are many towering wind turbines standing in a row by the seaside. Kî-thâu (Qitou) Village is a great place for water activities and diving and nearby there's an aquarium where you can observe a variety of vibrant marine life. Tshiah-khàm (Chikan) Village offers a rich and diverse seafood selection, including flatfish and pickled conch. In Thong-niû (Tongliang) Village, there's a vast grove of banyan trees, with lush branches and leaves. It's especially pleasant to visit in the summer when tourists can cool off under the shade of the trees. Pe̍h-sua (Baisha) Township is a fun-filled place where you can enjoy sand play and splashing about in the water, leaving you thoroughly enchanted.

Sai-sū-hiunn

西嶼鄉
Sai-sū Township

跨海大橋通橫礁　西嶼交通就好行　/　大路直通到外垵　隔壁燈塔嘛佇遐

外垵有个好港口　漁民趁錢起洋樓　/　西嶼『砲台』有歷史　防敵較實有工夫

內垵沙灘幼麵麵　熱天耍水當著時　/　小池日落上好看　彩霞變化萬百般

大菓葉玄武岩石壁　規排石柱徛佇遐　/　二崁古厝上完整　庄內樸實閣衛生

俗語褒歌蓋趣味　予人欣羨閣好奇　/　翁魚洞佇小門北　哪會挵甲遐大力

地質館的石頭濟　介紹汝知無問題　/　西嶼景致有夠濟　予人看甲暢心花

Khuà-hái-tuā-kiô thong Huînn-ta, Sai-sū kau-thong tiō hó-kiânn.
Tuā-lōo tit-thong kàu Guā-uann, keh-piah ting-thah mā tī hia.
Guā-uann ū tsit ê hó káng-kháu, hû-bîn thàn-tsînn khí iûnn-lâu.
Sai-sū "phàu-thâi" ū lik-sú, hông tik khah sit ū kang-hu.
Lāi-uann sua-than iù-mī-mī, juah-thinn sńg-tsuí tng-tiỏh-sî.
Sió-tî jit--lỏh siōng hó-khuànn, tshái-hâ piàn-huà bān-pah-puann.
Tuā-ké-hiỏh hiân-bú-giâm tsiỏh-piah, kui pâi tsiỏh-thiāu khiā tī hia.
Jī-khàm kóo-tshù siōng uân-tsíng, tsng lāi phoh-sit koh uē-sing.
Siỏk-gú po-kua kài tshù-bī, hōo-lâng him-siān koh hò-kî.
Ang-hû-tōng tī Sió-mn̂g pak, ná ē lòng kah hiah tuā-lat.
Tē-tsit-kuán ê tsiỏh-thâu tsuē, kài-siāu lú tsai bô-būn-tuê.
Sai-sū kíng-tì ū-kàu tsuē, hōo lâng khuànn kah thiòng sim hue.

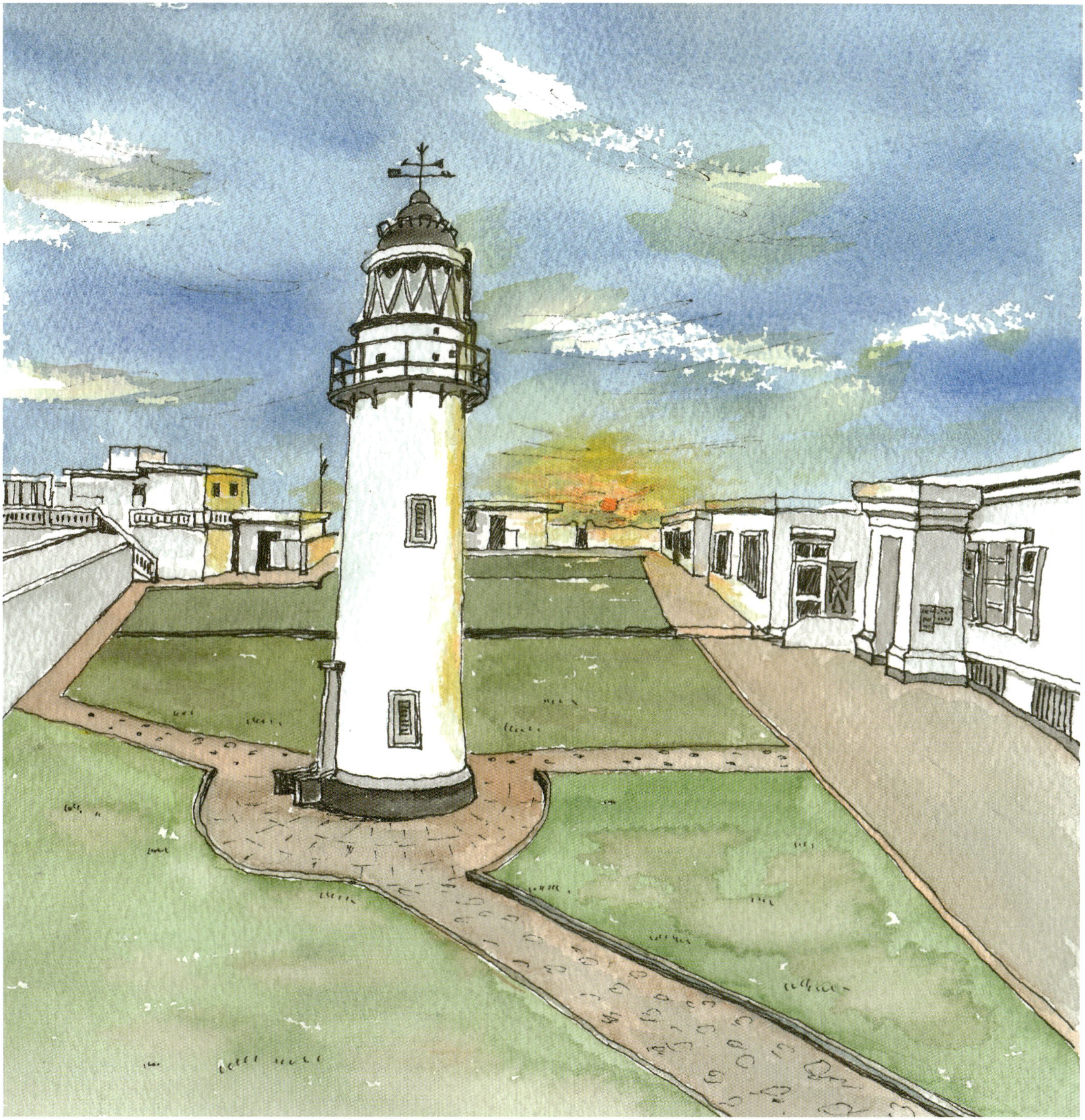

跨海大橋不僅連接了白沙島和西嶼，讓交通更便捷，兩端的半圓形拱門也成為遊客必訪的景點。

The Penghu Great Bridge not only connects Pe̍h-sua (Baisha) Island and (Sai-sū)Xiyu Island, making transportation more convenient, but the semi-circular arches at both ends have also become a must-visit attraction for tourists.

跨海大橋延伸到西嶼，大馬路延展至外垵，是在邀請每一位旅者前來探索。聳立西嶼的燈塔，守護著航行的人們。外垵的港口非常寬廣，討海人們辛勤地在海上拚搏捕魚，為了能賺取財富、蓋起洋樓，給家人過上舒適的生活。而西嶼的砲台則建得堅固又威武。內垵的沙灘成為夏季玩水的天堂。在小池角，日落景色美得驚人，彩霞在空中舞動，幻化迷人的色彩。大菓葉的玄武岩石壁整齊又壯觀，令人讚嘆。在二崁，壁頂上懸掛著各式各樣有趣的俗語褒歌，總令人駐足品味。小門北邊的鯨魚洞，是鯨魚撞出來的嗎？地質館裡的石頭琳瑯滿目，館內的介紹詳盡有趣。西嶼的好玩地方這麼多，等著每一個喜愛探索的朋友，明年記得再來喔！

・ ・ ・

The Penghu Great Bridge stretches toward Sai-sū (Xiyu) Township, with the road continuing to Guā-uann (Wai'an) Village, inviting travellers to explore. In Sai-sū, the lighthouse stands nearby, guiding those at sea like a bright beacon. The vast port in Guā-uann is bustling with hardworking fishermen striving to catch fish, hoping to earn wealth, build Western-style houses and enjoy a comfortable life. The fort in Sai-sū features a unique structure that adds to the area's charm. The beach in Lāi-uann (Nei'an) Village is a paradise for summer water play, while Sió-tî-kak (Xiaochijiao) Village is famous for its stunning sunsets, with colorful clouds dancing in the sky. In Tuā-ké-hio̍h (Daguoye), the basalt cliff is spectacular, leaving visitors in awe. In Jī-khàm (Erkan) Village, local sayings and ballads adorn the walls of ancient houses, tempting passersby to sing along. Just north of Sió-mn̂g (Xiaomen) Village lies the 'Whale Cave' — could it really have been made by a whale? With so many attractions in Sai-sū (Xiyu), it awaits all who love Penghu and the ocean to discover its wonders!

Kiat-puè-tshun
吉貝村
Kiat-puè Island

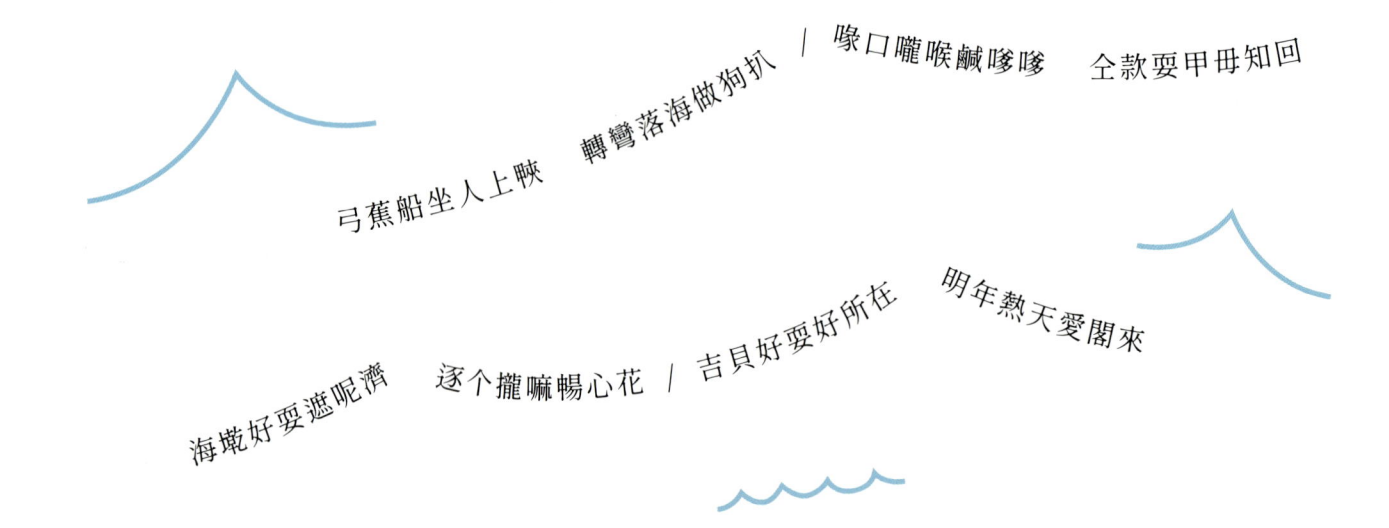

若講北海的吉貝

熱天耍水上笑詼

沙灘遊樂器材濟

海上騎駛『摩托車』

弓蕉船坐人上䆀　轉彎落海做狗扒　｜　喙口嚨喉鹹嗲嗲　全款耍甲毋知回

海墘好耍遮呢濟　逐个攏嘛暢心花　｜　吉貝好耍好所在　明年熱天愛閣來

Nā kóng Pak-hái ê Kiat-puè, juah-thinn sńg-tsuí siōng tshiò-khue.
Sua-than iû-lok khì-tsâi tsuē, hái-siōng khiâ-sái "môo-thóo-tshe".
King-tsio-tsûn tsē lâng siōng khueh, tńg-uan loh-hái tsò káu-á pê.
tshuì-kháu nâ-âu kiâm-teh-teh, kāng-khuán sńg kah m̄-tsai huê.
hái-kînn-á hó-sńg tsiah-nī-á tsuē, tak-ê lóng mā thiòng-sim-hue.
Kiat-puè hó-sńg hó sóo-tsai, mî-nî juah-thinn ài koh lâi.

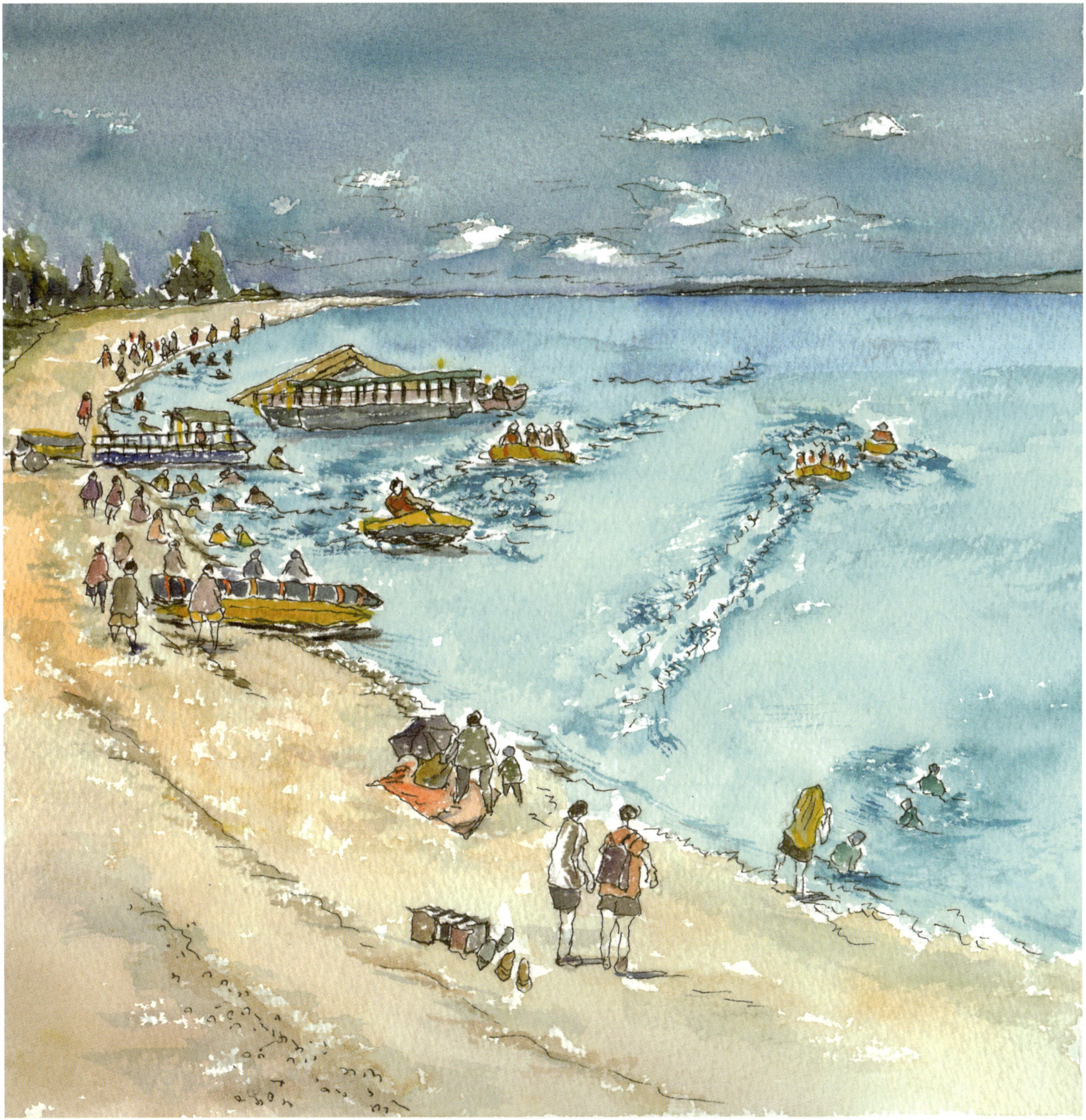

42 | 島嶼 TÓ-SŪ

吉貝的海邊全是白色的沙灘，是個充滿歡樂的地方，遊樂設施應有盡有。你可以嘗試海上摩托車，刺激無比的快感！坐上香蕉船，大家可以一起歡呼尖叫，當船大轉彎的時候，所有人可能都一起跌進海裡，像小狗一樣拍打著水面，狼狽可愛又開心。即使經常會喝到鹹鹹的海水，但這一切都是那麼刺激又好玩，於是大家都不想上岸休息，仍然希望能在這片歡樂的海洋裡盡情玩耍，享受每一刻的快樂！

• • •

Kiat-puè (Jibei) Island has beautiful white sandy beaches, making it a fun place with all kinds of entertainment. You can enjoy the exciting thrill of riding jet skis, which is amazing! When you and your friends get on a banana boat, cheers fill the air and as the boat turns, you might all fall into the sea, splashing around like playful puppies—awkward but really cute. Even if you swallow some salty seawater now and then, the fun is so great that no one wants to go ashore for a break; instead, everyone wants to keep playing in this happy ocean and enjoy every moment of fun!

Bāng-uann-hiunn

望安鄉
Bāng-uann Island

望安舊名叫八罩　本島親像大姊頭　／　全鄉戶口管透透　出生證明寄個兜

望安本島有較大　山頂出名天台山

草仔青青滿山嶺　飼牛牧場就佇遮

海墘上媠的海岸　就是孵龜的海沙

花宅古厝上完整　這社當時蓋文明

望安文石世界級　印鑑墜心粒粒珍

若有收藏上幸運　保恁平安有錢賰

Bāng-uann kū-miâ kiò Pueh-tàu, Pún-tó tshin-tshiūnn tuā-tsí-á-thâu.
Tsuân hiunn hōo-kháu kuán-thàu-thàu, tshut-sinn tsìng-bîng kià in-tau.
Bāng-uann Pún-tó ū khah tuā, suann-tíng tshut-miâ Thian-tâi-suann.
Tsháu-á tshinn-tshinn muá suann-niá, tshī gû bȯk-tiûnn tiō tī tsia.
Hái-kînn-á siōng suí ê hái-huānn, tiō-sī pū ku-á ê hái-sua.
Hue-thȯh kóo-tshù siōng uân-tsíng, tsit siā tong-sî kài bûn-bîng.
Bāng-uann bûn-tsiȯh sè-kài-kip, ìn-kàm tuī-sim-á liȧp-liȧp tin.
Nā ū siu-tsōng siōng hīng-ūn, pó lín pîng-an ū tsînn tshun.

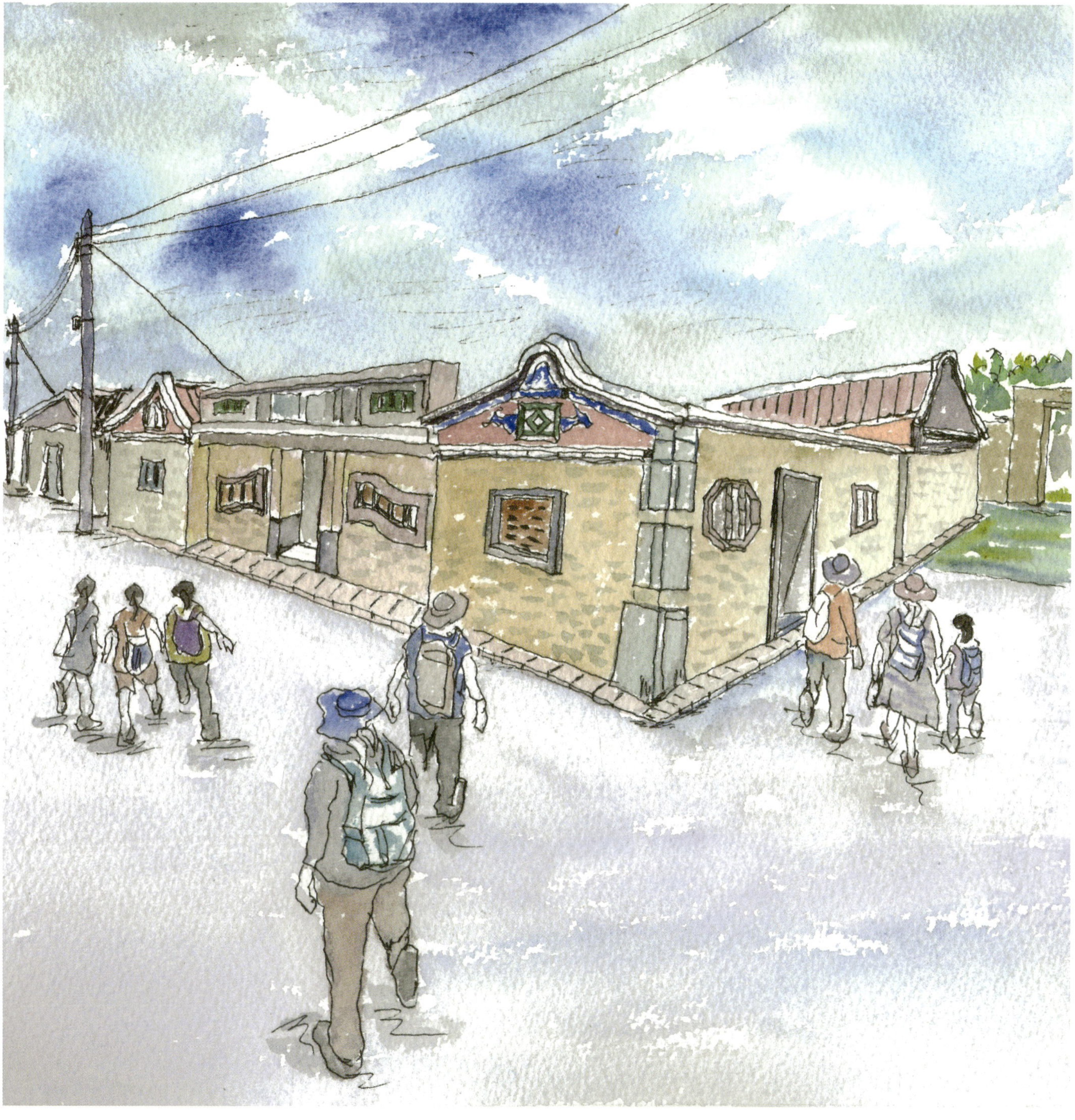

望安擁有多處沙灘，是綠蠵龜產卵的理想場所。其中，在東安社區活動中心旁的沙灘，還可以遠眺到東、西嶼坪的島嶼輪廓。

Bāng-uann (Wang'an) boasts numerous beaches, making it an ideal nesting site for green sea turtles. Among them, the beach next to the Tong-an (Dong'an) Community Activity Center offers a great view of the landscapes of Tang-sū-pîng (Dongyuping) and Sai-sū-pîng (Xiyuping) Islands.

望安以前叫做八罩，意思是這裡有八個小島，分別是望安本島、將軍澳嶼、東吉嶼、西吉嶼、花嶼、東嶼坪、西嶼坪和七美（大嶼）。望安本島上有一座美麗的天台山，那是全島最吸引人的地方。在山坡頂端，有一片綠油油的草地，總有牛兒在這裡悠閒地吃草。而在望安的海邊，延綿的白色沙灘成為海龜挖掘產卵洞的好地方。在花宅（中社村），有一些保存得很好又古老的房子，讓人彷彿走進歷史。望安的文石也很特別，和歐洲義大利的文石一樣有名，總讓人愛不釋手、想要擁有。

• • •

Bāng-uann (Wang'an) was formerly known as Pueh-tàu, which means 'the place of eight small islands'. These include the main island of Bāng-uann, Tsiong-kun-ò (Jiangjun'ao), Tang-kiat (Dongji), Sai-kiat (Xiji), Hue-sū (Huayu), Tang-sū-pîng (Dongyuping), Sai-sū-pîng (Xiyuping) and Tshit-bí (Qimei). On Bāng-uann Island, there is a beautiful hill called Tiantaishan, which is the most attractive spot on the island. At the top of the slope, there is a lush green meadow, perfect for cows to graze leisurely. Along Bāng-uann's coastline, the long stretches of white sandy beaches provide an ideal spot for sea turtles to dig their nests. In Hue-theh (Huazhai) Village, you'll find several well-preserved old houses that make you feel as though you have stepped back in time.

將軍兩个好港口　討海掠魚佮上勢
新進家私傳會到　海底珊瑚上勢鬮
冬天塗魠掠透透　輕鬆趁錢起洋樓
佮的海產嘛蓋濟　鰇魚小管佮龍蝦
鬚哥掠來煮酸瓜
芹菜切切炒狗蝦
九孔蒜頭豆油配　愛食巧味丁香膎
新鮮口味好落胃　欲食海產來遮提

Tsiong-kun-tshun

將軍村

Tsiong-kun-ò Island

Tsiong-kun ū nńg ê hó kang-kháu, thó-hái liảh-hû in siōng gâu.
Sin-tsìn ke-si tshuân ē kàu, hái-tué suan-ôo siōng gâu khau.
Tang-thinn thôo-thoh liảh-thàu-thàu, khin-sang thàn-tsînn khí iûnn-lâu.
In ê hái-sán mā kài tsuē, jiû-hû sió-kńg-á kah lîng-hê.
Tshiu-ko liảh lâi tsú sng-kue-á, khîn-tshài tshiat-tshiat tshá káu-hê.
Káu-kháng suàn-thâu tāu-iû phuè, ài-tsiảh khá-bī ting-hiunn-kuê.
Sin-sian kháu-bī hó lỏh-uī, beh tsiảh hái-sán tō lâi tsia thẻh.

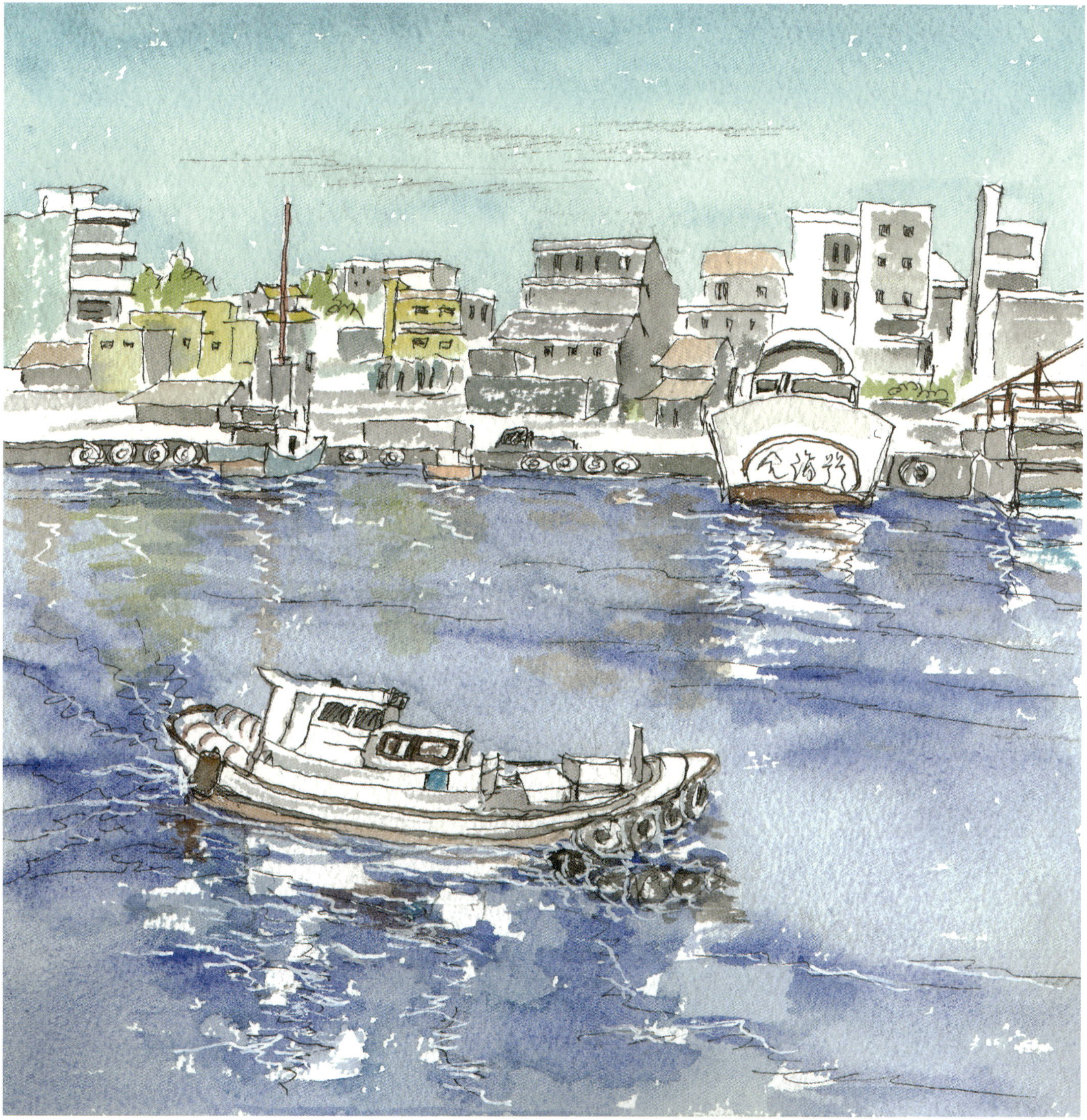

50 | 島嶼 TÓ-SŪ

將軍村的南北兩側，各有一個熱鬧的港口。這裡的漁民了解大海，他們會運用探魚機去找海底的魚群，每年冬天抓很多土魠魚。往昔漁民還會利用探魚機探索海底的珊瑚礁，將這些美麗的珊瑚採集回來，製作成價值非凡的藝術品。這使得將軍村成為外島上最早蓋起樓房的地方。漁民捕撈的魚類種類繁多，無論是鯀魚（魷魚）、小管（小卷），還是龍蝦，應有盡有，每一樣都美味好吃：用鬚哥魚加酸瓜仔煮成的湯，混合著芹菜炒狗蝦的清香，還有九孔沾醬油，稀飯搭配著丁香膎，每一道菜都令人垂涎三尺。在將軍村，海洋的禮物使每一餐都格外美味、珍貴。

• • •

Tsiong-kun-ò (Jiangjun'ao) Island has bustling ports on both its northern and southern sides. The fishermen here are very skilled at catching fish, as they use sonar equipment to locate schools of fish on the ocean floor, particularly catching a great deal of Spanish mackerel each winter. In the past, the fishermen also used sonar devices to explore the coral reefs below, collecting these beautiful corals to create valuable works of art. This made the island one of the earliest places in the Penghu archipelago to construct proper buildings. The variety of seafood caught by the fishermen is impressive, including squid, pencil squid and lobsters—there is something for everyone. On Tsiong-kun-ò Island, the gifts from the ocean make every meal especially delicious.

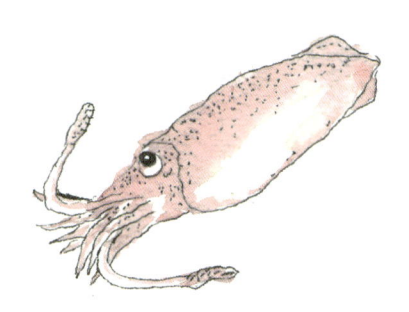

Tang-kiat-tshun

東吉村

Tang-kiat Island

電台就會　共　咱　傳

每工氣候　若　有　變

欲知天氣　無　困　難

島上有个　測　候　站

母驚駛船　無　目　標

四邊船隻看　會　到

燈光炤到　烏　水　溝

東吉出名　是　燈樓

Tang-kiat tshut-miâ sī ting-lâu, ting-kng tshiō kàu Oo-tsuí-kau.
Sì-pinn tsûn-tsiah khuànn ē kàu, m̄-kiann sái-tsûn bô bȯk-piau.
Tó siōng ū tsit ê tshik-hāu-tsām, beh tsai thinn-khì bô khùn-lân.
Muí kang khì-āu nā ū piàn, tiān-tâi tiō ē kā lán thuân.

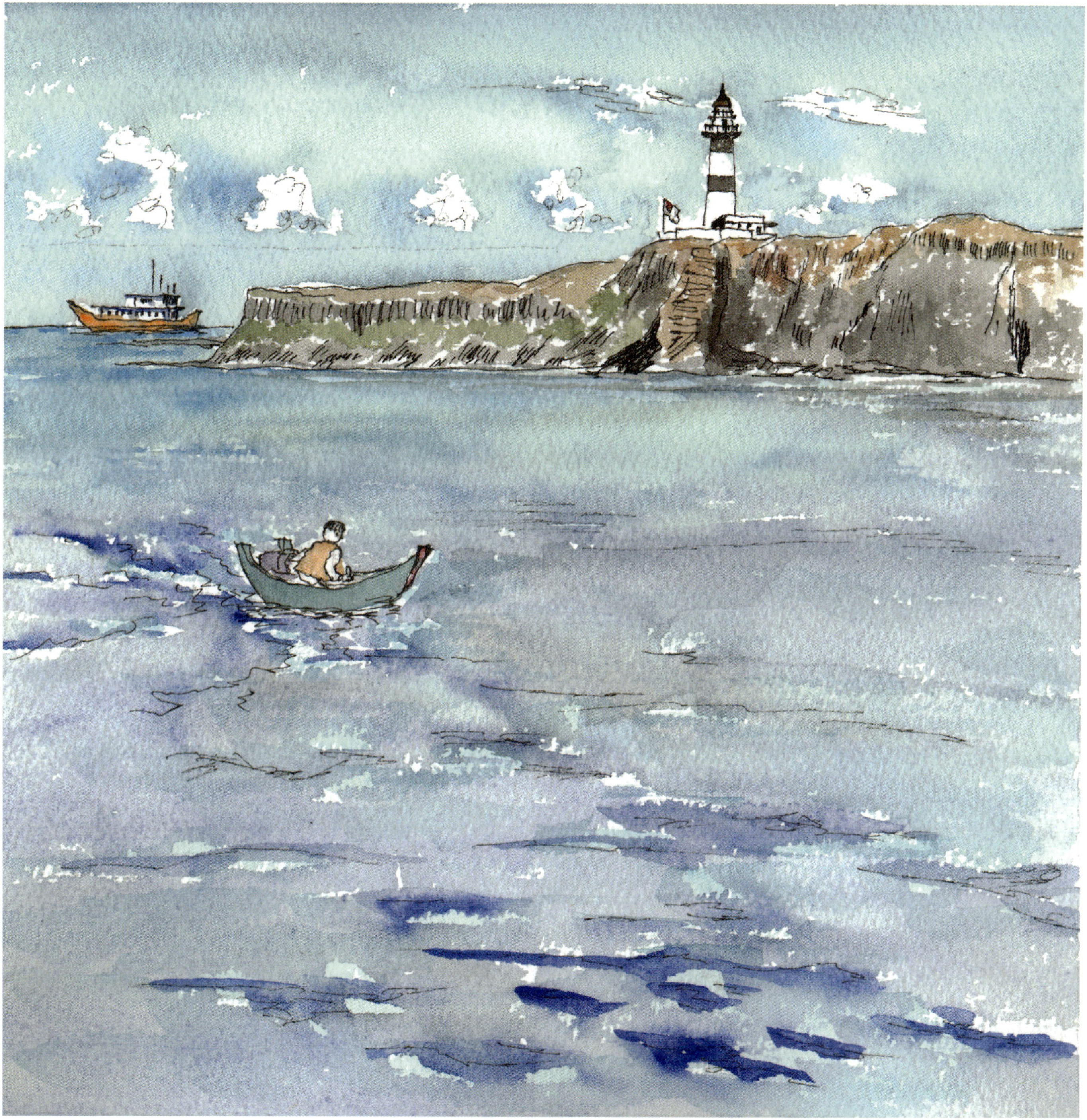

一座燈塔，一盞燈，東吉燈塔屹立百年，指引著黑水溝船隻，安定行船人的心。

The Tang-kiat (Dongji) lighthouse has stood for a century, guiding vessels navigating the Penghu Channel and providing peace of mind for sailors.

東吉村位於澎湖的東南方，與台灣隔著一條「黑水溝」。天氣惡劣時，狂風驟起，巨浪翻湧，湍急的水流使得海面更加危險。特別是在夜晚，若駕船不慎進入黑水溝，翻船的危險便隨之而來。為了保護航行的船隻，東吉村很早就設立一座燈塔，這道光芒指引著從澎湖、台南、高雄往返的船艘，讓他們找到回家的路。此外，東吉的氣象站肩負著預報的使命，每日觀測天氣狀況，並將這些信息傳送到氣象電台。漁民們透過收音機，便能及時獲知海上天氣，從而做出是否出海捕魚的選擇。

• • •

Tang-kiat (Dongji) Island is south east of the Penghu archipelago, separated from Taiwan by the Penghu Channel. During bad weather, strong winds create towering waves and fast currents make the sea perilous. At night, if a boat accidentally enters the Penghu Channel, the risk of capsizing increases. To protect vessels, a lighthouse was established on Tang-kiat Island long ago. Its light guides boats sailing to and from Penghu, Tainan and Kaohsiung. The Dongji Weather Station, located on Tang-kiat Island, monitors weather daily and relays this information to the meteorological radio station. Fishermen can tune in for timely updates about sea weather to make informed decisions about fishing.

Sai-kiat-tshun
西吉村
Sai-kiat Island

西吉生活 靠 討 海

歹天　無港 覕　風颱

這款生活
　　　無人愛　甘願遷村出外來

Sai-kiat sing-uah khò thó-hái, pháinn-thinn bô káng bih hong-thai.
Tsit-khuán sing-uah bô-lâng ài, kam-guān tshian-tshun tshut-guā lâi.

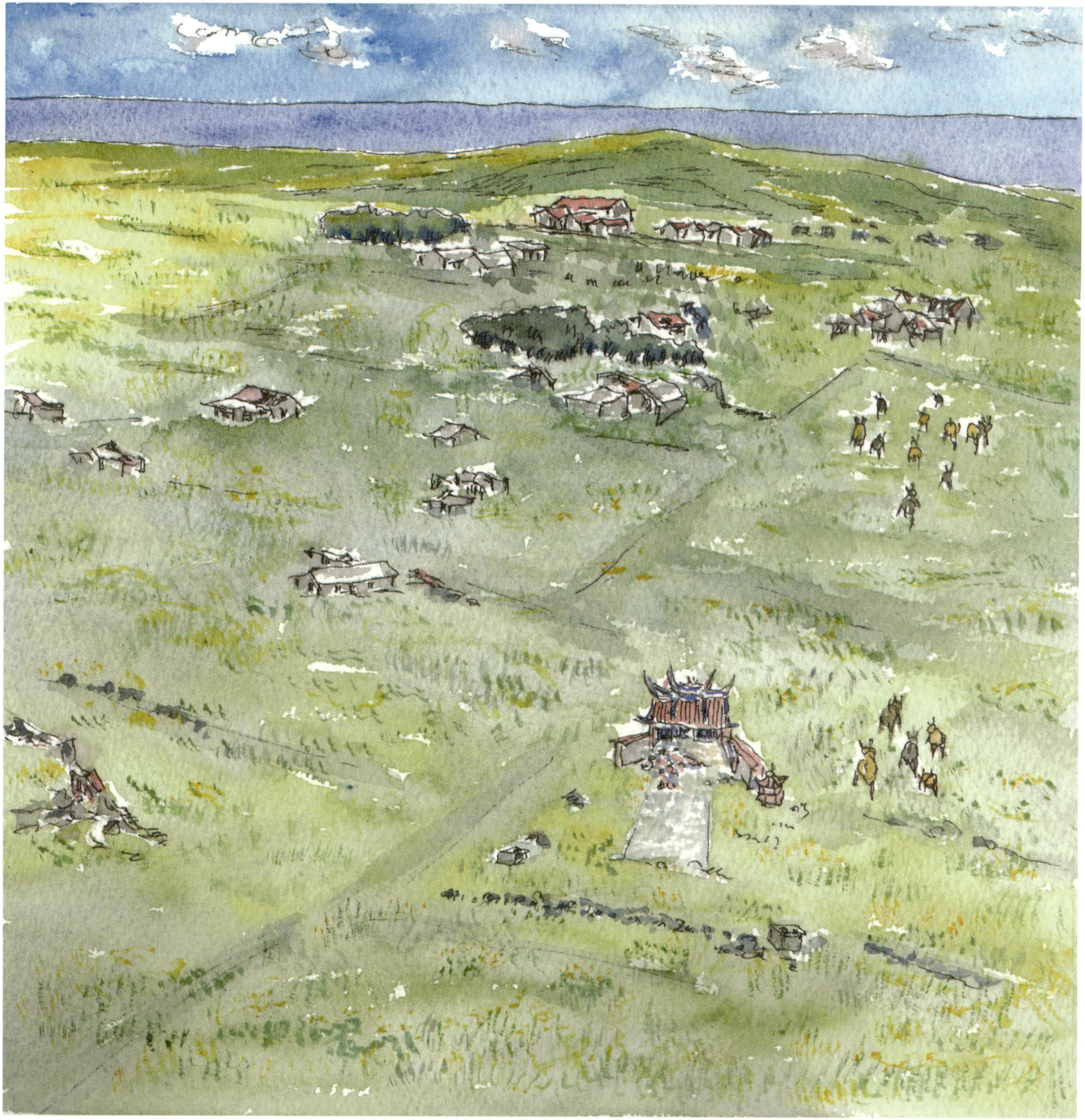

早年西吉嶼居住上百人,透過遷村計劃,1979 年正式裁撤西吉村。即使人去樓空,這些建築依然頑強地佇立在島嶼一隅,宛如時間的守望者。

In earlier years, Sai-kiat (Xiji) Island was home to over a hundred residents. However, because of a relocation plan, Sai-kiat Village was officially dismantled in 1979. Even with people gone, these buildings still stand in a corner of the island, like silent guardians of time.

西吉村因爲缺乏良好的港口，進出極爲不便。每當天氣不佳，船隻便無法找到安全的避風港，村民們仰賴著老天爺的臉色，村民都覺得很「驚惶」（kiann-hiânn）。這樣的處境使得居民渴望遷往更安全、更方便、更爲安穩的處所。

· · ·

Because of the lack of a good harbor, access to Sai-kiat (Xiji) Island became inconvenient. When the weather was poor, boats struggled to find a safe harbor, leaving the villagers at the mercy of the elements and causing them anxiety. This situation led local residents to feel that they did not want to live there and yearned to relocate to safer, more secure homes.

Tang-pîng-tshun

東坪村

Tang-sū-pîng Island

查埔查某上意愛　逐家招來耍小牌　若贏算汝蓋厲害　若輸後遍才閣來

若有興趣去藏沫　順細掠蟳佮掠蠘

驚熱毋免走去覕　阮的海水冷吱吱

冬天漁船無出海　麻雀群胡攏總來

踮佇東坪嘛四序　每工會當食鮮魚

冬天海釣大耳　熱天暗時舵鰱魚

Tuà tī Tang-pîng mā sù-sī, muí-kang ē-tàng tsiah tshinn-hî.
Kiann juah m̄-bián tsáu khù bih, gún ê hái-tsuí líng-ki-ki.
Tang-thinn hû-tsûn-á tiò tuā-hīnn, juah-thinn àm-sî-á tuā jiû-hî.
Nā ū hìng-tshù khù tshàng-bī, sūn-suà liah tsîm kah liah tshih.
Pháinn-thinn hû-tsûn-á bô tshut-hái, muâ-tshiok khûn-ôo-á lóng-tsóng lâi.
Tsa-poo tsa-bóo siōng ì-ài, tak-ke tsio lâi sǹg sió-pâi.
Nā iânn sǹg lú kài lī-hāi, nā su āu-piàn tsiah koh lâi.

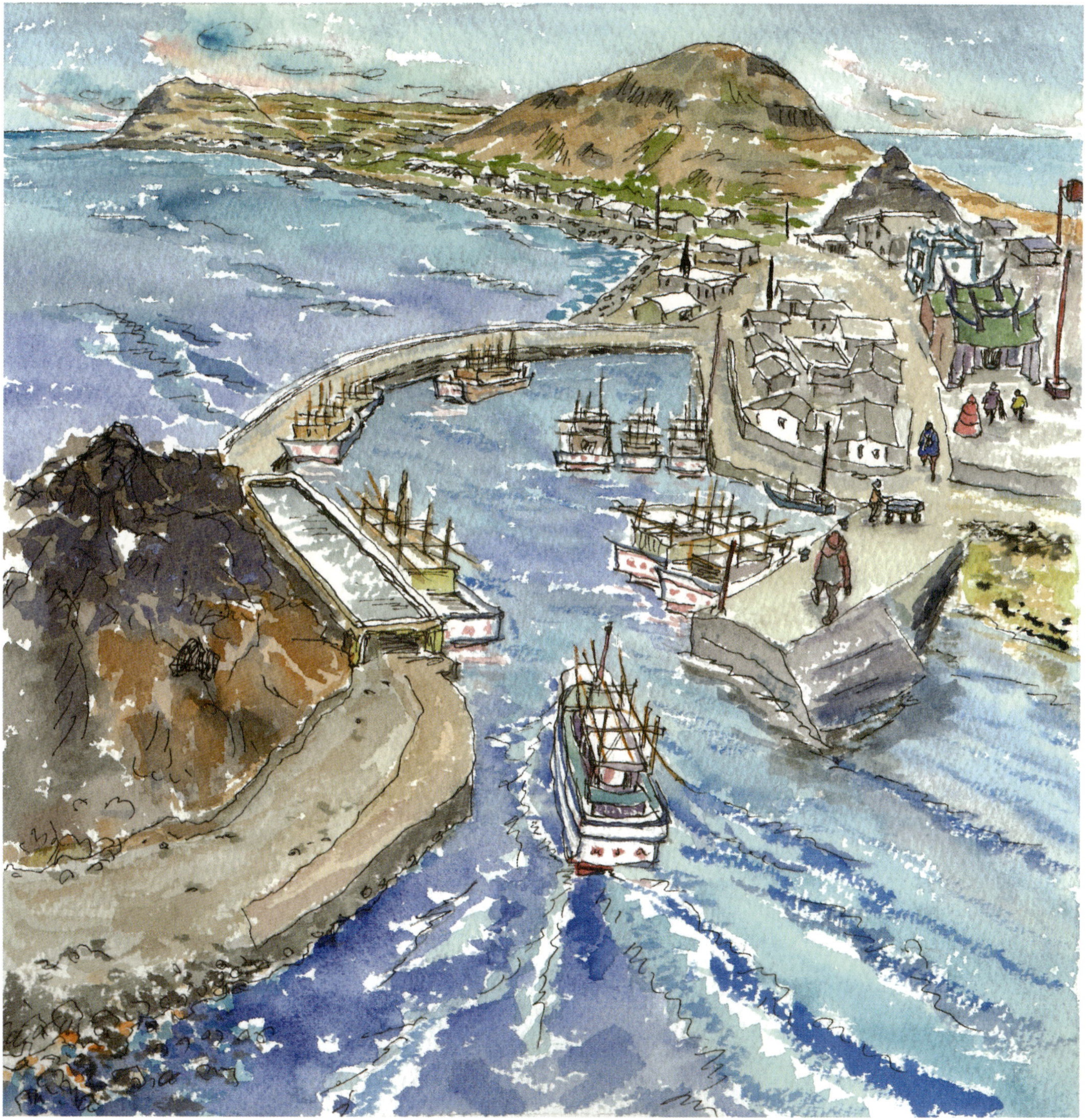

東嶼坪周圍的大海是嶼坪人的冰箱,運氣好的時候,小船就能有滿滿的漁獲。

The sea acts like a refrigerator for the island's residents; on lucky days, small boats return with a bountiful catch.

住在東嶼坪的日子眞的很愜意，每天都有新鮮的魚蟹可以享用，炎熱的時候就去海邊戲水。冬天如果天氣好，漁船就會出海釣大耳（馬鮫）；夏天的晚上，大家會出海釣魷魚。白天若有興致，可以潛水欣賞那美麗的海底世界，順便抓些蟳和蠘等蟹類回家。但是如果碰上壞天氣不能出海，村裡的人就會相約一起玩四色牌或麻將。贏的自然被大家稱讚，運氣眞好；而輸的人也不用煩憂，因爲總有下次的機會，再來拚一拚。這樣簡單質樸而快樂的生活，眞是「無懷氏，葛天氏之民也。」

・・・

Living on Tang-sū-pîng (Dongyuping) Island was wonderful. Every day we had fresh fish and during hot weather we would swim at the beach. In winter, if the weather was good, fishing boats would go out to catch Chinese mackerel (Scomberomorus sinensis); during summer evenings, everyone would go out to catch squid. If we had free time during the day, we could dive in and admire the stunning underwater world while catching some crabs to take home. However, if bad weather prevented us from going out to sea, the villagers would gather to play cards or mahjong. This simple life, when I think back, was filled with endless joy.

Sai-pîng-tshun
西坪村
Sai-sū-pîng Island

若蹛西坪上蓋好　遊山玩水好迌迌　／　欲食海魚家己釣　海坪嘛有肥石蚵

西坪好漢坡上崎　上山逐家攏愛行

全村的厝起山頂　厝頂看海上蓋清　／　夏秋睏佇磚坪頂　看著天星粒粒明

這个所在是仙境　親像神仙徛天庭　／　有錢袂曉按怎用　無煩無惱心清清

我會講甲遮詳細　故鄉永遠是咱的　／　有閒著愛轉去揣　伊是咱的老祖家

Nā tuà Sai-pîng siōng-kài hó, iû-san-uân-suí hó tshit-thô.
Beh tsiàh hái-hî-á kai-kī tiò, hái-phiànn mā ū puî tsiòh-ô.
Sai-pîng Hó-hàn-pho siōng kiā, tsiūnn-suann tàk-ke lóng ài kiânn.
Tsuân tshun ê tshù khí suann-tíng, tshù-tíng khuànn hái siōng-kài tshing.
Hā tshiu khùn tī tsng-pînn tíng, khuànn tiòh thinn-tshinn liàp-liàp bîng.
Tsit-ê sóo-tsai sī sian-kíng, tshin-tshiūnn sin-sian khiā thian-tîng.
Ū-tsînn buē-hiáu án-tsuánn īng, bô-huân-bô-ló sim tshing-tshing.
Guá ē kóng kah tsiah siông-sè, kòo-hiong íng-uán sī lán ê.
Ū-îng tiòh ài tńg-khù tshē, i sī lán ê lāu-tsóo-ke.

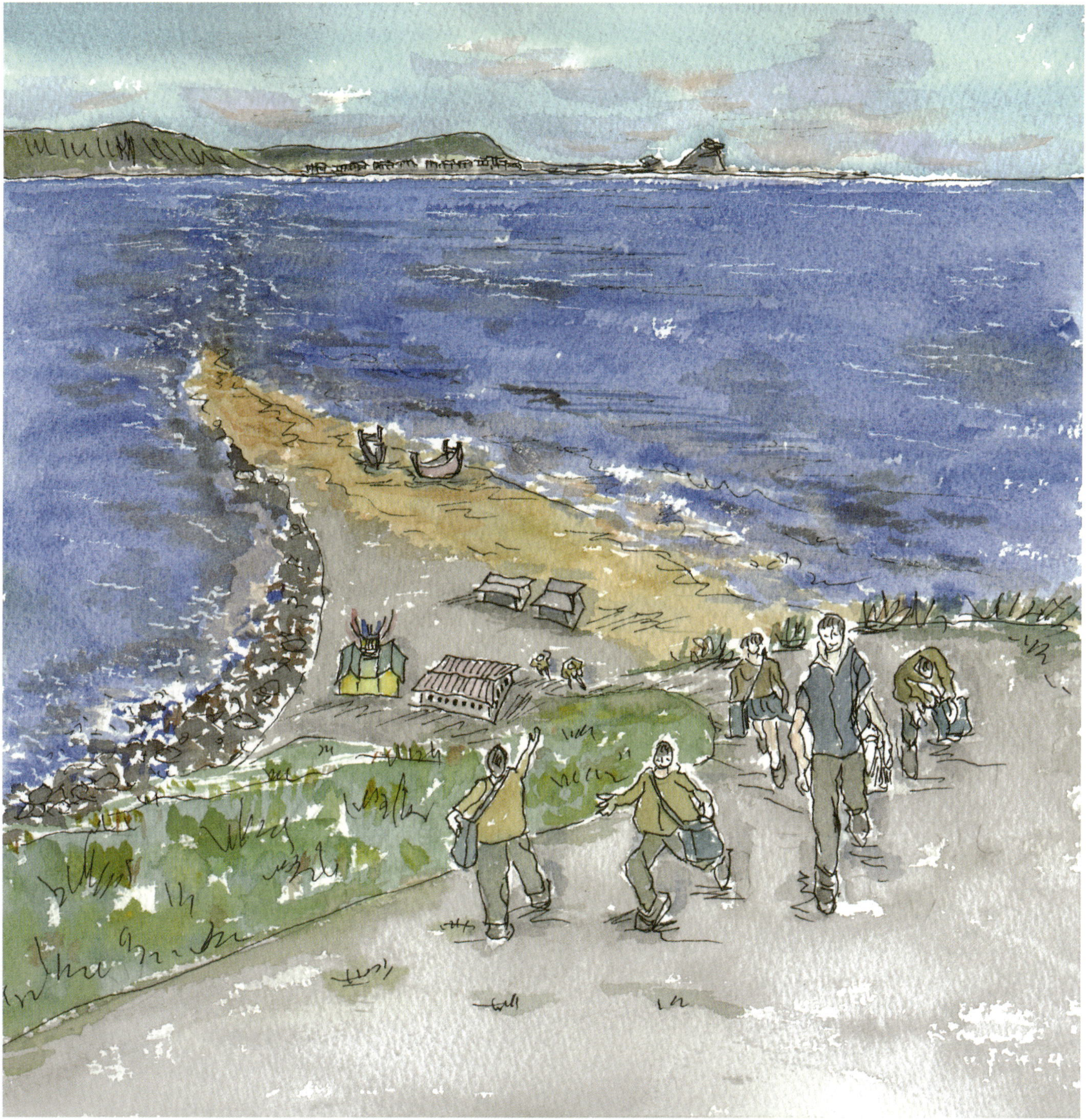

平坦的屋頂看似樸實無華,卻是西嶼坪村民白天觀景和晚上休息的好地方。

The flat rooftops may seem ordinary but they serve as excellent vantage points for villagers to enjoy the view during the day and rest at night.

西嶼坪真是個好地方，無論是戲水踏浪、釣魚，還是抓螃蟹和攕（tshiám）蚵仔，都充滿了樂趣。整個村子坐落在山頂，護龍的屋頂是磚坪頂，白天可以欣賞四周沿海的壯麗景色；而在夏秋的夜晚，到屋頂上睡覺，滿天的星星近在咫尺。由於這裡是三級離島，交通不便，村民們倚靠自然資源就地取材，就能自足，因此生活開銷不高。居民們似乎都沒有太多煩惱，彷彿生活在世外桃源中。故鄉永遠是我們的根，出外打拚的遊子，有時間就應當回去看看，重溫那份最熟悉的簡樸之美。

・・・

The shores of Sai-sū-pîng (Xiyuping) Island were filled with joy whether one was splashing in the water, fishing or catching crabs and oysters. The village was situated on a hilltop where traditional houses had flat brick roofs. During the day one could sit atop these roofs and enjoy the stunning coastal scenery; in summer and during autumn nights it was lovely to sleep under a sky full of stars that seemed within reach. As this was a remote island with limited transport the villagers relied on local resources, resulting in low living costs. The residents appeared to have few worries as if they were living in paradise. Regardless of the time, our hometown always held a special place in our hearts and for those who had moved away, it was important to return whenever possible to experience that familiar simplicity and beauty once again.

花嶼石頭坪的紫菜

煮塗魠湯頭有夠哈

煮臭肚湯頭嘛袂穤　欲食一碗著趕緊來

一碗若食落腹肚內　鮮甜的滋味才會知

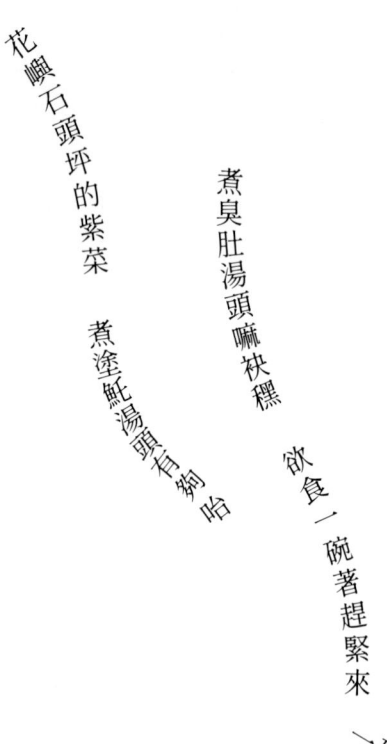

目睭䀹金比大拇指　食福的感覺是按呢

Hue-sū-tshun

花嶼村

Hue-sū Island

Hue-sū tsiȯh-thâu-phiânn ê tsí-tshài, tsú thôo-thoh thng-thâu ū-kàu hai.
Tsú tshàu-tōo-á thng-thâu mā buē-bái, beh tsiȧh tsit uánn tȯh kuánn-kín lâi.
Tsit uánn nā tshiȧh lȯh pak-tóo lāi, tshinn-tinn ê tsu-bī tsiah ē tsai.
Bȧk-tsiu thí-kim pí tuā-bó-tsáinn, tsiȧh-hok ê kám-kak sī án-ne.

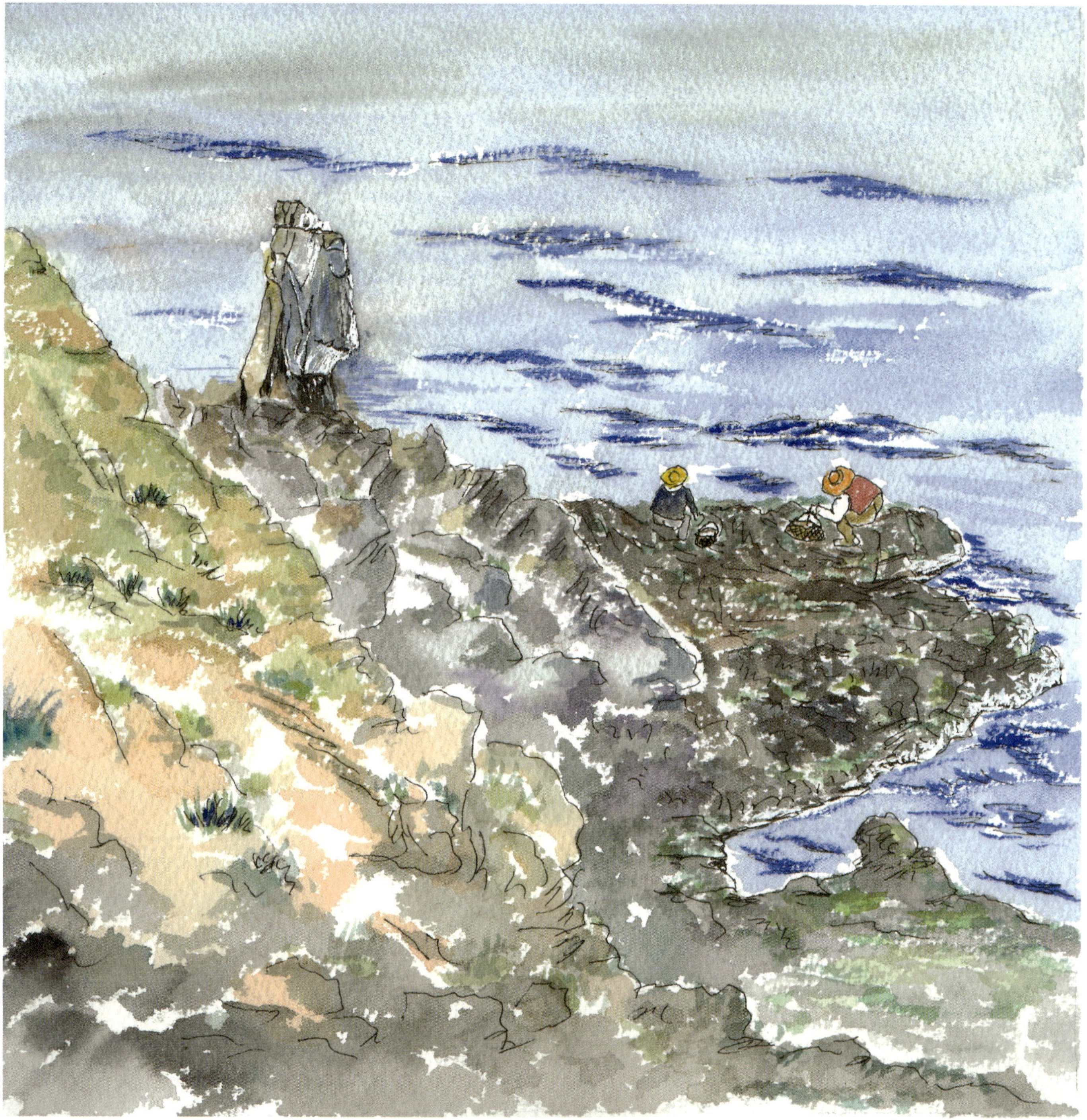

70 | 島嶼 TÓ-SŪ

花嶼海面的海蝕平台很平坦,在那裡剾(khau)起來的紫菜質佳味醇,沒有一粒砂石參雜其間。無論是用來煮土魠魚、龍尖魚還是臭肚仔魚,湯頭總是清甜可口,紫菜更是滑順美味,品嚐過的人就知道什麼是幸福的滋味。

• • •

The coastal platform of Hue-sū (Huayu) Island is flat and the water quality is excellent, resulting in high-quality seaweed free from grains of sand. When used to make fish soup, it provides a sweet and delectable flavor, while the seaweed is smooth and delicious, earning praise from all who have tasted it.

Tshit-bí-hiunn

七美鄉

Tshit-bí Island

七美舊名叫大嶼　遠遠看去遐大bu／個用石頭來起厝　嘛用石頭圍園坵

查某種作兼顧厝　查埔骨力去掠魚　　為欲生活較富裕　家家飼牛佮飼豬

　　豬仔細隻賣出去　　　　　　犁園種作留大牛

雙心石滬有夠媠　全用石頭疊來圍　　魚仔趖入滬內覕　母知走出靠滬邊

　　七美人塚人情味　　　　　　予咱想起古早時

　　女人貞節上在意　　　　　　甘願犧牲毋夆欺

七个招招跳入井　生根發葉長樹枝　　望恁靈聖來保庇　全島平安萬萬年

Tshit-bí kū-miâ kiò Tuā-sū, hn̄g-hn̄g khuànn--khù tsiah tuā bu. / In iōng tsio̍h-thâu lâi khí-tshù, mā iōng tsio̍h-thâu uî hn̂g-khu.
Tsa-bóo tsìng-tsoh kiam kòo-tshù, tsa-poo kut-la̍t khù lia̍h-hû. / Uī beh sing-ua̍h khah hù-jū, ke-ke tshī gû kah tshī tu.
Tu-á-kiánn suè-tsiah buē tshut-khù, luê-hn̂g tsìng-tsoh tsiah lâu tuā-gû.
Siang-sim-tsio̍h-hōo ū-kàu suí, tsuân iōng tsio̍h-thâu thia̍p lâi uî. / Hû-á sô jip hōo lāi bih, m̄-tsai tsáu tshut khuà hōo pinn.
Tshit-bí Jîn-thióng jîn-tsîng-bī, hōo lán siūnn-khí kóo-tsá-sî.
Lú-jîn tsing-tseh siōng tsài-ì, kam-guān hi-sing m̄ hông khi.
Tshit ê tsio-tsio ê thiàu jip tsínn, sinn-kun huat-hio̍h tióng tshiū-ki. / Bāng lín lîng-siànn lâi pó-pì, tsuân tó pîng-an bān-bān nî.

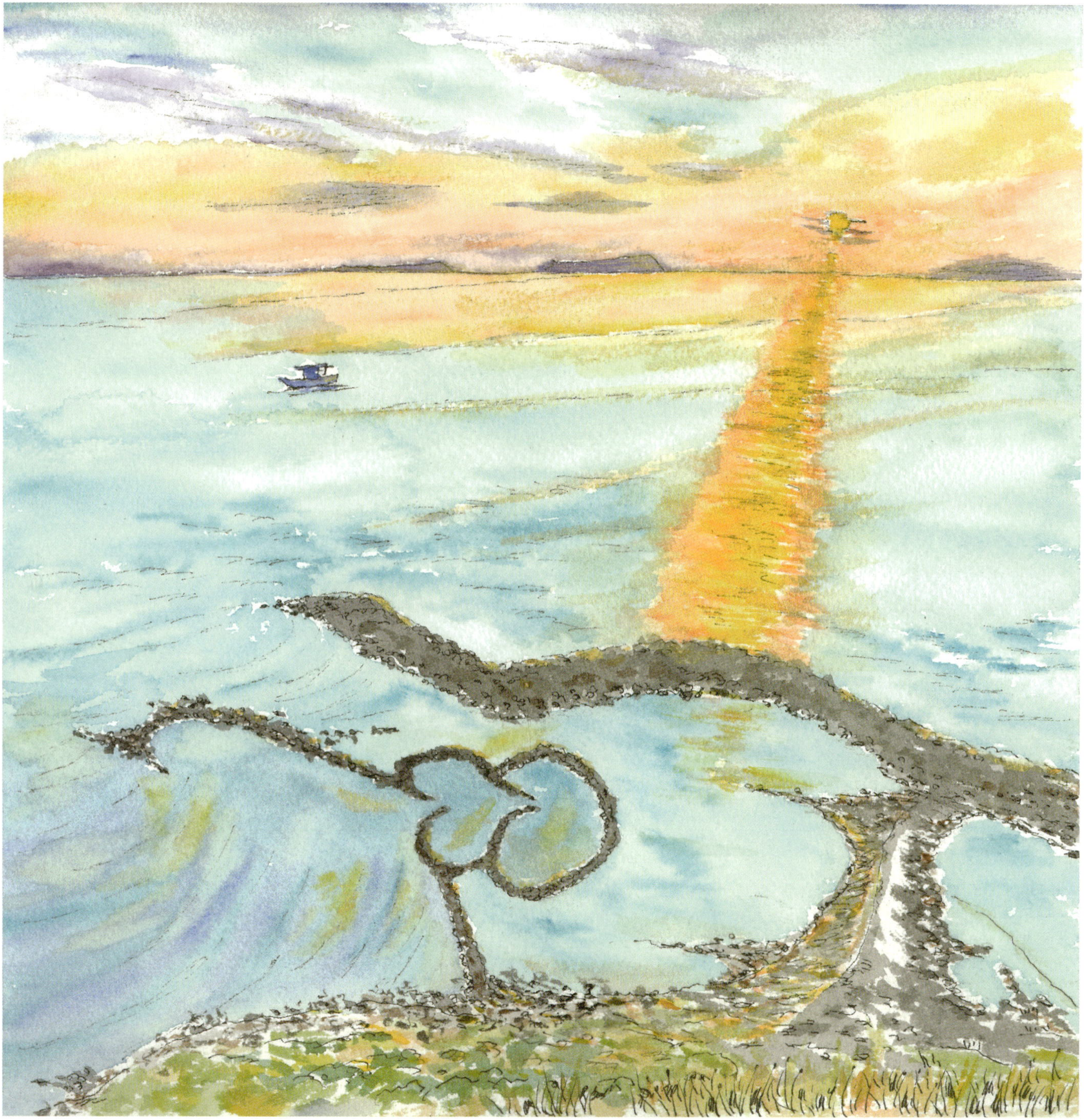

74 | 島嶼 TÓ-SŪ

七美鄉這座島眞的很大，過去叫做大嶼。這裡的男人們主要負責出海捕魚，而女人們則忙著種田和照顧家庭。爲了改善家庭經濟，大嶼人養豬，拍種（phah-tsíng，交配）後會生出很多小豬，所以其他離島的人想養豬，都會來大嶼購買。大嶼的東北海邊，有一個石滬叫做雙心石滬，漲潮時，水流進另一個石滬，退潮時，大魚往往搞不清楚就留在石滬裡，而小魚則能地從石頭縫溜回大海，眞是智慧又環保。不過，七美的歷史中也有悲傷的故事。據傳以前有倭寇想要侮辱七位美麗的姑娘，不願受辱的姑娘們一起投井自殺，後來這裡長出七棵樹。人們把這裡叫做七美人塚，後來就成爲人人敬仰懷念的觀光勝地，同時也把「大嶼」改名爲「七美」。

・ ・ ・

Tshit-bí (Qimei) Island is indeed quite large; it was formerly known as 'Tuā-sū', meaning 'big island'. In the past, the men here primarily fished at sea, while the women busied themselves with farming and taking care of the household. To improve their economy, the islanders kept pigs, allowing them to breed and produce many piglets. As a result, people from smaller islands would come to Tshit-bí Island to buy pigs. On the north eastern coast, there is a stone weir called 'Twin-Hearts Stone Weir'. During high tide, water flows into another stone weir and when the tide recedes, large fish often lose their sense of direction and become trapped, while smaller fish can slip through the gaps back into the sea. This method of fishing is clever and sustainable. However, Tshit-bí Island's history also holds sad stories. It is said that in the past, pirates sought to dishonor seven beautiful maidens. Refusing to be humiliated, the maidens jumped into a well to take their own lives. Seven trees later grew in that place, leading people to call it 'Seven Beauty Mound' and to change 'Tuā-sū' to 'Tshit-bí (Qimei)'.

TUĒ-KÍNG

地景

　　自從故鄉在 2014 年被劃爲澎湖南方四島國家公園後，呂坤翰體驗到「家園」轉變爲「公園」的變與不變。國家公園在海洋、生態和歷史等領域的研究成果，豐富了他對知識的渴望；東嶼坪的手作步道，不僅讓原本崎嶇陡峭的路變得更好走，更串連起島上的人文與自然地景。而他的家鄉，依舊以素樸的面貌，靜靜守護著這片土地。對他而言，「地景」成爲他對澎湖海陸兩域與家園心靈的抒發。

　　〈澎湖島嶼海產濟〉、〈海上漁田──箱網現流上鮮〉、〈珍貴海產──海膽〉等作品生動刻畫澎湖島嶼豐富的海洋資源，彷彿大海就是澎湖人的冰箱。而在〈澎湖南方四島蓋神奇〉、〈東坪山勢第一奇〉、〈嶼坪好山景〉三首作品中，無論是描繪陸地上的梯田景觀，或是海底瑰麗的珊瑚礁世界，都讓我們深切感受到他對土地紋理的細膩觀察。

　　此外，他也將返鄉參與修築步道的經過，寫出〈鋪路做義工〉、〈小王子平台〉兩首作品，唱出來自各地的志工，如何爲東嶼坪築出一條永續且充滿人文精神的手作步道。對於生態地景，〈澎湖縣花──天人菊〉和〈澎湖茗茶──風茹草〉展現了他的獨到觀察。最後，透過這些年的返家、凝視與回望，他寫下〈阮兜〉與〈三口井的故事〉，充分表達他對家的思念與對土地所承載記憶的深刻情感。

　　讓我們跟呂坤翰的作品，看見蘊藏在島嶼的時間足跡，並聽見來自地景的迴聲。

LANDSCAPE

Since his hometown was designated as the South Penghu Marine National Park in 2014, Lu Kun-Han has witnessed the transformation of 'homeland' into 'park', reflecting both changes and constants. The research from the national park on marine, ecological and historical aspects has given him a deeper insight into his homeland. The Eco-friendly Trail on Tang-sū-pîng (Dongyuping) Island not only eases the previously steep paths but also connects the island's cultural and natural heritage. Nevertheless, his homeland retains its simple charm. For him, these landscapes serve as a way to express his connection to his roots.

Works such as 'Rich and Diverse Seafood of the Penghu Islands', 'From Cage to Table: The Freshness of Fish Cage Farming', and 'Precious Seafood: Sea Urchin' vividly highlight the rich marine resources of the Penghu Islands, making the ocean seem like a larder for the islanders. Additionally, the terraced landscapes described in 'Four Rare Islands in Southern Penghu', 'Special Hills of Sū-pîng Islands' and 'Stunning Landscapes of Tang-sū-pîng Island', along with the breathtaking coral reefs beneath the waves, showcase his keen observations of the environment.

Moreover, he has chronicled his experiences in helping to build the pathways in pieces such as Inspiring 'Tales of Eco-Friendly Trail Volunteers on Tang-sū-pîng Island' and 'The Little Prince Viewing Platform', recounting how volunteers from various backgrounds joined forces to create a sustainable and culturally enriching Eco-friendly Trail on Tang-sū-pîng Island. His works 'My Homeland' and 'The Tale of the Three Wells' express his profound longing for his homeland and the deep emotions tied to it.

Let us explore the footprints of time etched in the island through Lu Kun-Han's works and listen to the echoes that resonate from the landscape.

島嶼上鮮是海產　落海欲提無困難　/　欲食龍蝦家己網　欲食海螺有青胭

熱天小管　配　海　膽
　冬天　紫菜　煮　龍　尖

　　　嘛有魚卵佮魚肱　上肥　塗魠　提　來　煎
　　　　　逐家　食了　會　思　念
　　　　　　　通人　呵咾　無　人　嫌

Phînn-ôo Tó-sū Hái-sán Tsuē

澎湖島嶼海產濟

Rich and Diverse Seafood
of the Penghu Islands

Tó-sū siōng tshinn sī hái-sán, lòh-hái beh thèh bô khùn-lân.
Beh tsiàh lîng-hê kai-kī bāng, beh tsiàh hái-lê-á ū tshinn-ian.
Juah-thinn sió-kńg-á phè hái-tám, tang-thinn tsí-tshài tsú lîng-tsiam.
Mā ū hû-nn̄g kah hû-kiān, siōng puî thôo-thoh thèh-lâi tsian.
Tak-ke tsiàh liáu ē su-liām, thong-lâng o-ló bô lâng hiâm.

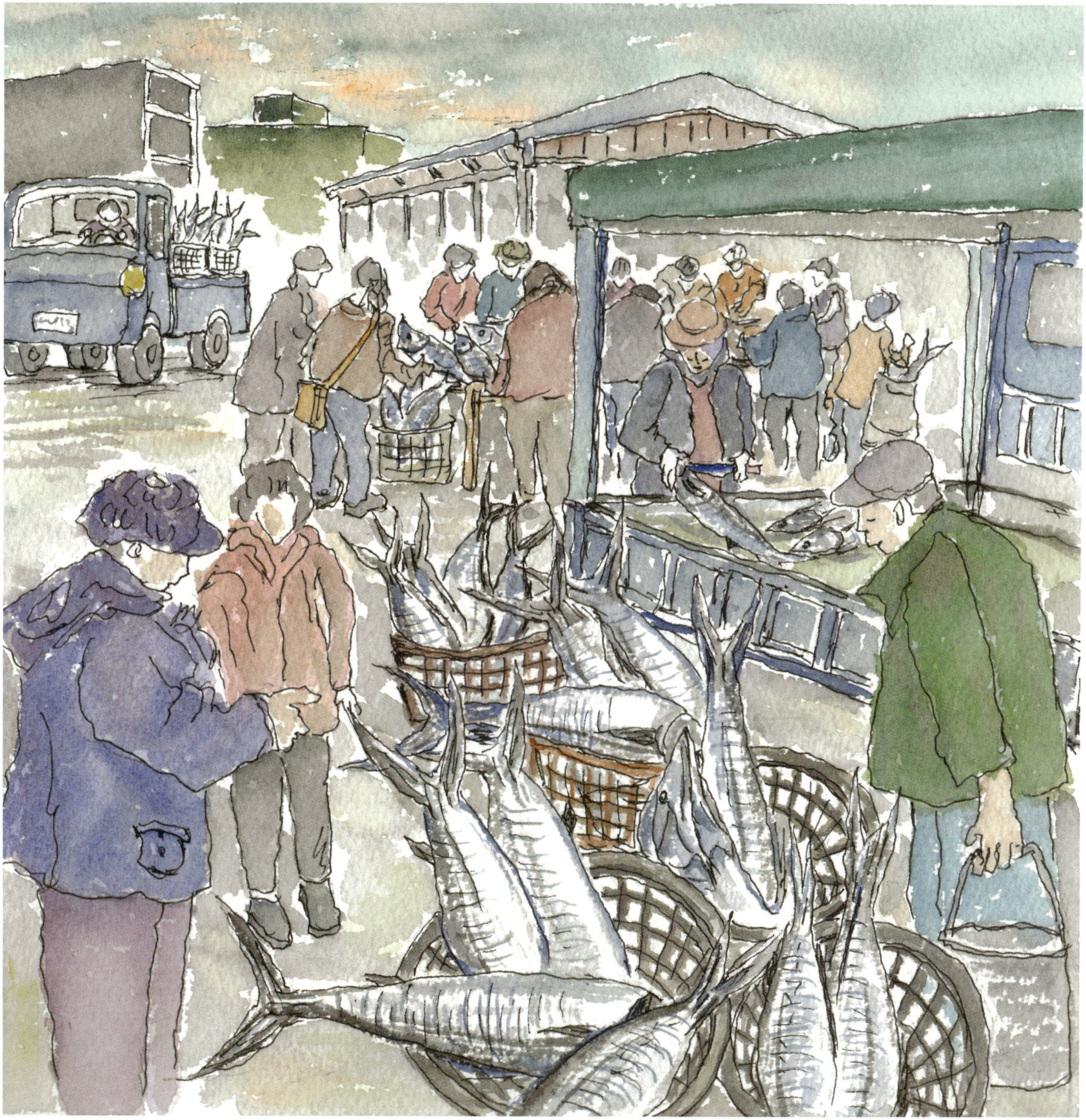

早年沒有冰箱，居民習慣將漁獲醃漬、曬乾、用日照和海風的方式封存食材，方便儲存。

Before the era of refrigerators, preserving food was challenging. As a result, residents would cure their catches and dry them in the sun and sea breeze, extending the shelf life of their food.

澎湖島嶼擁有豐富的海洋資源，想吃新鮮的海鮮，去海裡找，準沒錯。如果你喜歡龍蝦，可以自己去捕捉；如果愛吃螺仔，只需在海邊或海蝕平台上仔細尋找，就能撿到青胭（黑鐘螺）。到了夏天，小管和海膽盛產，正是享受海鮮的好時機。而冬天時，紫菜則成為了主角，尤其是搭配煮龍尖或土魠，湯頭鮮美得讓人直呼好吃。各種魚卵和魚腱也非常美味，每一口都讓人忍不住再來一口。在澎湖，這片豐富的海域讓每一餐都充滿期待，讓人徹底沉醉於美妙的海洋風味中。

· · ·

The Penghu Archipelago are blessed with abundant marine resources. If you are in the mood for fresh seafood, you can't go wrong by looking in the ocean. If you fancy lobsters, you can catch them yourself; if you love conch, just search carefully along the shore or on the rocky platforms. Summer is the peak season for pencil squid and sea urchins, making it the perfect time to indulge in seafood. In winter, seaweed combined with Spanish mackerel creates a broth that is simply exquisite. Various fish roe and fish tendons are also incredibly delicious, with each bite tempting you to take another. In Penghu, the rich marine resources make every meal a source of excitement and surprise, allowing you to immerse yourself fully in the wonderful flavours of the sea.

澎湖島嶼海產濟 Phînn-ôo Tó-sū Hái-sán Tsuē

Hái-siōng Hû-tshân – Siunn-bāng Hiān-lâu-á Siōng Tshinn

海上漁田——箱網現流上鮮

From Cage to Table: The Freshness of Fish Cage Farming

澎湖內海無汙染　海水清氣袂死鹹
來飼鹹水魚上讚　箱網圍海做漁田
一坵一坵來定點　坵
　　　　　　　　坵
　　　　　　　　網
　　　　　　　　線
　　　　　　　縛
　　　　　　相
　　　　　連
石斑海鱺飼規片　青喙加志佮龍尖
欲愛去撈便有現　清湯紅燒隨恁煎
現流的魚上新鮮　好食就是無人嫌
帶動觀光來發展　生理永遠接袂完

Phînn-ôo lāi-hái bô u-jiám, hái-tsuí tshing-khì buē sí-kiâm.
Lâi tshī kiâm-tsuí-hû siōng tsán, siunn-bāng uî hái tsò hû-tshân.
Tsit khu tsit khu lâi tīng-tiám, khu-khu bāng-suànn pa̍k sio liân.
Tsio̍h-pan hái-lē-á tshī kui phiàn, tshinn-tshuì-á ka-tsì kah lîng-tsiam.
Beh ài khù hôo piān ū hiān, tshing-thng âng-sio suî lín tsian.
Hiān-lâu ê hû siōng sin-sian, hó-tsia̍h tio̍h-sī bô-lâng hiâm.
Tài-tōng kuan-kong lâi huat-tián, sing-lí íng-uán tsiap buē uân.

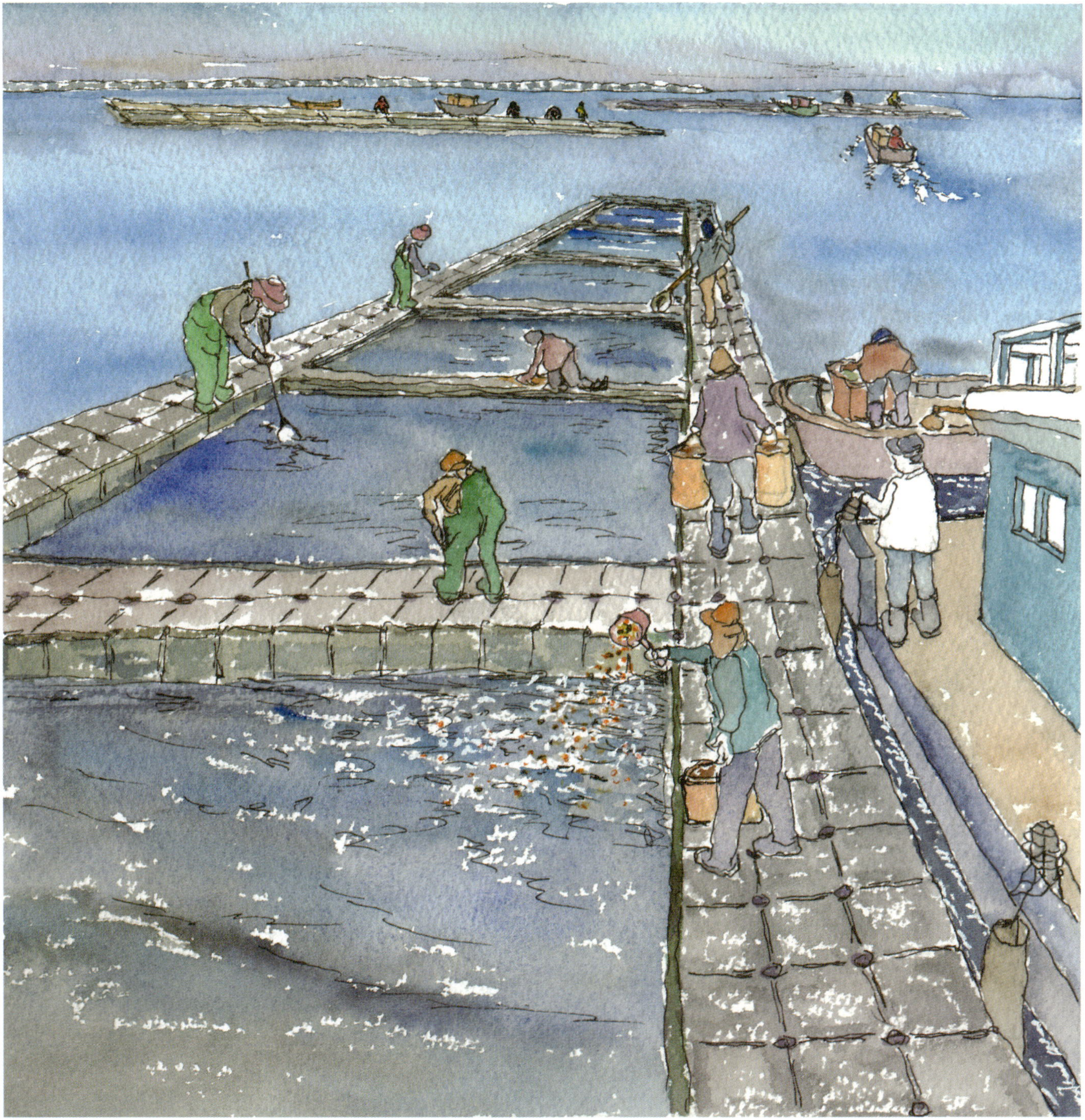

84 | 地景 TUĒ-KÍNG

澎湖因為沒有設立工業區，所以海水格外清澈，特別是內海，更是養殖鹹水魚的理想之地。在這裡，漁民們用魚網圍成箱型，將不同區域的箱網綁在一起，形成了一個個生機勃勃且海洋永續的養殖區，培育著各種美味的魚類，如石斑、海鱺、青嘴、加志和龍尖等。若想品嚐鮮魚，馬上去撈就有，現流最新鮮美味，觀光客最喜歡，商機當然暢旺長紅！

・・・

Penghu, having no designated industrial areas, boasts particularly clear waters, especially in the inner sea, which is an ideal location for cultivating saltwater fish. Here, fishermen use nets to create box-like enclosures, forming a sustainable marine farming area that nurtures a variety of delicious fish. If you fancy tasting fresh fish, you can simply go and catch some right away!

Tin-kuì Hái-sán – Hái-tám

珍貴海產——海膽
Precious Seafood: Sea Urchin

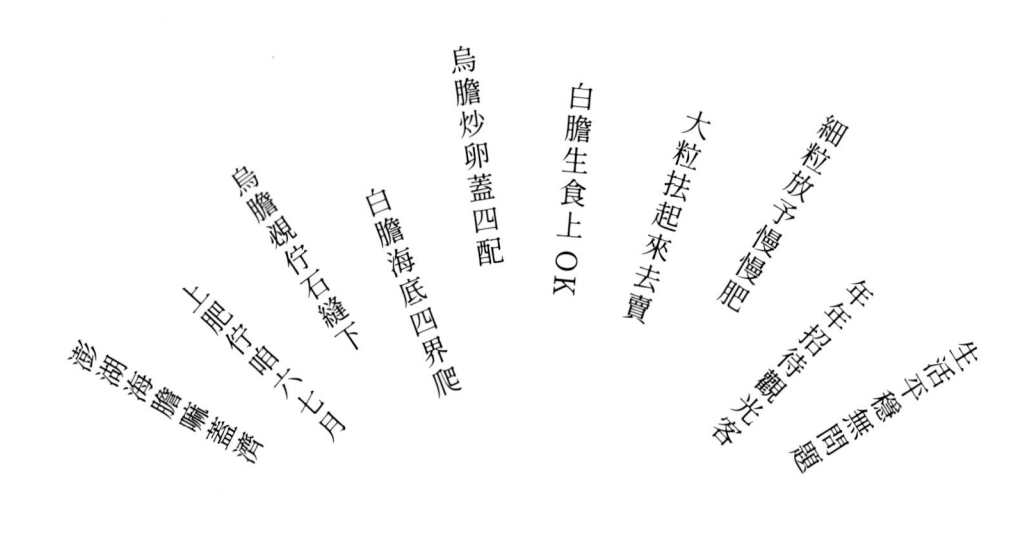

烏膽視行石縫下
上肥芛是六七月
澎湖海膽蕉薑齊

白膽海底四界爬
烏膽炒卵蓋四配

大粒抾起來去賣
白膽生食上 OK

細粒放予慢慢肥
年年招待觀光客

生活平穩無問題

Phînn-ôo hái-tám mā kài tsuē, siōng puî tī lán la̍k-tshit ge̍h.
Oo-tám bih tī tsio̍h-phang ē, pe̍h-tám hái-tué sì-kuè pê.
Oo-tám tshá nn̄g kài sù-phuè, pe̍h-tám tshinn-tsia̍h siōng "óo-khe".
Tuā-lia̍p-ê khioh khí lâi-khù buē, suè-lia̍p-ê pàng hōo bān-bān-á puî.
Nî-nî tsiau-thāi kuan-kong-kheh, sing-ua̍h pîng-ún bô-būn-tuê.

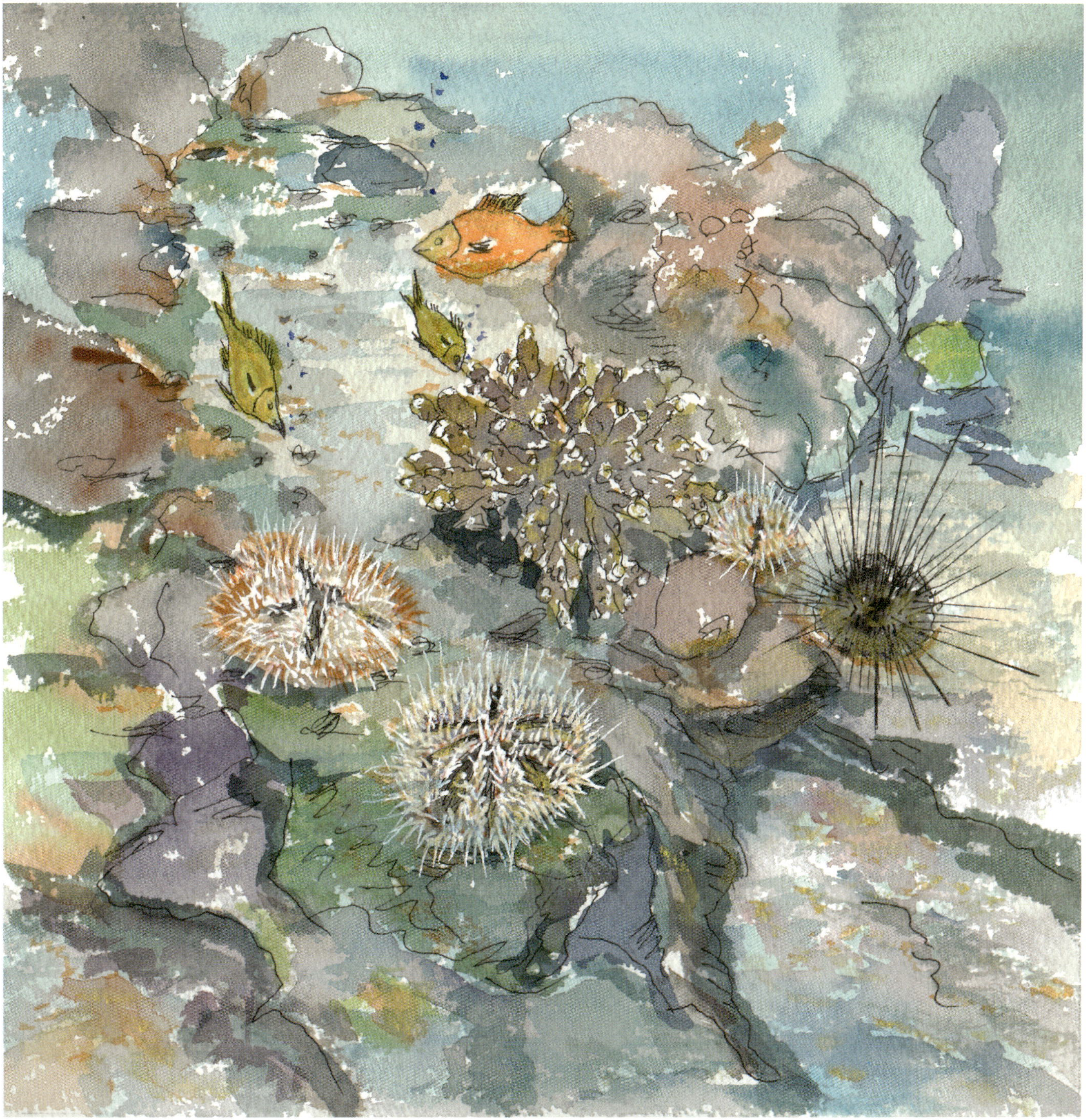

88 ｜地景 TUĒ-KÍNG

海膽營養豐富，味道甘甜、口感極佳，但價格也不便宜。每年農曆六、七月，正是海膽最肥美的季節，這段時間政府會開放漁民下海採收。海膽有兩種常見的種類：黑膽刺長，叫做長刺海膽，它們躲在石縫中，肉質較香，最適合拿來炒蛋或炒高麗菜干，風味絕佳。白膽刺短叫做馬糞海膽，常在海底覓食，肉質甘甜，無論生吃還是搭配冬菜、冬粉煮湯，都非常美味。每年夏天，來到澎湖的觀光客們，最愛品嚐的就是這美味的海膽，讓人一試圈粉，回味無窮。

• • •

Sea urchins are highly nutritious, with a sweet flavor and excellent texture, but they come at a price. Each year, during the lunar months of June and July, it is the peak season for delicious sea urchins and the government allows fishermen to harvest them. There are two common types. One is the black sea urchin, characterised by its long spines, known as the long-spined sea urchin. They hide in rock crevices and are perfect for frying with eggs or stir-frying with dried cabbage, yielding exceptional flavor. In contrast, the white sea urchin, with short spines, is known as the red sea urchin and is often found foraging on the sea floor. Whether eaten raw or used in a soup with seaweed, it is incredibly delicious. Each summer, tourists visiting Penghu particularly enjoy these delectable sea urchins, which leave a lasting impression and keep them coming back for more.

Phînn-ôo Lâm-hong-sì-tó Kài Sîn-kî

澎湖南方四島蓋神奇
Four Rare Islands in Southern Penghu

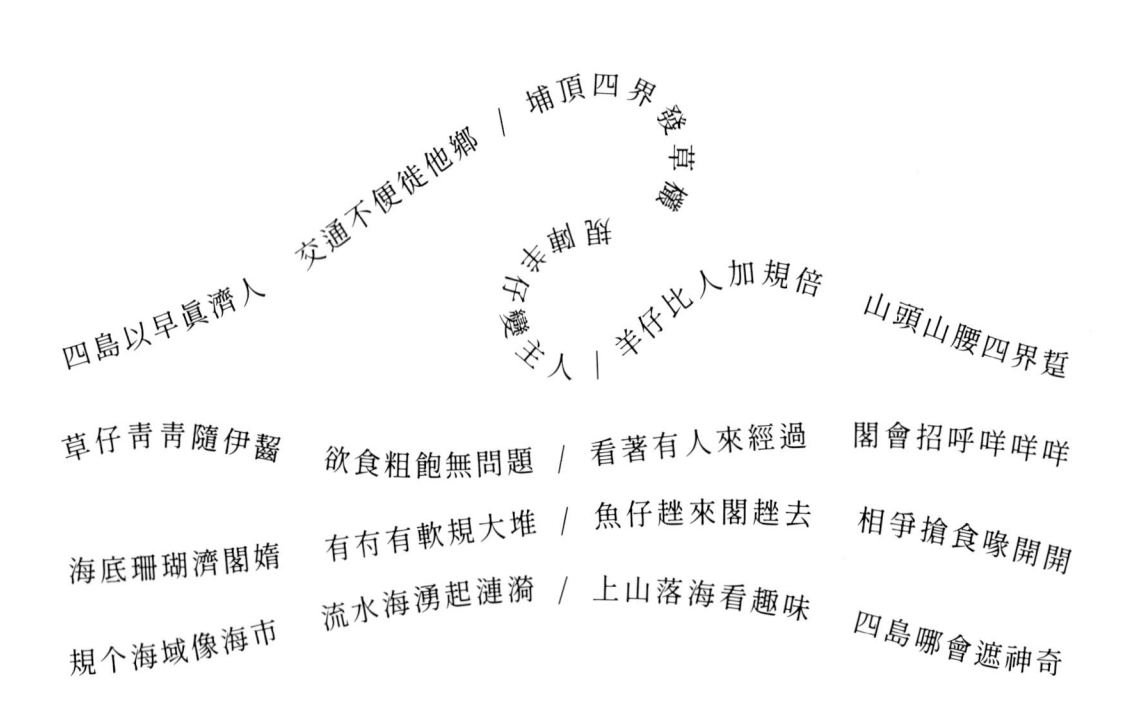

四島以早真濟人 ／ 交通不便徙他鄉 ／ 埔頂四界發草欉
草仔青青隨伊齧 ／ 欲食粗飽無問題 ／ 看著有人來經過 ／ 閣會招呼咩咩咩
海底珊瑚濟閣媠 ／ 有兇有軟規大堆 ／ 魚仔趖來閣趖去 ／ 相爭搶食喙開開
規个海域像海市 ／ 流水海湧起漣漪 ／ 上山落海看趣味 ／ 四島哪會遮神奇

羊欄女主人 ／ 羊仔比人加規倍 ／ 山頭山腰四界踅

Sì-tó í-tsá tsin tsuē lâng, kau-thong put-piān suá tha-hiong.
Poo-tíng sì-kuè huat tsháu-tsâng, kui tīn iûnn-á piàn tsú-lâng.
Iûnn-á pí lâng ke kui-á puē, suann-thâu suann-io sì-kuè sėh.
Tsháu-á tshinn-tshinn suî i khuè, beh tsiảh tshoo-pá bô-būn-tuê.
Khuànn-tiỏh ū-lâng lâi king-kuè, koh ē tsio-hoo me--me--me.
Hái-tué suan-ôo tsuē koh suí, ū tīng ū nńg--ê kui-tuā-tui.
Hû-á sô lâi koh sô khì, sio-tsinn tshiúnn-tsiảh tshuì khui-khui.
Kui-ê hái-hik tshiūnn hái-tshī, lâu-tsuí hái-íng khí liân-i.
Tsiūnn-suann lỏh-hái khuànn tshù-bī, Sì-tó ná ē tsiah sîn-kî.

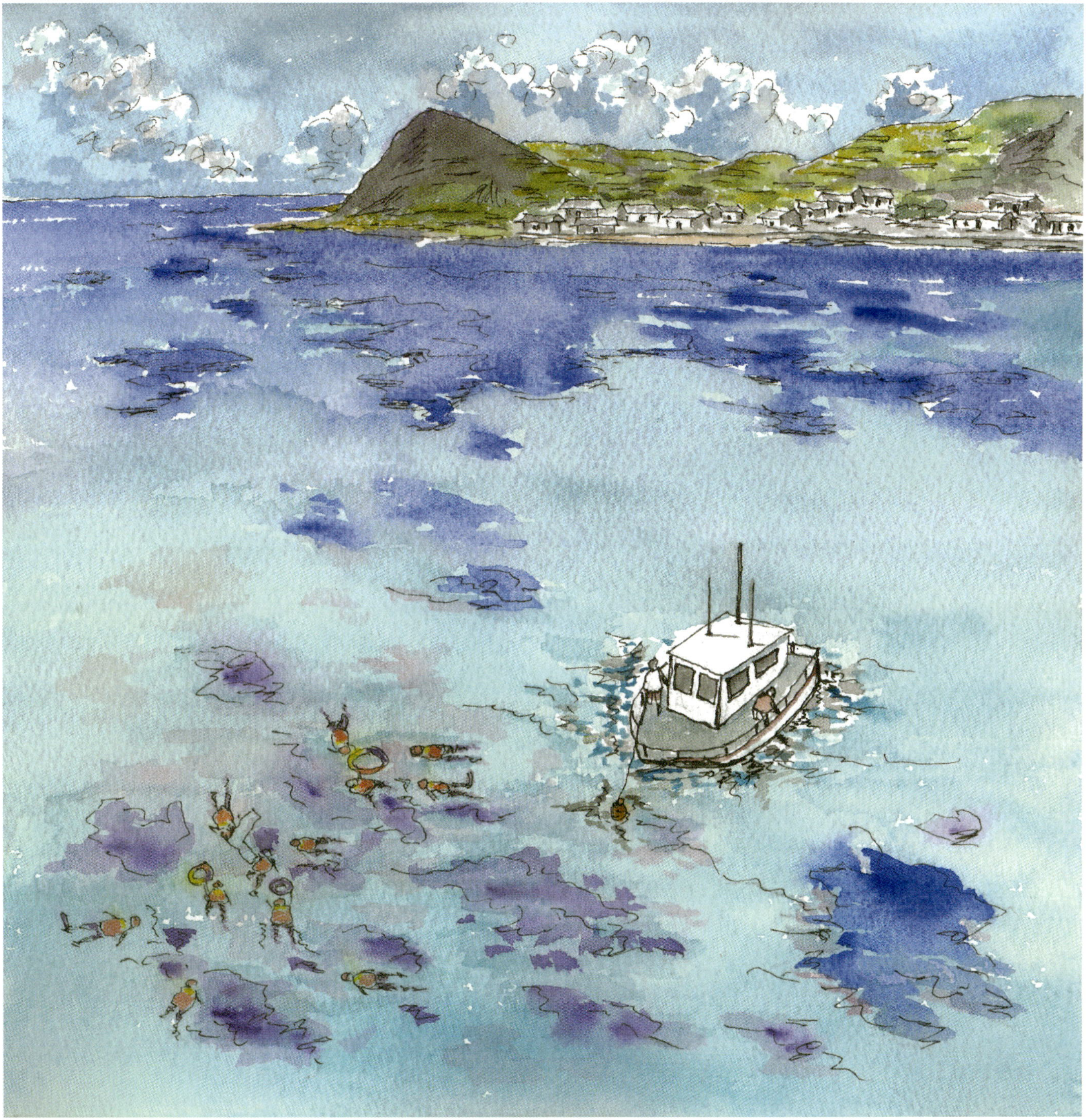

羊群是東嶼坪島上無法忽略的動物，試著從牠們的視野與足跡閱讀島嶼，往往會發現很多有趣的視角。

The goats are an unmistakable presence on the island. By viewing the world from their perspective and following their trails, one often uncovers a wealth of intriguing discoveries.

澎湖南方四島曾經有不少居民，然而，由於交通不便，人們相繼遷往外地。隨著居民的離去，島上長滿了野草，山羊們也因此自由自在地在島上生活與繁殖，甚至數量已超過島上的村民。每當遊客爬上坪頂的小山丘，遇見羊群時，羊兒們會發出咩咩的叫聲，彷彿在熱情地歡迎這些客人呢。南方四島的海底是一片瑰麗的珊瑚礁世界，無論是硬的或軟的，數量之多令人驚嘆。熱帶魚們成群結隊，在水中嬉戲，嘴巴張得大大的，互相爭搶著食物，場面頗為有趣！整個海底熱鬧非凡，再加上海流和波浪的流動與拍打，彷彿一座繁榮的海底城市。

• • •

The four islands of southern Penghu used to be home to many residents but because of inconvenient transport, people gradually moved away. As the inhabitants left, the islands became overgrown with wild grass, allowing goats to roam freely and reproduce, eventually surpassing the number of islanders. Whenever visitors climb the small hills of Tang-sū-pîng (Dongyuping) Island and encounter the flocks of goats, their bleating seems to welcome these guests warmly. Beneath the waters surrounding these islands lies a beautiful underwater world of coral reefs. Tropical fish swim in schools, playfully darting around with their mouths wide open, competing for food in an amusing display! The entire seabed is bustling with life and combined with the currents and waves, it resembles a captivating underwater city.

Tang-pîng Suann-sè Tē-it Kî
東坪山勢第一奇
Special Hills of Tang-sū-pîng Island

東坪前山有較崎　彎彎斡斡行上山　雖然行甲大粒汗　歡喜自然佇心肝

埔頂視野較曠闊　島嶼粒粒佇天跤　/　徛佇山頂向北看　後山是塊大斜坪

先人園仔一直搵　為顧腹肚度生活　/　園內嘛有種塗豆　番薯生湠盤過溝

高粱飽穗粒粒紅　番麥煤熟有夠芳　/　園仔看去有夠媠　一層一層若樓梯

『馬丘比丘』好名字　名共號甲會觸舌　/　徛佇埔頂看出去　遮是澎湖第一奇

Tang-pîng Tsîng-suann ū khah kiā, uan-uan-uat-uat kiânn tsiūnn-suann. / Sui-jiân kiânn kah tuā-liàp-kuānn, huann-hí tsū-jiân tī sim-kuann.
Poo-tíng sī-iá khah khòng-khuah, tó-sū liàp-liàp tī thinn-kha. / Khiā tī suann-tíng hiòng pak khuànn, Āu-suann sī tsit tè tuā tshuâ-phiânn.
Sian-jîn hn̂g-á it-tit iah, uī kòo pak-tóo tōo sing-uàh. / Hn̂g-lāi mā ū tsìng thôo-tāu, han-tsû sinn-thuànn puânn kuè kau.
Ko-liâng pá-suī liàp-liàp âng, huan-bèh sàh-sik ū-kàu phang. / Hn̂g-á khuànn khù ū-kàu suí, tsit tsàn tsit tsàn ná lâu-thui.
"Mā-tshiu-pī-tshiu" hó miâ-jī, miâ kā hō kah ē tak-tsih. / Khiā tī poo-tíng khuànn tshut-khì, tsiâ sī Phînn-ôo tē-it kî.

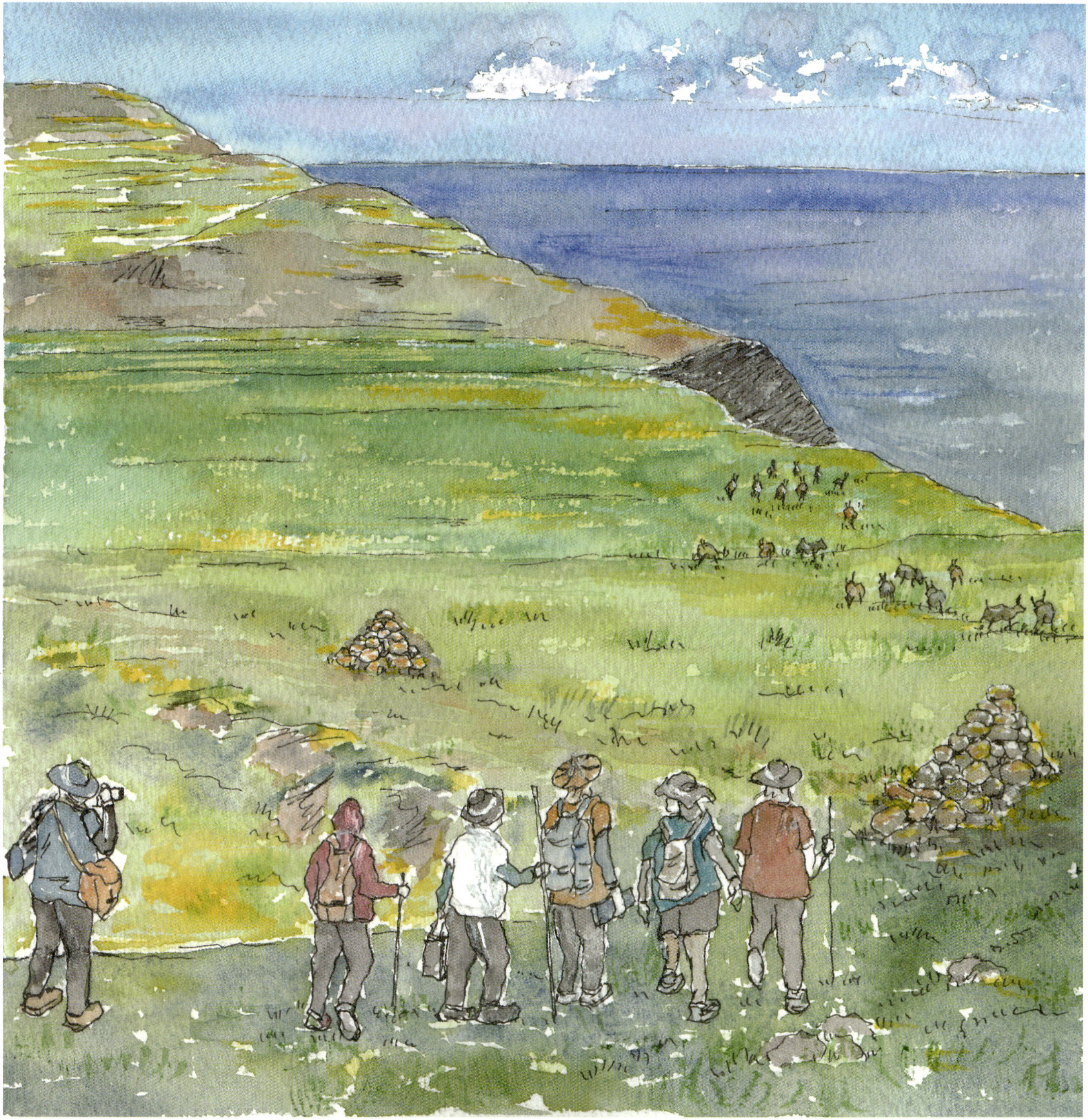

呂坤翰老師手指的方向是東嶼坪的梯田，日治時期，居民挑著玄武岩上山，堆砌成梯田，規模之大，宛如巨人的階梯。

The path indicated by Mr Lu Kun-Han leads to the terraces on Tang-sū-pîng Island. During the Japanese colonial period, residents carried pieces of basalt up the mountain to construct these terraces, creating a striking landscape that resembles a giant's staircase.

東嶼坪的前山陡峭險峻，行走其上需小心翼翼，踏著石階沿著蜿蜒的步道緩步攀登。因此，一步一步向坪頂挺進的遊客，都汗水淋漓。當抵達高處，眼前的美景瞬間將所有的辛勞化為清風；視野開闊，四周的島礁盡收眼底，壯麗的風光宛若一幅幅生動的島嶼畫卷，令人心曠神怡。

站在前山的制高點，向北眺望，映入眼簾的是後山那片綿延廣闊的斜坡。為了在這片土地上永續生活，先民們開墾了無數梯田，栽種花生、蕃薯、高粱與玉米。這些梯田遠望去，層層疊疊，猶如巨人的階梯，格外引人注目。外地遊客為此賦予台版「馬丘比丘」的名號，這特別的名稱無疑的，也是澎湖地區獨特的自然與人文景觀之一！

・・・

The small hill on the southern side of Tang-sū-pîng (Dongyuping) Island is quite steep. As a result, visitors tend to walk slowly upwards, sweating as they go. However, when they finally reach the summit, the breathtaking view makes them forget their earlier exertion. The expansive panorama reveals island reefs all around, creating a magnificent landscape that resembles a picturesque painting, refreshing the spirit. From the highest point of the front hill, gazing north, one is greeted by the sight of vast, rolling land. To sustain their lives on this soil, the earlier inhabitants cultivated countless terraces, planting peanuts, sweet potatoes, sorghum and corn. Viewed from a distance, these terraces rise in layers like giant staircases, capturing the attention of all. Many visitors refer to this place as Taiwan's 'Machu Picchu', a distinctive name that highlights one of the most special natural and cultural landscapes in the Penghu region!

Sū-pîng Hó Suann-kíng
嶼坪好山景
Stunning Landscapes of Sū-pîng Islands

東坪　西坪　好山景
龍虎東西分　兩　爿

毋驚大風　佮大湧
年年　護阮　過太平

Tang-pîng Sai-pîng hó suann-kíng, lîng-hóo tang-sai hun nñg-pîng.
M̄-kiann tuā-hong kah tuā-íng, nî-nî hōo gún kuè thài-pîng.

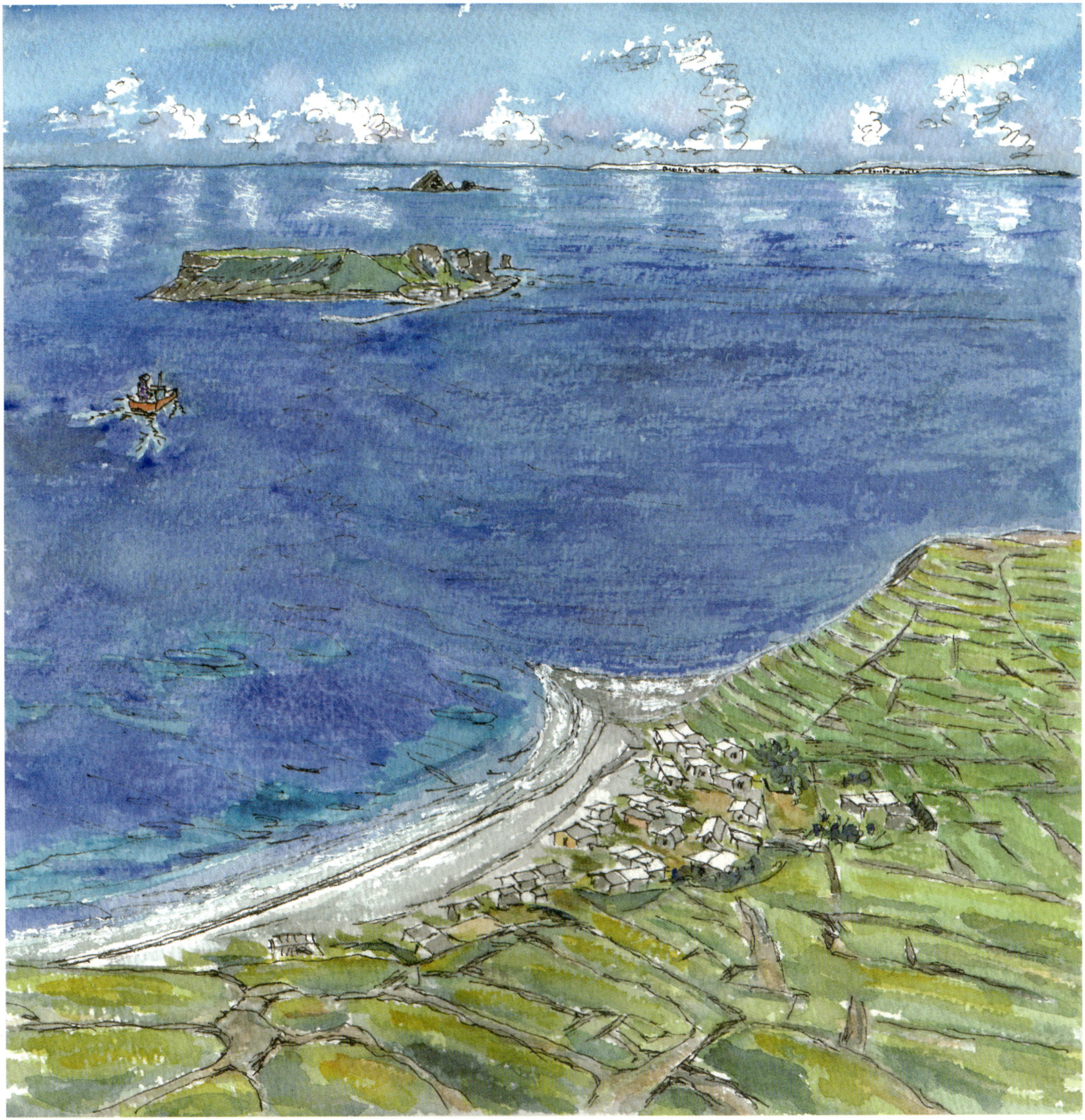

在東、西嶼坪兩島相隔的七百公尺之間，由於水淺、海流湍急，與地形交互作用之後，產生向南奔流的半月形浪潮，相當特殊。

Seven hundred meters wide, the strait between Tang-sū-pîng Island and Sai-sū-pîng Island features shallow waters and swift currents that interact with the terrain to create a unique southward-flowing crescent-shaped wave.

澎湖南方四島上有兩個小島，分別叫做東嶼坪和西嶼坪，當地人也稱東坪和西坪。兩座島相距只有七百公尺，彼此凝望。站在西嶼坪向東眺望，映入眼簾的是東嶼坪北側如同蟠龍般雄偉的山勢；而站在東嶼坪向西眺望，西嶼坪東側山丘則恰似一隻睥睨的老虎，靜靜守護著這片土地。這兩座島嶼的龍虎，不僅構成壯麗的自然景觀，各自守護著自己的島嶼，也象徵對家園的庇佑，讓人感受到精神上有所寄託。無論是伴隨著強勁東北風而來的洶湧浪潮，還是夏季肆虐的颱風，這兩座象徵著龍、虎的島嶼，始終庇佑著島上的村民生活平安順利。

・・・

Among the four islands in the southern Penghu region are two small islands known as Tang-sū-pîng (Dongyuping) and Sai-sū-pîng (Xiyuping), which are just 700 metres apart. The locals also refer to them as Tang-pîng (Dongping) and Sai-pîng (Xiping). Standing on Sai-sū-pîng Island and gazing east, one is greeted by the majestic mountains on the northern side of Tang-sū-pîng Island, which resemble the head of a dragon. Conversely, from Tang-sū-pîng Island looking west, the hills on the eastern side of Sai-sū-pîng appear like a tiger in repose, quietly guarding the land. This not only creates a magnificent natural landscape but also symbolises protection over the homeland, instilling a sense of spiritual solace. Whether it is the crashing waves brought by north east winds in winter or the raging typhoons in summer, these two landforms, symbolising the dragon and tiger, consistently safeguard the lives of the island's inhabitants, ensuring their safety and well-being.

Phoo-lōo Tsò Gī-kang
鋪路做義工
Inspiring Tales of Eco-Friendly Trail Volunteers on Tang-sū-pîng Island

九月三號好日子　逐家見面　笑微微

七早八早就距起　毋知是欲弄啥物

鋤頭掘仔帶帶去　嘛有手套佮畚箕

逐家攏是心自願　歡喜鬥陣做義工

東坪埔頂有較崎　上山確實　真歹行

路若做予平坦坦　阿婆來距嘛毋驚

國家公園逐家的　路草好行四界踅　/　美麗風景隨咱看　歡喜自然佇心肝

Káu-geh sann-hō hó jit-tsí, tak-ke kìnn-bīn tshiò-bi-bi. / Tshit-tsá-pueh-tsá tiō peh-khí, m̄-tsai sī beh lōng siánn-mih.
Tû-thâu kut-á tuà-tuà-khì, mā ū tshiú-thò kah pùn-ki. / Tak-ke lóng sī sim tsū-guān, huann-hí tàu-tīn tsò gī-kang.
Tang-pîng poo-tíng ū khah kiā, tsiūnn-suann khak-sit tsin pháinn kiânn. / Lōo nā tsò hōo pînn-thánn-thánn, a-pô-á lâi peh mā m̄-kiann.
Kok-ka-kong-hn̂g tak-ke ê, lōo-tsháu hó kiânn--luè sì-kuè seh. / Bí-lē hong-kíng suî lán khuànn, huann-hí tsū-jiân tī sim-kuann.

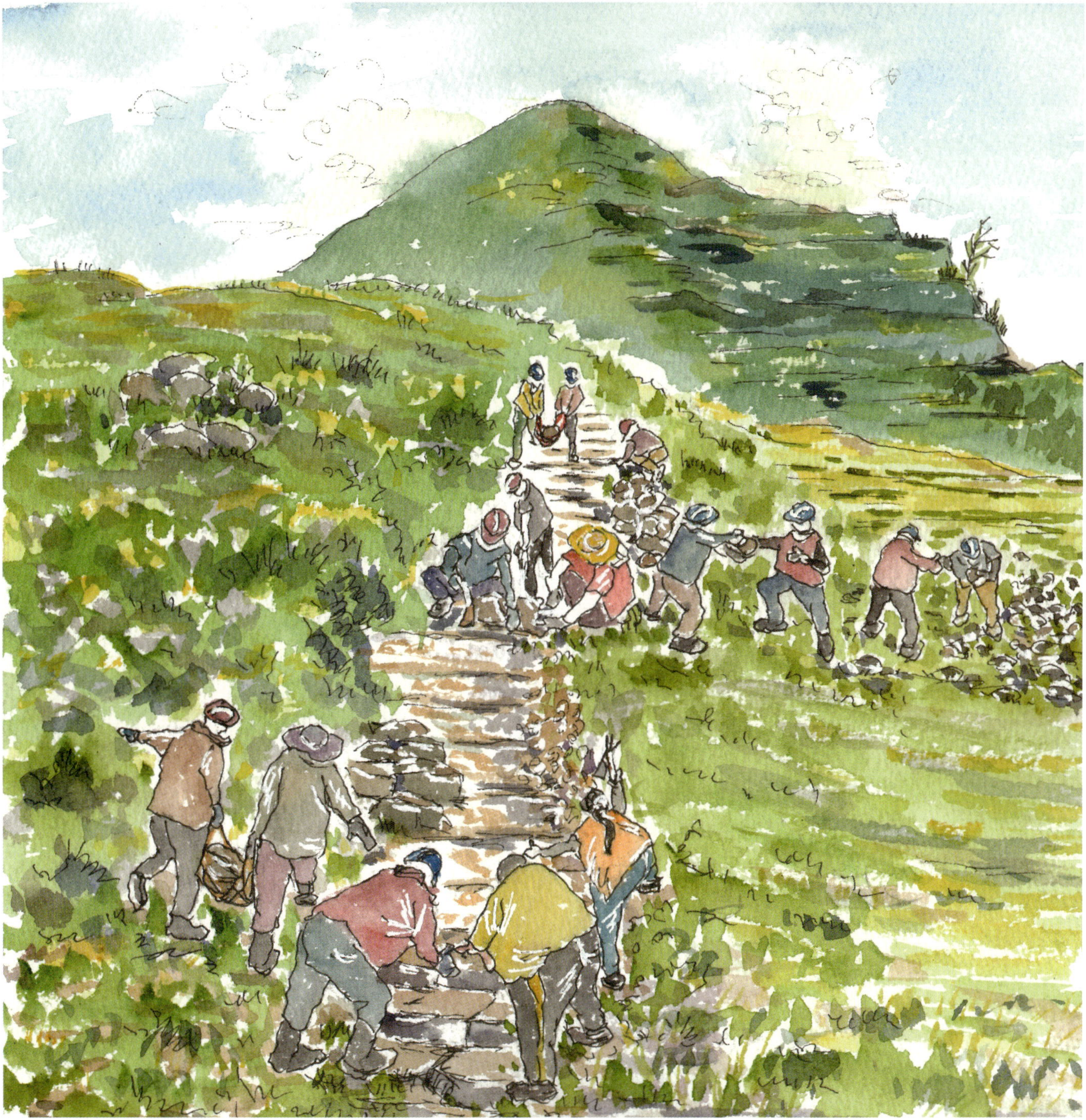

志工們攜帶各式工具，踏上東嶼坪前山步道，共同手護小島之路。

Volunteers come together with various tools to build and protect this eco-friendly trail with their own hands.

在清晨破曉之前，看到一群人早早上工，呂坤翰心中不禁充滿好奇，想知道他們在忙些什麼。只見他們每個人神情愉悅、精神抖擻，聽著步道師的指導，戴上手套、扛著大鋤頭、拿起畚箕和小掘子，朝著東嶼坪的前山而行。於是，呂坤翰也忍不住加入他們的行列，想要為家鄉出一份力。雖然上山的路陡峭不好走，但他的心中充滿使命感，心想：如果大家能把這條路修得更好走，即使是 80 歲的阿婆也能放心地走上來！這座國家公園是大家的，只要路好走，我們就能輕鬆享受四周的美景，感受與大自然融為一體的樂趣。

• • •

Before dawn, Lu Kun-Han noticed a group of people preparing to head out, which sparked his curiosity. He watched as they, filled with cheerful spirits, listened attentively to the trail leader's instructions. Putting on their work gloves, shouldering hefty spades, and gathering shovels and dustpans, they made their way towards a small hill in the southern area of Tang-sū-pîng (Dongyuping) Island to work on the path. Unable to resist the urge to join them, Lu Kun-Han decided to lend a hand for the sake of his hometown. The path was indeed steep and unwelcoming, yet for Lu Kun-Han, it felt like a mission. He thought to himself, "If we can make this path more accessible, even an 80-year-old grandmother could confidently make her way up here!" This national park belongs to everyone; as long as the pathway is well-built and eco-friendly, we can all enjoy the stunning surroundings and relish the joy of being immersed in nature.

Sió-ông-tsú Pîng-tâi
小王子平台
The Little Prince Viewing Platform

身徛小王子平台
美麗景色報恁知　/　早看日頭
海面起　日落彩霞半天邊　/　港邊有座
關公塔　往西閣有二塭礁　/　遠遠東南有鐘仔
近近校邊鐘座跤　/　東面閣有香爐礁　廟南嘛有四角跤　/
王子平台視野好　歡迎逐家來𨑨迌

Sin--khiā Sió-ông-tsú Pîng-tâi, bí-lē kíng-sik pò lín tsai.
Tsá--khuànn jit-thâu hái-bīn khí, jit--lȯh tshái-hâ puànn thinn-pinn.
Káng-pinn ū tsō Kuan-kong-thah, óng sai koh ū Lī-un-á-ta.
Hñg-hñg tang-lâm ū Tsing-á, kīn-kīn hāu pinn Tsing-tsō-á-kha.
Tang-bīn koh ū Hiunn-lôo-ta, Biō lâm mā ū Sì-kak-á-kha.
Ông-tsú Pîng-tâi sī-iá hó, huan-gîng tȧk-ke lâi tshit-thô.

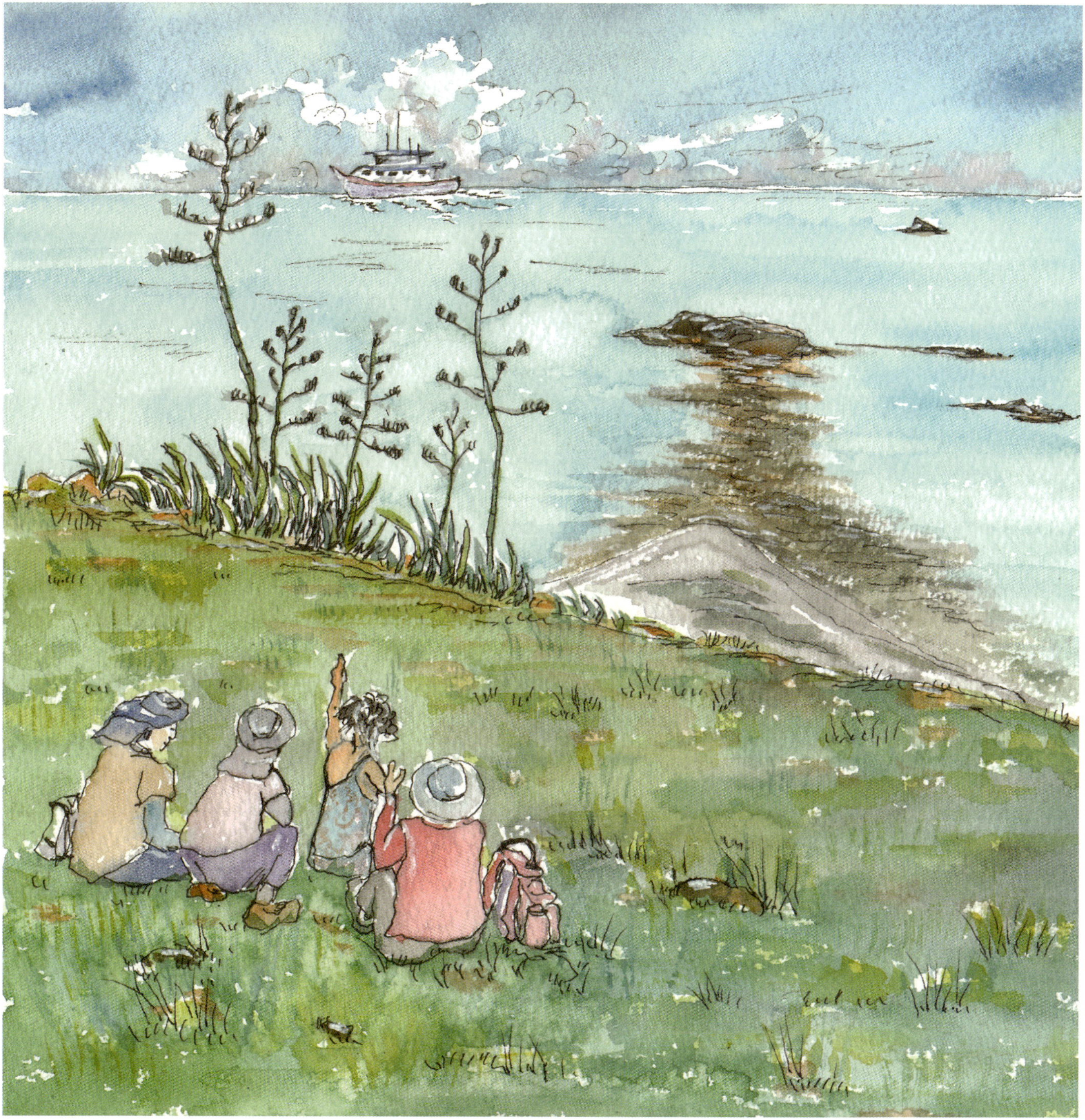

在「小王子平台」，同時欣賞日出與日落的絕美景色，左側是塔仔，右側則是二塭。

At the 'Little Prince Viewing Platform', one can enjoy the breathtaking views of both sunrise and sunset.

在東嶼坪前山的半山腰，有一片向南延伸的平台田地，這裡視野開闊，三面環景，讓人無限遐想。向東望去，東吉和西吉的美景映入眼簾，而近處的豬母礁和香爐礁形狀獨特，讓人不禁聯想到它們的名字。東南方可看到鐘仔，南方有南塭，西南方則遠看七美。西方視野遠看貓嶼，近看二塭、塔仔（關公石）及鐘座仔（青蛙石），西北方花嶼在遠處，西嶼坪近在咫尺。日出前，還有機會看到台灣本島的高山。步道師徐銘謙和其他志工們發現這片平台，宛如《小王子》中所提到的 B612 星球。「小王子平台」這個名字，讓呂坤翰直呼：是佳妙的聯想。

・・・

On a small hill in the south of Tang-sū-pîng (Dongyuping) Island, there is a viewing platform extending southward. This area offers expansive views, with beautiful scenery on three sides. Looking east, the picturesque sights of Tang-kiat (Dongji) Island and Sai-kiat (Xiji) Island come into view, while the nearby Tu-bó-ta (Zhumujiao) Reef and Hiunn-lôo-ta (Xianglujiao) Reef feature unique shapes. To the southeast lies Tsing-á (Zhongzi) Reef, to the south is the Lâm-un-á (Nanwen) Reef and to the south west stands Tshit-bí (Qimei) Island. In the west, Niau-sū (Maoyu) Isle is visible with the Lī-un-á (Lijian) Reef, the Thah-á (Tazi) Reef, and the Tsing-tsō-á (Zhongzuozi) Reef (Frog Rock) in the foreground, while Hue-sū (Huayu) Island can be seen to the north west and Sai-sū-pîng (Xiyuping) Island is just a stone's throw away. Just before sunrise, there's also a chance to glimpse the towering mountains of Taiwan. Trail Master Hsu Ming-Chien and the other volunteers discovered this viewing platform, likening it to the B612 planet mentioned in *The Little Prince*. The name 'Little Prince Viewing Platform' left Lu Kun-Han absolutely delighted!

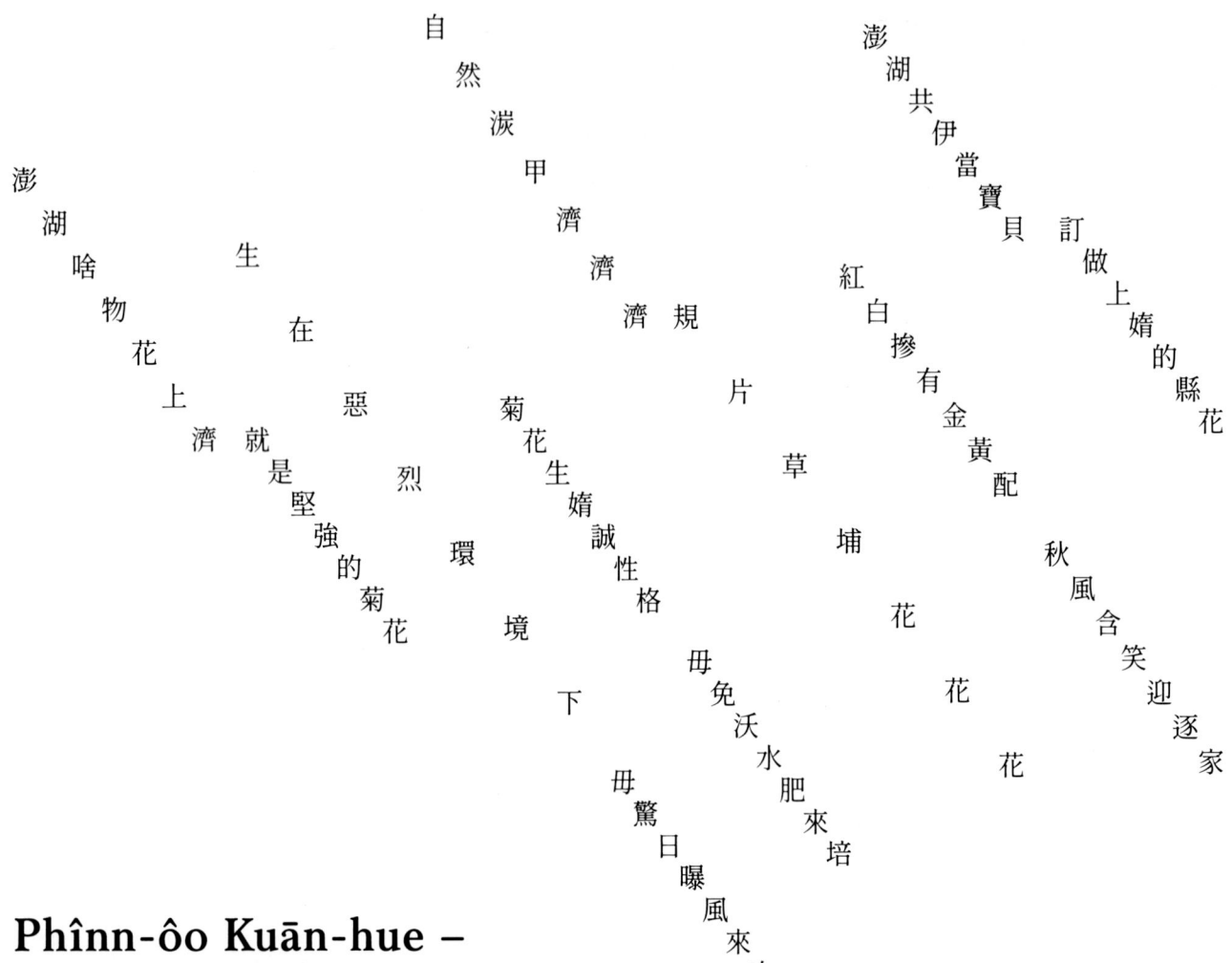

澎湖啥物花上濟 就是堅強的菊花
生在惡烈環境
自然湠甲濟濟濟規片
菊花生婿誠性格 母免沃水肥來培
母驚日曝風來吹
紅白摻有金黃配 秋風含笑迎逐家
澎湖共伊當寶貝 訂做上婿的縣花

Phînn-ôo Kuān-hue – Thian-jîn-kiok

澎湖縣花──天人菊

The County Flower of Penghu: Blanket Flower

Phînn-ôo siánn-mih hue siōng tsuē, tiō-sī kian-kiông ê kiok-hue.
Sinn tsāi ok-liát huân-kíng ē, m̄-kiann jit--phák hong lâi tshue.
Kiok-hue sinn suí tsiânn sìng-keh, m̄-bián ak-tsuí koh puî lâi puê.
Tsū-jiân thuànn kah sī tsuē-tsuē-tsuē, kui phiàn tsháu-poo sī hue-hue-hue.
Âng-péh tshàm ū kim-hông phuè, tshiu-hong hâm-tshiò gîng ta̍k-ke.
Phînn-ôo kā i sī tòng pó-puè, tīng tsuè siōng suí ê kuān-hue.

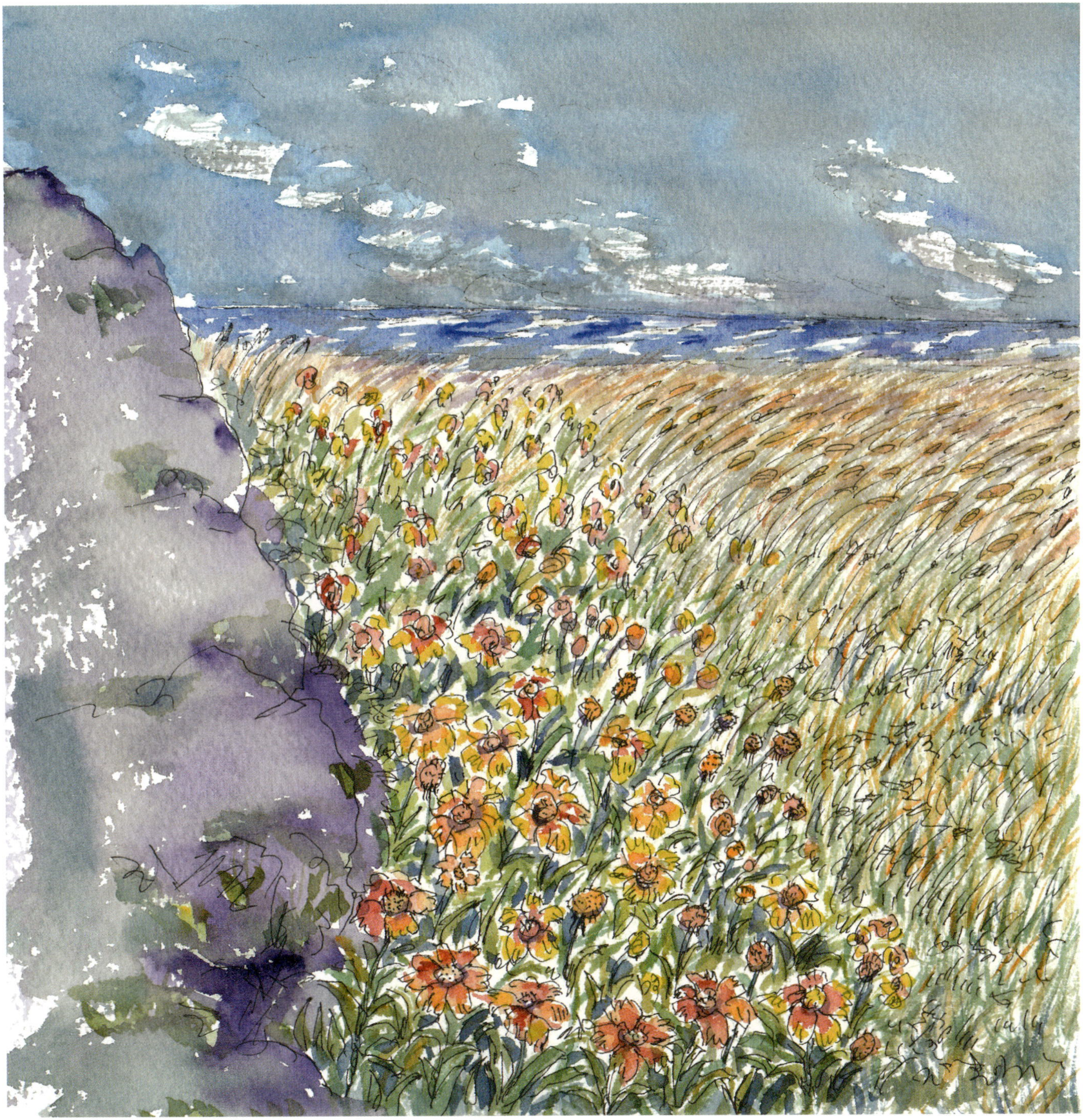

地景 TUĒ-KÍNG

澎湖最有名的花是什麼呢？是堅韌的天人菊。澎湖沒有高山屏障，冬天來的時候，強風和大浪把鹹水鬚（kiâm-tsuí-tshiu）吹得到處都是，路邊的草木都枯死了。即使在這樣惡劣的環境下，天人菊卻依然長得很自在。夏天雖然陽光強烈，雨水又少，但它們依然開得非常美麗。天人菊的花色有紅的、白的，還有金黃色的花蕊，尤其在秋天的時候，隨著秋風一吹，整片草坪上的天人菊「搖搖弄弄」（iô-iô-lāng-lāng），彷彿在熱情迎接大家。因此，澎湖人珍愛天人菊，選它作為縣花。

• • •

What is the most famous flower in Penghu? It is the resilient Blanket Flower. The landscape of Penghu lacks high mountains and during winter, strong winds and large waves carry salty moisture everywhere, causing the grass and plants by the roadside to wither. Yet, even in such harsh conditions, the Blanket Flowers continue to thrive. In summer, although the sun is intense and rainfall scarce, these flowers bloom beautifully. The Blanket Flowers appear in shades of red and white, with bright yellow at the centre. In autumn, when the breeze blows, the carpet of Blanket Flowers moves with the wind, warmly welcoming everyone. For this reason, the people of Penghu cherish the Blanket Flowers and have chosen them as the county flower.

Phînn-ôo Bîng-tê – Hong-jû-tsháu

澎湖茗茶——風茹草
Glossogyne tenuifolia: The Famous Tea of Penghu

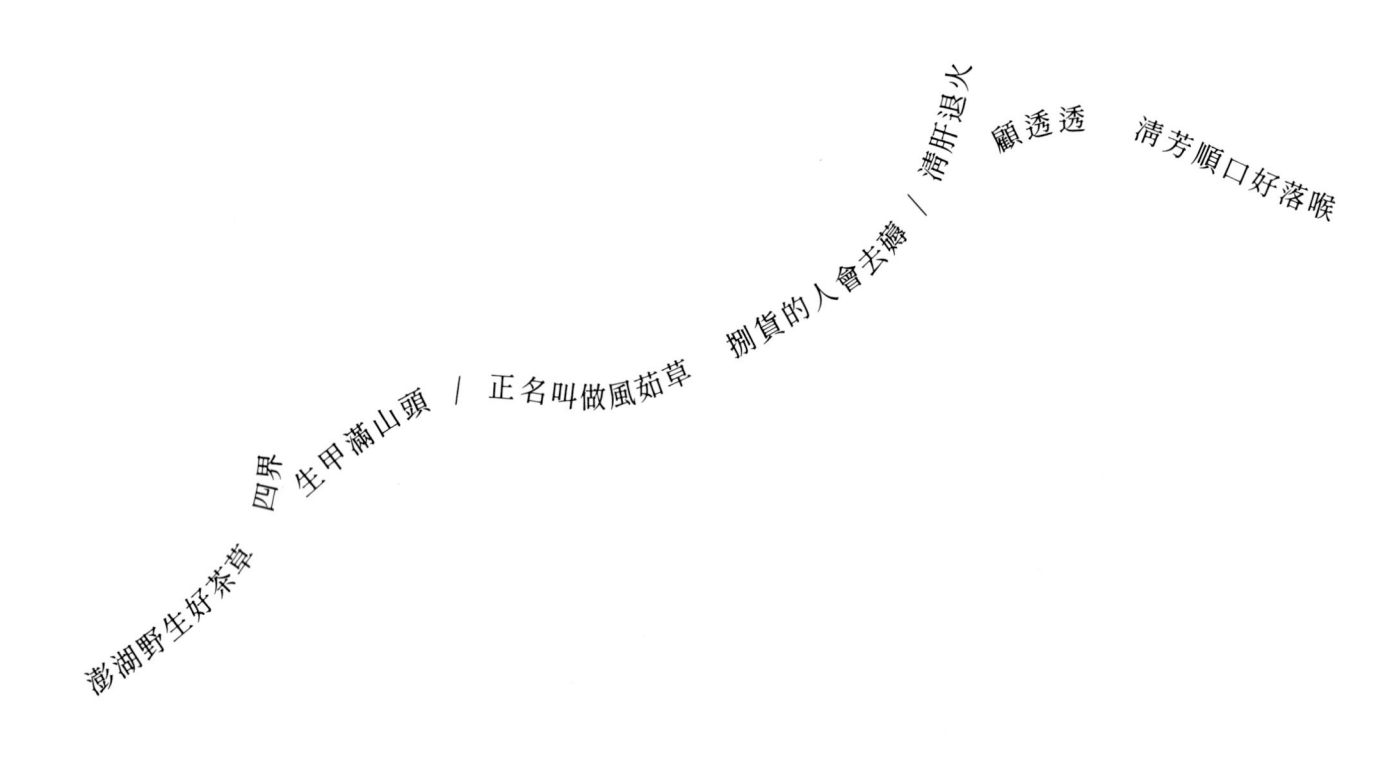

澎湖野生好茶草　四界　生甲滿山頭　∕　正名叫做風茹草　捌貨的人會去搜　∕　清肝退火　顧透透　清芳順口好落喉

Phînn-ôo iá-sing hó tê-tsháu, sì-kè sinn kah muá suann-thâu.
Tsiànn-miâ kiò-tsò hong-jû-tsháu, bat-hè ê lâng ē khù khau.
Tshing-kuann thuè-hé kòo-thàu-thàu, tshing-phang sūn-kháu koh hó lòh-âu.

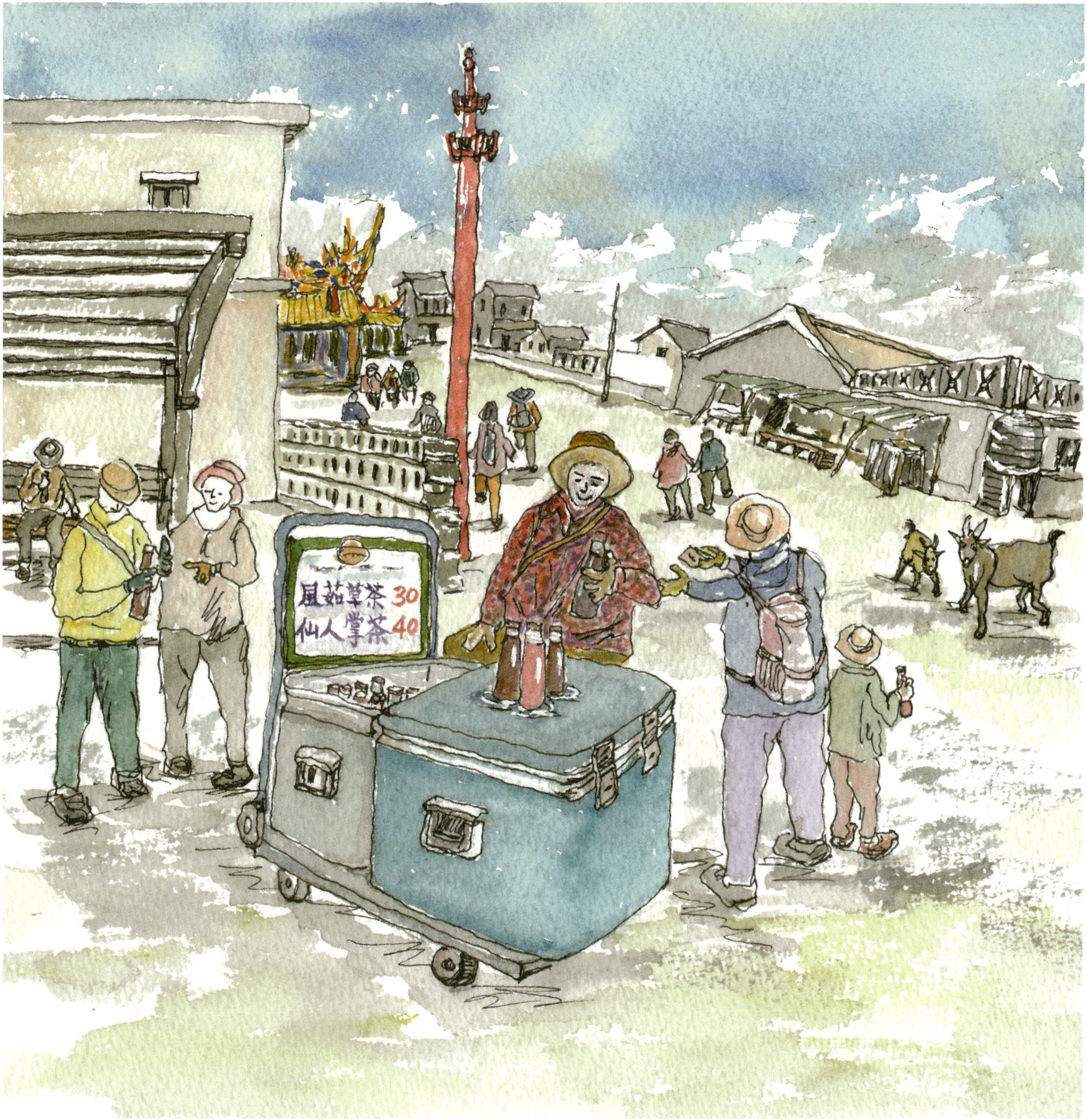
風茹草茶 30
仙人掌茶 40

風菇草茶 30
仙人掌茶 40

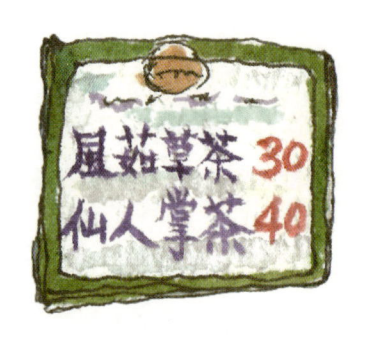

澎湖有一種野生的草,叫做風茹草,加水煮沸後不管是熱飲還是冷飲,味道都甘美。如果你到山坡頂去尋找,一定能找到這種草。內行人都會把它挖回去「燃茶」(hiânn-tê)。風茹草是一種有助於清肝退火、解毒治中暑的茶草,氣味清香,入口順滑,越喝越「紲喙」(suà-tshuì)。

• • •

In Penghu, there is a wild grass called hong-jû-tsháu (Glossogyne tenuifolia). When boiled, it makes a delightful hot or cold drink. If you visit the hills in search of it, you are sure to find it. Locals often dig it up to brew tea. Hong-jû-tsháu is known for its ability to cleanse the liver and relieve heat. It has a pleasant aroma and smooth taste, making it a favorite drink among the people of Penghu.

Gún-tau
阮兜
My Homeland

西坪西溝是阮兜　　厝後懸懸是山頭

兩爿園仔種塗豆　　厝前有條大水溝

溝前水井有三口　　井泉溝水日日流

後山前水好地理　　囝孫代代出頭天

Sai-pîng Sai-kau sī gún-tau, tshù-āu kuân-kuân sī suann-thâu.
Nňg-pîng hn̂g-á tsìng thôo-tāu, tshù-tsîng ū tsit tiâu tuā-tsuí-kau.
Kau-tsîng tsuí-tsínn ū sann kháu, tsínn-tsuânn kau-tsuí ji̍t-ji̍t lâu.
Āu suann tsîng tsuí hó tuē-lí, kiánn-sun tāi-tāi tshut-thâu-thinn.

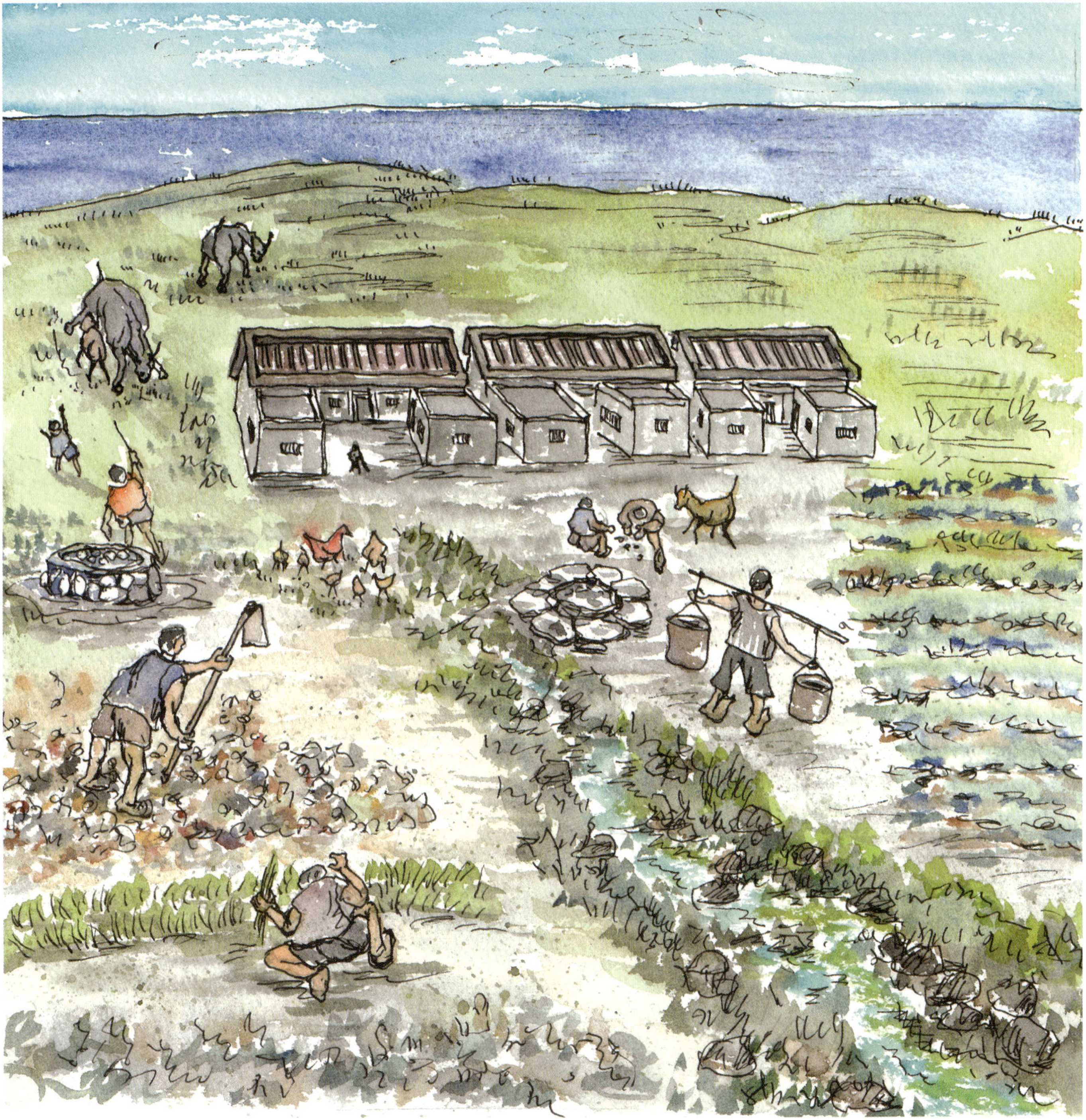

呂坤翰老師所踏的地方是他的家。當他服完兵役返回東嶼坪任教時，原本的家已被拆除。幸運的是，他的姪子呂水上透過畫作重現了老家的風貌，讓他在重返家園時，能夠感受到那份熟悉與思念。

The place where Mr Lu Kun-Han stands is his home. However, when he returned to Tang-sū-pîng (Dongyuping) Island to teach after completing his military service, he found that his original home had been demolished. Thankfully, his nephew, Lu Shui-Shang, recreated the appearance of the old house through paintings, allowing him to feel a sense of familiarity and nostalgia upon his return.

呂坤翰的老家，位於西嶼坪的西溝，背後是一座小山丘，面前則流淌著清澈的小溪流。附近兩旁都是田地，家人們勤奮耕作，過著自給自足的生活，一家幸福美滿。父親愛讀書，無論是《古文觀止》還是《四書五經》，都能深刻剖析其中的道理，因此也結交了許多知識淵博的朋友。大哥更是聰明伶俐，學業向來認真，每一科都表現出色。呂坤翰表示，自己也愛讀書，我學的是華語。成為一名老師後，他選擇回到家鄉，教導孩子們學習知識和禮儀道德。他自信地說：「阮嘛共庄內的囡仔教甲誠勢（gâu），誠捌（bat）禮數，大漢出社會，嘛攏誠有成就。」

・・・

Lu Kun-Han's family home is on the west side of Sai-sū-pîng (Xiyuping) Island, nestled behind a small hill and overlooking a clear stream. Surrounded by fields, his family works diligently to maintain a self-sufficient lifestyle. His father was an avid reader of classical literature, skilled at analysing its principles. His elder brother was exceptionally bright and excelled in his studies. Lu Kun-Han also enjoyed reading, particularly focusing on Mandarin Chinese literature. After becoming a teacher, he returned to his hometown to educate children in knowledge and ethics, hoping they would contribute meaningfully to society.

Sann Kháu Tsínn ê Kòo-sū
三口井的故事
The Tale of the Three Wells

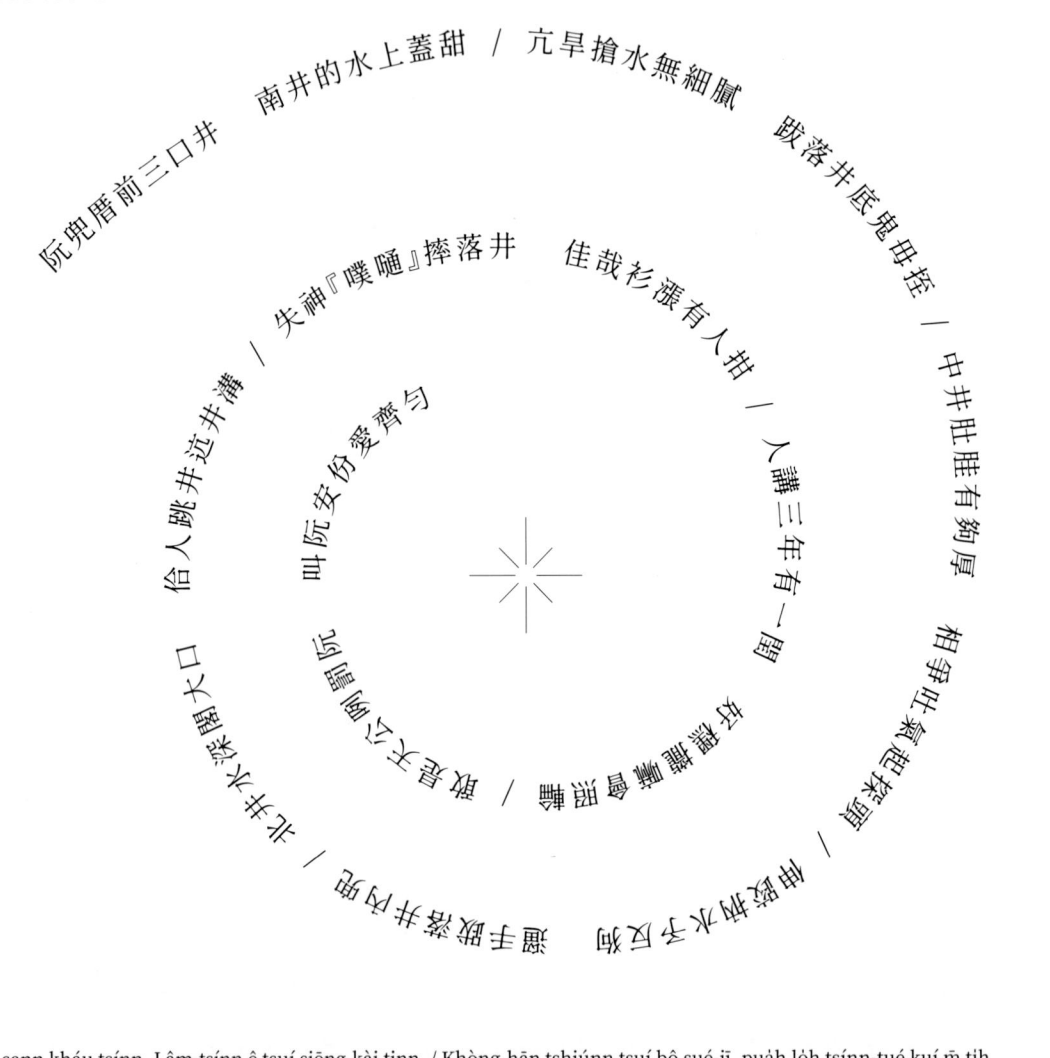

阮兜厝前三口井　南井的水上蓋甜　/　亢旱搶水無細膩　跋落井底鬼申捼　/　中井肚胿有夠厚　相爭挹水相觸頭　/　阮翁跤躼水予朋桊　煞遛手跋落井內兜　/　北井水深閣大口　佮人跳井迒井溝　/　失神『噗咚』摔落井　佳哉衫漲有人扛　/　人講三年有一閏　好䆀攏嘛會照輪　/　敢是天公仔咧罰阮　叫阮安份愛齊勻

Gún-tau tshù tsîng sann kháu tsínn, Lâm-tsínn ê tsuí siōng-kài tinn. / Khòng-hān tshiúnn tsuí bô sué-jī, puah lo̍h tsínn-té kuí m̄ tih.
Tiong-tsínn tōo-kuai-á ū-kàu kāu, sio tsinn thóo-khuì lóng khé thàm-thâu. / Gún iōng kha lā-tsuí hōo--pîng-káu, suah liù-tshiú puah lo̍h tsínn lāi tau.
Pak-tsínn tsuí tshim koh tuā-kháu, kah lâng thiàu tsínn hānn tsínn-kau. / Sit-sîn "phuh-thong" siak-lo̍h tsínn, ka-tsài sann--tiùnn ū-lâng khînn.
Lâng kóng sann nî ū tsit lūn, hó-bái lóng mā ē tsiàu-lûn. / Kám sī Thinn-kong-á leh huat--gún, kiò gún an-hūn ài tsiâu-ûn.

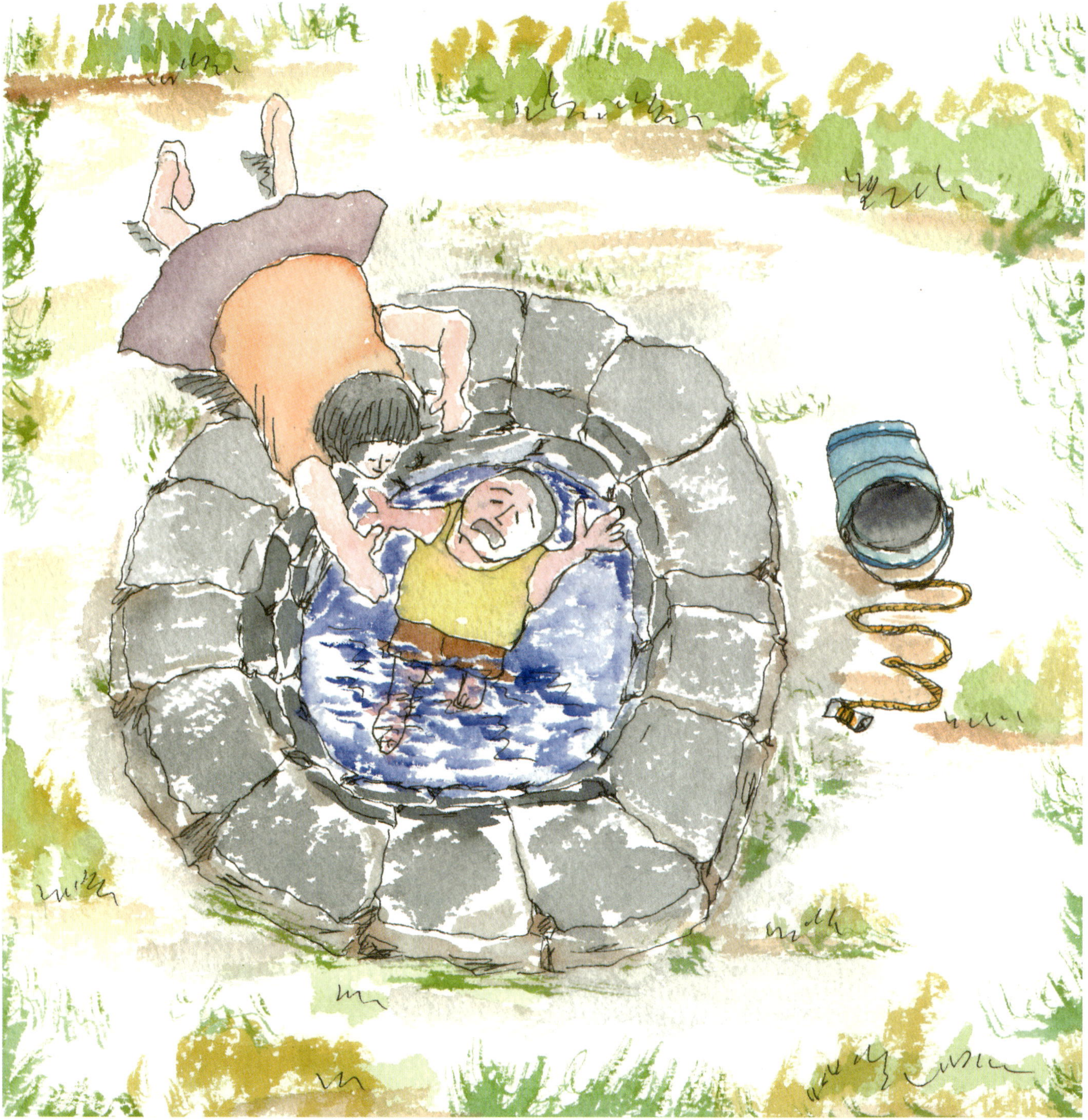

照片中央的井是「南井」，因爲水質好而深受村民喜愛。此外，這裡還承載著呂坤翰兒時因爲乾旱搶水而落井的難忘回憶。

The well in the center of the photo, known as the 'South Well', was cherished by the villagers for its excellent water quality. It also holds unforgettable memories for Lu Kun-Han from his childhood, as he once fell into the well while trying to get water during a drought.

呂坤翰家的附近有三口井，中井的水最淺，深度約及一位成年人的腰部。1949 年夏天，下過雨後，他發現井裡有蝌蚪，牠們不斷游到水面探頭呼吸，十分有趣。興奮之下，他用雙手抓住井邊的石頭，用一腳在水中划動，試圖讓蝌蚪翻滾，就在哈哈大笑，想要鼓掌叫好的時候，兩手一鬆就掉下去了。幸運的是，堂姐恰好在旁，一把拉起來，要不然已經小命不保。

北井是新開挖的，深約三丈，井中有三分之二的水。1951 年夏天，呂坤翰跟著大哥哥們一起放牛，一起玩跨越井口的遊戲。結果因爲個子小跨不過對岸，又跌入井裡了！所幸身上的衣服有浮力，在井中載浮載沉。兩位大哥哥見狀，立刻下井救人，又一次逃過了險境，眞是幸運！

南井的水質最爲甘甜，是全村人最愛的飲水來源。然而，1957 年恰逢乾旱，整年鮮少雨水，全村的井底都在仰望天空。要想從井中舀起一些水，往往需要漫長的等待，可以想見當時搶水的情況有多麼激烈。在這樣的慌忙中，呂坤翰急著取水，再度不小心跌入井中，並且失去知覺。當他再次醒來時，發現自己竟然活著，眞是奇蹟，還好閻羅王大概不打算收走他！幾次事件，呂坤翰自省，一定是做事不夠仔細，不安分，怪不得上天要處罰。

Near Lu Kun-Han's home, there were three wells: the North Well, the Central Well and the South Well. The Central Well was the shallowest, reaching waist height for an adult. In the summer of 1949, after some rain, he discovered tadpoles in the well. Playfully, he dipped a foot into the water, trying to make the tadpoles tumble. Just as he was about to clap in delight, he accidentally fell in! Fortunately, his cousin was nearby and pulled him out, saving his life.

The North Well was newly dug and about an adult's height in depth. In the summer of 1951, Lu Kun-Han herded cows with older boys and they played a game of jumping over the well. However, being smaller, he couldn't reach the opposite side and fell in again! Luckily, his clothes were buoyant, allowing him to float. The older boys quickly jumped in to rescue him and once again, he escaped danger—a true miracle!

The South Well provided the sweetest water and was the village's favorite source of drinking water. However, in 1957, a drought struck and rainfall was scarce. The village wells were drying up, making competition for water fierce. In the rush to collect water, Lu Kun-Han accidentally fell into the well again and lost consciousness. When he woke up, he was surprised to find he was still alive; it seemed the King of Hell had no intention of claiming him yet! Reflecting on these incidents, Lu Kun-Han realised he had been careless and reckless and it was no wonder that fate seemed to punish him.

信 SÌN-GIÓNG 仰

　以捕魚爲生的澎湖人民，面對海上的無常，總是虔誠祈求神明庇佑，保護生命安危。信仰不僅是島民生活與勞動的寄託，面臨困難時的精神支柱，信仰也讓彼此的心更緊密相連。

　在〈澎湖天后宮〉這首作品中，讚頌了全台最古老廟宇的悠久歷史，承載無數信徒的期盼與祝福，使其成爲澎湖文化的靈魂。接著在〈澎湖上元節〉，描繪澎湖人對每年元宵節的期待，並透過「乞龜」（khit-ku）儀式展現出熱鬧的祈福氛圍。〈東吉村中元普渡〉則歌頌來自東吉的遊子，在中元節前搭船返鄉祭拜時，所流露出對故土的深厚情感。而在「東嶼坪池府王爺生日」中，則是生動的唱出漁民駕船進港的壯闊景象，各處歸鄉的島民，在噓寒問暖間回味起昔日的家鄉。

　這些褒歌深情吟誦著澎湖島嶼信仰的故事，也串起人們心中對故土的回憶與思念。

FAITH

The fishermen of Penghu always pray sincerely to the gods for protection, hoping to navigate the challenges posed by the sea safely. For the people of Penghu, faith is not just a source of support in their daily lives and work; it is also a spiritual pillar that connects their hearts. In the ballad Penghu Matsu Temple, Taiwan's oldest temple is celebrated for its long history, embodying the hopes and blessings of countless believers and serving as the heart of Penghu's culture. The ballad 'Penghu Lantern Festival' captures the excitement that the community feels for the annual festival, showcasing a vibrant atmosphere of prayer through the 'khit-ku' ritual. 'Dongii Village's Ghost Festival' honors the residents returning home to Dongji Island to pay their respects during this important celebration, expressing their deep affection for their hometown. In the 'Ritual of Wangye Chifu Worship on Dongyuping Island', the grand sight of fishermen entering the harbor and the islanders gathering together is vividly depicted as they reminisce about the beautiful moments of their past. These ballads convey the stories of faith in Penghu, connecting people's memories and their longing for their homeland.

Phînn-ôo Thian-hiō-kiong

澎湖天后宮
Penghu Matzu Temple

澎湖較早 歹討趁　逐家攏是散赤人　/　明朝媽祖來晟咱　歷史超過四百冬

助咱討海有錢趁　助咱出海攏平安

助咱種作收成讚　助咱生理接袂完

廟內 香火　日日旺　　人 人　誠心　奉香檨

媽祖助咱來發展　帶動外地來觀光

家家戶戶有錢趁　生活富裕閣平安

Phînn-ôo khah-tsá pháinn thó-thàn, ta̍k-ke lóng sī sàn-tsiah lâng.
Bîng-tiâu Má-tsóo lâi tshiânn lán, li̍k-sú tshiau-kè sì-pah tang.
Tsōo lán thó-hái ū tsînn thàn, tsōo lán tshut-hái lóng pîng-an.
Tsōo lán tsìng-tsoh siu-sîng tsán, tsōo lán sing-lí tsiap buē uân.
Biō lāi hiunn-hué ji̍t-ji̍t ōng, lâng-lâng sîng-sim hōng hiunn-tsâng.
Má-tsóo tsōo lán lâi huat-tián, tài-tōng guā-tuē lâi kuan-kong.
ke-ke-hōo-hōo ū tsînn thàn, sing-ua̍h hù-jū koh pîng-an.

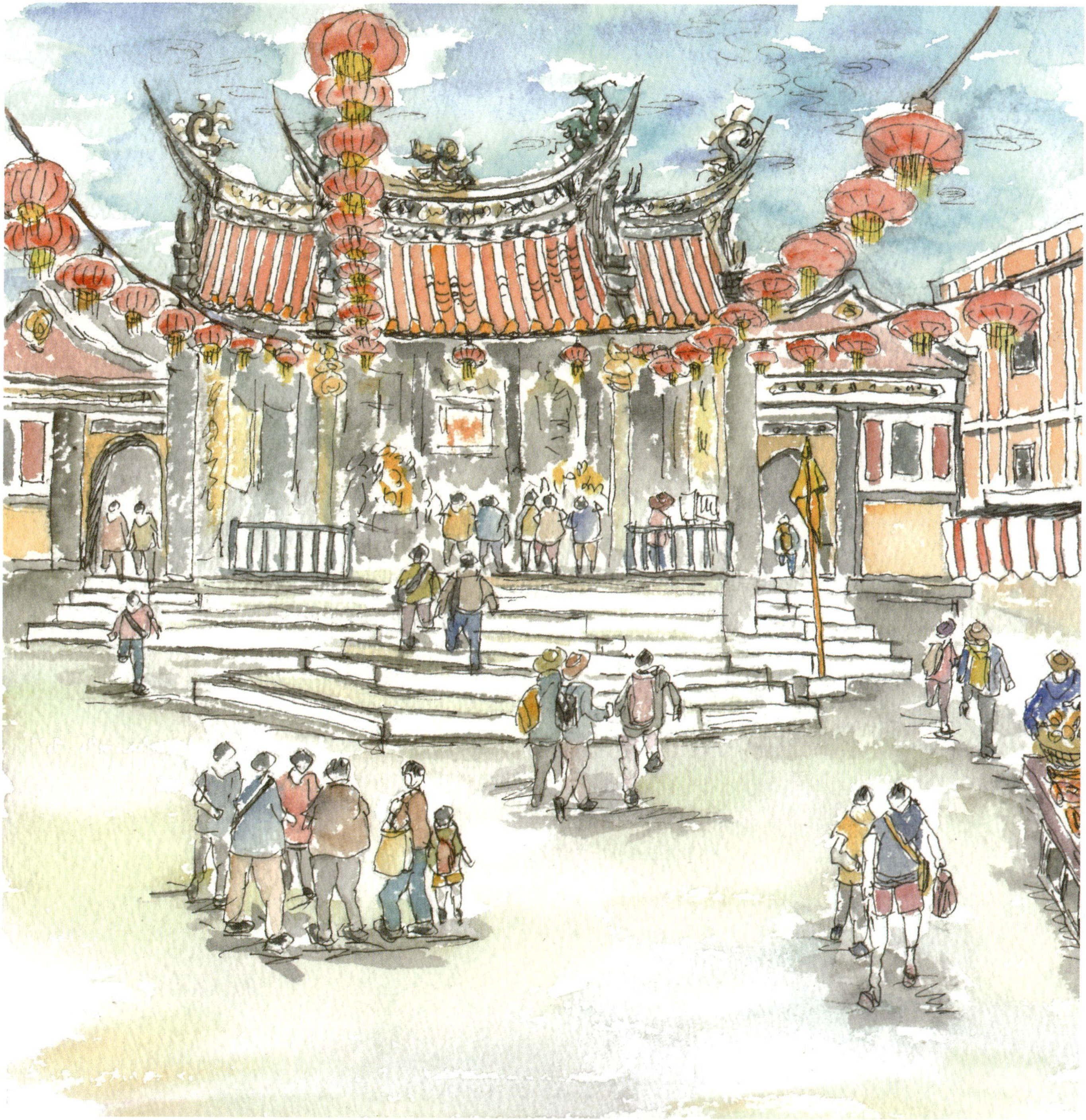

130 ｜ 信仰 SÌN-GIÓNG

澎湖人以前討海渡生活，海上的風浪很大，常常會有意外發生，所以大家都特別希望能獲得神明的保護，保障漁民的生命安全。澎湖天后宮在明朝萬曆32年（1604年）建立，至今已四百多年歷史，是全台灣最古老的廟宇。島上居民對這座廟非常虔誠，深信神明會保佑大家出海時的安全，且讓漁獲豐富、耕作順利，做生意也能賺錢。此外，他們也希望媽祖吸引更多外地的遊客來觀光消費，為居民的生活帶來富裕和安定。

• • •

In the past, the people of Penghu made their living through fishing but the often rough seas led to many accidents. As a result, everyone hoped for protection from the gods to ensure the safety of the fishermen. The Penghu Matzu Temple was established as early as the 32nd year of the Ming Empire's Wanli period, in 1604, making it over 400 years old and the oldest temple in Taiwan. The local community is deeply religious regarding this temple and firmly believes that the gods will bless them with safety while fishing. This not only leads to a bountiful catch and successful farming but also helps local businesses thrive. Furthermore, they hope to attract more visitors from outside, which would increase spending and bring wealth and stability to the lives of the locals.

Phînn-ôo Siōng-guân-tsueh
澎湖上元節
Penghu Lantern Festival

正月十五好日子　上蓋鬧熱上元時
這是一層大代誌　　澎湖的人笑微微
規工攏嘛真歡喜　家家戶戶食湯圓
日猜燈謎真趣味　暗捔花燈鬧規暝
外垵煙火放袂離　五花十色衝上天
全村燈火光爍爍　鬧熱親像咧過年
廟內乞龜人上興　排隊跋桮求神明
麵龜紅片龜攏揀　逐家求甲蓋虔誠
乞龜是欲食平安　會記明年著愛還
這是事先的心願　　加大還了心自安
保庇年年有錢趁　生理永遠接袂完

Tsiann-gėh tsȧp-gōo hó jit-tsí, siōng-kài lāu-jiȧt siōng-guân sî.
Tse sī tsit tsân tuā-tāi-tsì, Phînn-ôo ê lâng tshiò-bi-bi.
Kui kang lóng mā tsin huann-hí, ke-ke-hōo-hōo tsiȧh thng-înn.
Jit tshai ting-mî tsin tshù-bī, àm kuānn hue-ting nāu kui mî.
Guā-uann ian-hé pàng buē lī, ngóo-hue-tsȧp-sik tshiong tsiūnn-thinn.
Tsuân tshun ting-hé kng-sinnh-sinnh, lāu-jiȧt tshan-tshiūnn leh kuè-nî.
Biō lāi khit-ku lâng siōng hìng, pâi-tuī puȧh-pue kiû sîn-bîng.
Mī-ku hông-phiàn-ku lóng kíng, tȧk-ke kiû kah koh kài khiân-sîng.
Khit-ku sī beh tsiȧh pîng-an, ē-kì ê mî-nî tiȯh ài hân.
Tse sī sū-sian ê sim-guān, ka-tuā hân liáu sim tsū an.
Pó-pì nî-nî ū tsînn thàn, sing-lí íng-uán tsiap buē uân.

帝德高風

134 | 信仰 SÌN-GIÓNG

澎湖一年四季中，最熱鬧的日子非正月十五的元宵節莫屬。在這一天，各地的澎湖人，家家戶戶都會祭拜神明和祖先。人們會一起聚在一起，享用湯圓、猜燈謎、賞花燈，還會到廟裡「乞龜」。澎湖的廟宇會準備許多不同的「龜」，讓信徒來祈求和許願。

元宵節的夜晚，西嶼外垵整個村莊燈火通明，甚至比過年還要熱鬧。村民們一起放煙火、賞花燈、猜燈謎和「乞龜」，讓人感受到濃厚的節日氛圍和鄉情的溫暖。這一夜，澎湖的人們聚在一起，共同歡慶，留下了許多美好的回憶。

• • •

In Penghu, the busiest day of the year is the Lantern Festival, celebrated on the 15th day of the first lunar month. On this day, families across Penghu honor the gods and their ancestors. People gather to enjoy sweet rice balls, solve riddles, admire lanterns and participate in a tradition known as 'khit-ku'. Here, 'khit' is the Taiwanese pronunciation for 'to pray', while 'ku' sounds like the word for 'turtle'. In Mandarin, 'turtle' has a similar pronunciation to the word for 'return'. This reflects the hope for a safe return home. Thus, on this day, the temples in Penghu prepare many turtle-shaped cakes as offerings for people to pray and make wishes. During the Lantern Festival in 2021, Guā-uann (Wai'an) Village in Sai-sū (Xiyu) Township was illuminated, creating an atmosphere even livelier than during the Lunar New Year. Villagers set off fireworks, enjoyed lantern displays, solved riddles and took part in 'khit-ku', fostering a strong festive spirit and a sense of warmth within the community. That night, the people of Penghu came together to celebrate, creating many wonderful memories.

六月十六好日子　就是池府王爺生 ／ 這是一層大代誌　嶼坪的人笑微微
逐家趕緊來準備　豬公上桌來祝生 ／ 五牲魚肉滿滿是　果菜排甲桌滿墘
出外漁船回鄉里　船頂插著神明旗 ／ 規陣漁船出港口　迎請神明趖沙溝
鼓聲炮聲一直鬧　船後海湧白泡泡 ／ 規个沙溝趖透透　全部船仔才回頭
規陣船仔入港內　廟埕嘛是鬧猜猜 ／ 逐家招招緊來拜　祈求平安大發財

Tang-sū-pîng Tî-hú-ông-iâ Sinn-ji̍t

東嶼坪池府王爺生日

Ritual of Tî Ông-iâ Worship on Tang-sū-pîng Island

La̍k-ge̍h tsa̍p-la̍k hó jit-tsí, tiō-sī Tî-hú-ông-iâ sinn. / Tse sī tsit tsân tuā-tāi-tsì, Sū-pîng ê lâng tshiò-bi-bi.
Ta̍k-ke kuánn-kín lâi tsún-pī, tu-kong tsiūnn-toh lâi tsiok-sing. / Ngóo-sing hû-bah muá-muá-sī, kó-tshài pâi kah toh buán-kînn.
Tshut-guā hû-tsûn huê hiong-lí, tsûn tíng tshah tio̍h sîn-bîng-kî. / Kui tīn hû-tsûn-á tshut káng-kháu, ngiâ-tshiánn sîn-bîng se̍h sua-kau.
Kóo-siann phàu-siann it-ti̍t nāu, tsûn āu hái-íng pe̍h-phau-phau. / Kui-ê sua-kau-ê se̍h thàu-thàu, tsuân-pōo tsûn-á tsiah huê-thâu.
Kui tīn tsûn-á ji̍p káng lāi, biō-tiânn mā sī nāu-tshai-tshai. / Ta̍k-ke tsio-tsio ê kín lâi pài, kî-kiû pîng-an tuā huat-tsâi.

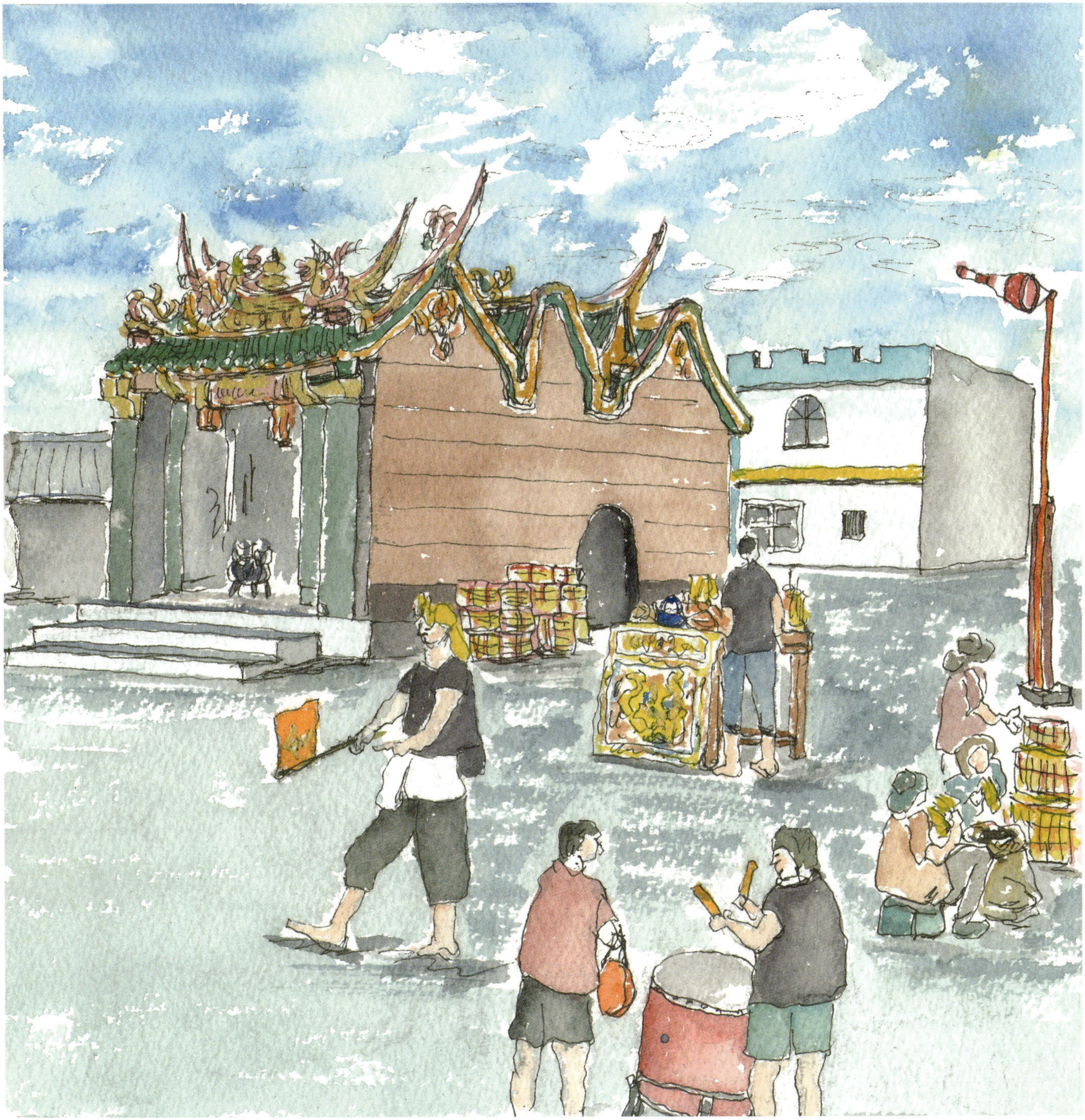

東嶼坪港內停滿了插著神明旗的漁船，場面十分壯觀。

The harbour of Tang-sū-pîng Island is filled with fishing boats adorned with flags representing the deities, creating a truly spectacular sight.

農曆六月十六日是池府王爺的生日，這對東嶼坪的居民來說，是一個令人期待的大日子。大家都會用心準備慶祝的貢品，像是用來祭拜的豬公、五牲魚肉、蔬菜水果、餅乾、飲料、罐頭，金紙等豐盛的祭品擺了滿桌。

在這一天，出海的漁船會陸續回來參加慶祝，船頂上插著神明的旗幟，向神明致敬。所有的船隻會繞過沙溝，再進港參拜。此時，鼓聲和炮聲響起，場面熱鬧得就像過年一樣，令人目不暇接！大家都希望王爺能夠保佑每個家庭平安順遂，生意興隆。東嶼坪的廟內有兩尊主神，另一尊是蕭府王爺，祂的生日在農曆十月十日。每到慶生的時候，住在外地的村民們也都會回來參加熱鬧的慶祝，因為村民們都感念王爺信仰護衛大家勇敢奮鬥；也珍惜這份信仰團結大家，深厚彼此的情感。

• • •

Each year, on the sixteenth day of the 16th lunar month, the residents of Tang-sū-pîng (Dongyuping) Island celebrate the birthday of Tî Ông-iâ, a revered deity known for offering protection and blessings. This eagerly awaited day sees the community preparing a variety of rich offerings to honor him. Fishing boats returning from the sea participate in the worship ceremonies, proudly displaying flags with Ông-iâ's name as a sign of respect. These boats circle around the western side of the island before entering the harbor to partake in the celebrations. The air is filled with the lively sounds of drums and firecrackers, reminiscent of the Lunar New Year festivities. On this special occasion, everyone hopes for Ông-iâ to bless their families with safety and prosperity in their businesses.

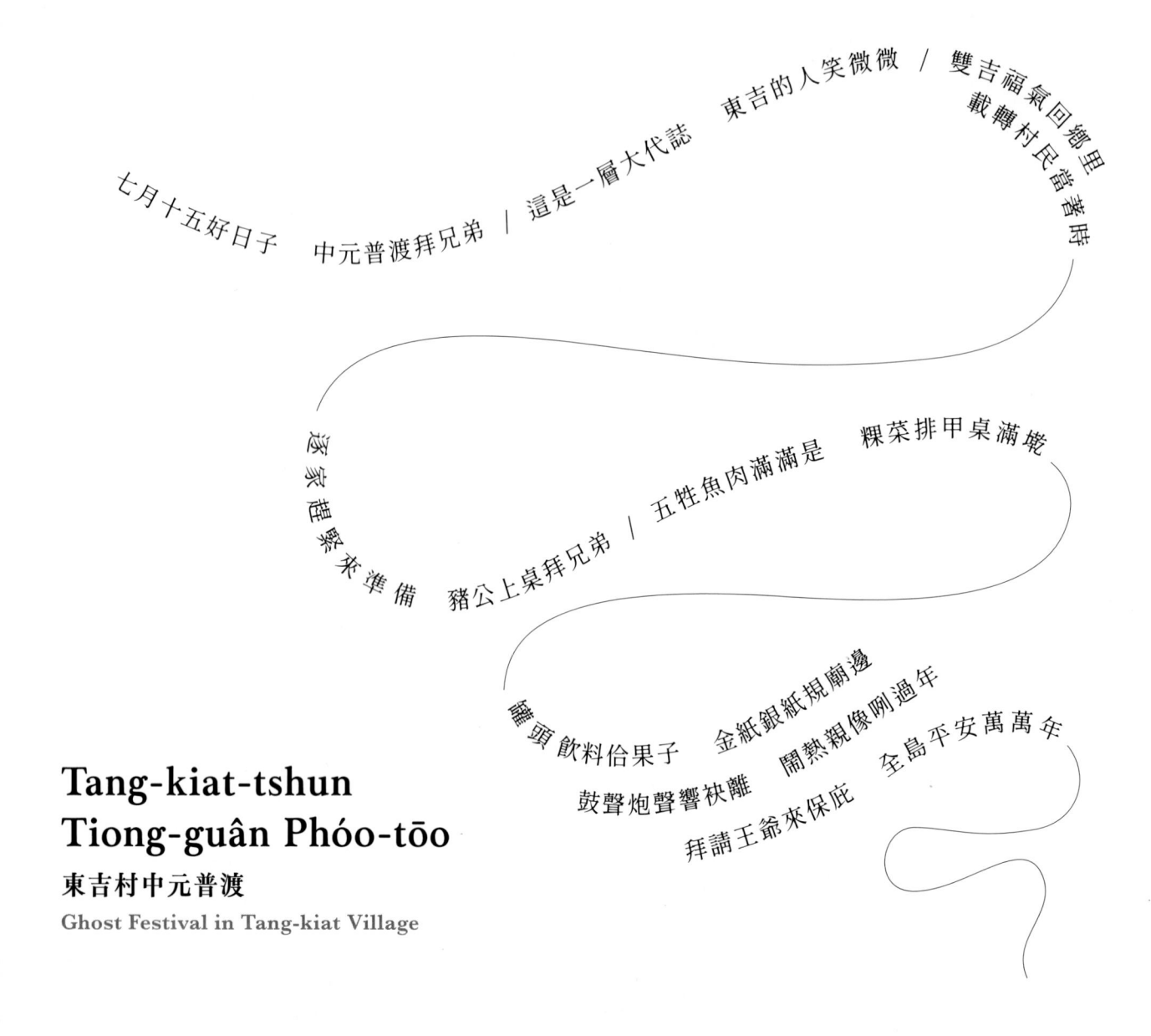

七月十五好日子　中元普渡拜兄弟　／　這是一層大代誌　東吉的人笑微微　／　雙吉福氣回鄉里　載轉村民當著時

逐家趕緊來準備　豬公上桌拜兄弟　／　五牲魚肉滿滿是　粿菜排甲桌滿墘

罐頭飲料佮果子　金紙銀紙規廟邊　鬧熱親像咧過年
鼓聲炮聲響袂離　拜請王爺來保庇　全島平安萬萬年

Tang-kiat-tshun Tiong-guân Phóo-tōo
東吉村中元普渡
Ghost Festival in Tang-kiat Village

Tshit-ge̍h tsa̍p-gōo hó jit-tsí, tiong-guân phóo-tōo pài hiann-tī. / Tse sī tsit tsân tuā-tāi-tsì, Tang-kiat ê lâng tshiò-bi-bi.
Siang-kiat-hok-khì huê hiong-lí, tsài tńg tshun-bîn tng-tio̍h-sî. / Ta̍k-ke kuánn-kín lâi tsún-pī, tu-kong tsiūnn-toh pài hiann-tī.
Ngóo-sing hû-bah muá-muá-sī, ké-tshài pâi kah toh buán-kînn. / Kuàn-thâu ím-liāu kah ké-tsí, kim-tsuá gûn-tsuá kui biō pinn.
Kóo-siann phàu-siann hiáng buē lī, lāu-jia̍t tshin-tshiūnn leh kuè-nî. / Pài-tshiánn Ông-iâ lâi pó-pì, tsuân tó pîng-an bān-bān nî.

140 | 信仰 SÌN-GIÓNG

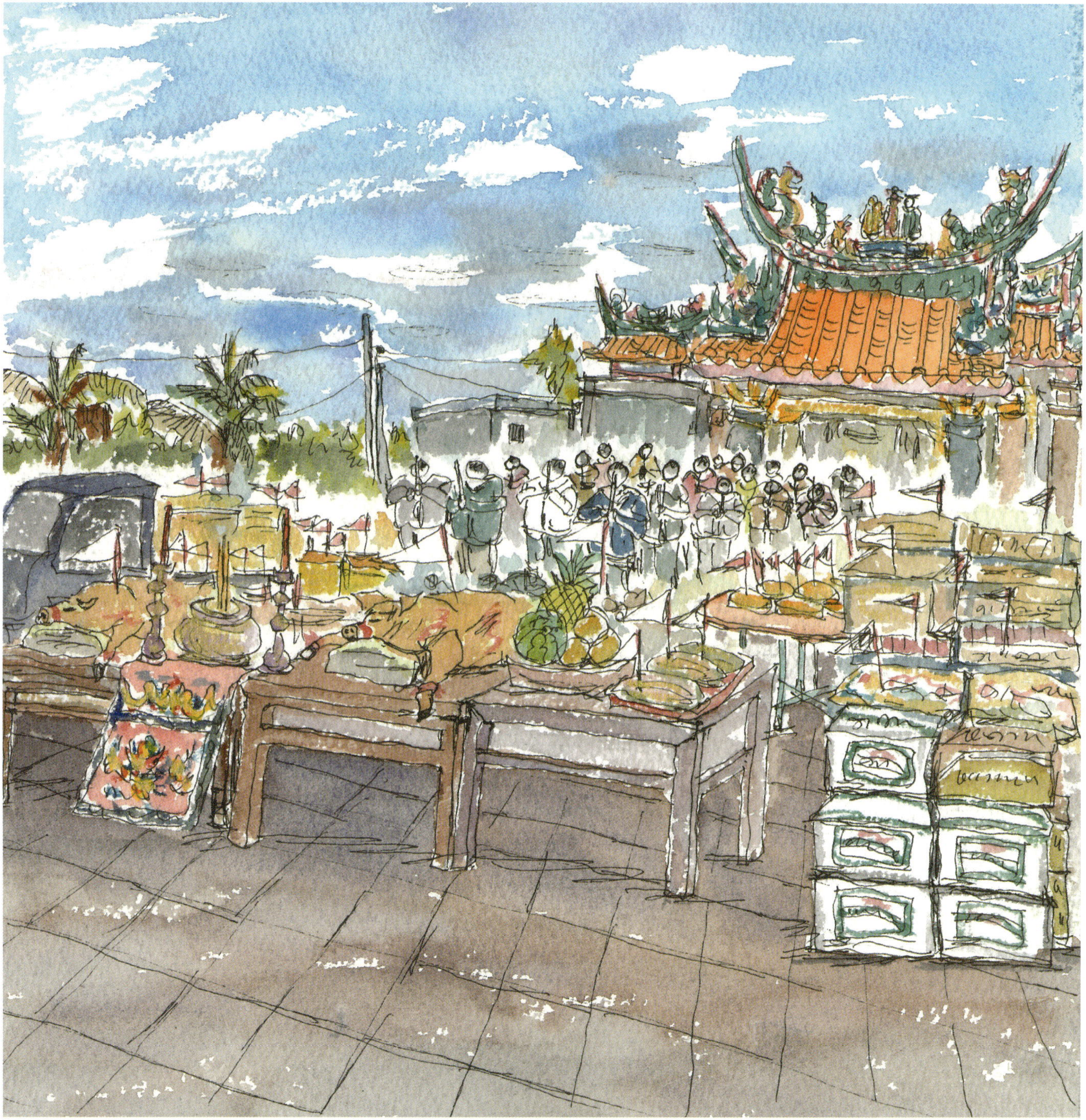

許多遷居馬公、台南、高雄等地的居民，都會返鄉參與這個小島大事，晚間在啟明宮的廟埕前吃辦桌，洋溢著歡樂的氣氛。

Many residents who have settled in places like Má-kíng (Magong), Tainan and Kaohsiung return to their hometown to participate in this ritual activity. In the evenings, everyone gathers in front of the temple, sitting around circular tables to enjoy delicious dishes together, creating a warm and joyful atmosphere that fills the island.

在東吉村，每年農曆七月十五中元節祭拜好兄弟，無論是居住在島上的村民，還是移居在外的遊子，滿心期盼的便是這一天的到來。雙吉福氣號的交通船會把住在台灣本島的村民們接回來，全村的人忙著準備祭祀活動，殺豬公來祭拜王爺和好兄弟。大家準備了豐富的祭品，包括五牲魚肉、蔬菜水果、餅乾和飲料，桌子上擺滿村民的心意，廟前的金紙和銀紙也堆得滿滿的。此時，鼓聲和鞭炮聲此起彼落，就像過年一樣熱鬧。人們虔誠地拜請王爺和好兄弟保佑，希望全村居民能夠平平安安，生意興隆，賺到大錢！

・・・

In Tang-kiat (Dongji) Village, the Ghost Festival, celebrated on the 15th day of the seventh lunar month, is a significant occasion for paying respects to the spirits. This day is eagerly awaited by both the villagers who live on the island and those who have moved away. The ferry, aptly named Double Lucky, transports villagers back from the main island of Taiwan and the entire community busily prepares for the ceremonies. Residents prepare a generous array of offerings, including pork, chicken, duck, fish, vegetables, fruits, cookies and beverages. At the temple, piles of spirit money are set out in tribute. As the festivities unfold, the air is filled with the vibrant sounds of drums and firecrackers, creating an atmosphere reminiscent of Lunar New Year celebrations. Villagers earnestly pray to Ông-iâ and the spirits, seeking peace and safety for everyone, prosperity for their businesses and an abundance of wealth.

SING-UÁH

生

活

　　歷經時光的淬煉,澎湖居民自然地發展出一套與土地和大海的共生之道。

　　作品中,〈澎湖較早的生活情〉、〈以早的東嶼坪〉以及〈落雨天歹起火〉分別生動描繪了早期澎湖人駕舟撒網、撿螺拾貝,順應自然就地取材的生活寫照。冬天特別嚴峻,當強風與巨浪襲來時,鹹水的霧氣瀰漫整個島嶼,青草枯萎,樹木也難以存活,大地一片荒蕪。面對這樣的困境,居民們靈活應對,巧妙利用當地資源,搭建硓𥑮石圍牆以抵擋風沙,圍牆內的蔬菜得以茁壯成長,最終獲得豐收,展現出生活的智慧。

　　在〈掠魚、生囝〉中,男人主要負責出海捕魚,而女人則在家裡照顧家庭並且耕作,真實的生活情境展現無遺,而〈哪會按呢〉則為生活中的戀愛趣味。〈克難學校〉述說了呂坤翰家鄉小學的艱辛故事,彰顯對教育的珍惜與追求。最後,〈快樂的澎湖人〉和〈澎湖人愛褒歌〉則傳遞出島嶼人民的樂觀精神,以及用褒歌唱出對生活的熱情與面對困難時的幽默。

　　讓我們在哼唱著這些褒歌的同時,走進聚落,細聽那些取材於日常的動人故事。

LIFE

Over the years, the people of Penghu have formed a strong emotional bond with the land and sea. The works 'The Early Life in Penghu', 'The Former Tang-sū-pîng Island', and 'It's Difficult to Light a Fire on Rainy Days' show their early experiences of sailing to fish and foraging for shellfish while living in harmony with nature. Winter brings challenges; strong winds and huge waves cover the island in salty mist, causing plants to die and leaving the land dry. In response, the residents cleverly use local resources, gathering coral stones from the beach to build walls that protect them from sandstorms. Behind these walls, their crops grow well, showing their smart thinking. 'Fishing and Having Children' shows traditional family roles, where men go out to sea while women take care of the home and farms. 'How Could This Happen?' adds a touch of romance to daily life, while 'Difficult Times at a Remote Primary School' tells the inspiring story of a primary school in Lu Kun-Han's hometown, highlighting his dedication to education. Finally, 'The Happy People of Penghu' and 'The People of Penghu Love to Sing Ballads' express the islanders' hopefulness, enjoyment of life and sense of humor in tough times. We invite you to explore these stories rooted in everyday life.

Phînn-ôo Khah-tsá ê Sing-uah-tsîng
澎湖較早的生活情
The Early Life in Penghu

澎湖出名風湧大　冬天若來風飛沙

鹹水鬚若飛上岸　園內種作眞歹活

石頭硞砧圍田岸　圍予懸懸閘風沙　/　菜子提來圍內掖　冬天種菜有通食

牛屎浞浞做屎餅　擗佇圍牆曝予焦　/　煮飯炒菜兼滷肉　這是上好的火柴

豬屎嘛是好肥料　全部攏囥佇豬牢　/　秋天種作收了後　豬仔全部放出牢

放予四界去食草　順紲將肥埋田溝　/

雞仔放伊四界走　食蟲食草伊上勢　/　每工草埔巡透透　伊的腹肚哪會枵

雞公燖補上有效　雞母生卵上蓋勢

這是庄跤的現象　生活特殊姑不將　/　鄉下生活共恁講　毋通笑阮草地倯

Phînn-ôo tshut-miâ hong-íng tuā, tang-thinn nā lâi hong-pue-sua. / Kiâm-tsuí-tshiu nā pue tsiūnn-huānn, hn̂g-lāi tsìng-tsoh tsin pháinn uah.
Tsióh-thâu lóo-kóo-á uî tshân-huānn, uî hōo kuân-kuân tsah hong-sua. / Tshài-tsí thueh-lâi uî-á-lāi iā, tang-thinn tsìng-tshài tō ū-thang tsiah.
Gû-sái tshiok-tshiok-ê tsò sái-piánn, phiak tī uî-á-tshiûnn phak hōo ta. / Tsú-pn̄g tshá-tshài kiam lóo-bah, tse sī siōng-hó ê hé-tshâ.
Tu-sái mā sī hó puî-liāu, tsuân-pōo lóng tún tī tu-tiâu. / Tshiu-thinn tsìng-tsoh nā siu liáu-āu, tu-á tsuân-pōo pàng tshut tiâu.
Pàng hōo sì-kè khù tsiah tsháu, sūn-suà tsiong puî tâi tshân-kau. / Ke-á pàng i sì-kuè tsáu, tsiah thâng tsiah tsháu i siōng gâu.
Muí kang tsháu-poo sûn thàu-thàu, i ê pak-tóo ná ē iau. / Kue-kang tīm-póo siōng ū-hāu, Kue-bó sinn nn̄g siōng-kài gâu.
Tse sī tsng-kha ê hiān-siōng, sing-uah tik-sû koo-put-tsiong. / Hiunn-ē sing-uah kā lín kóng, m̄-thang tshiò gún tsháu-tuē-sông.

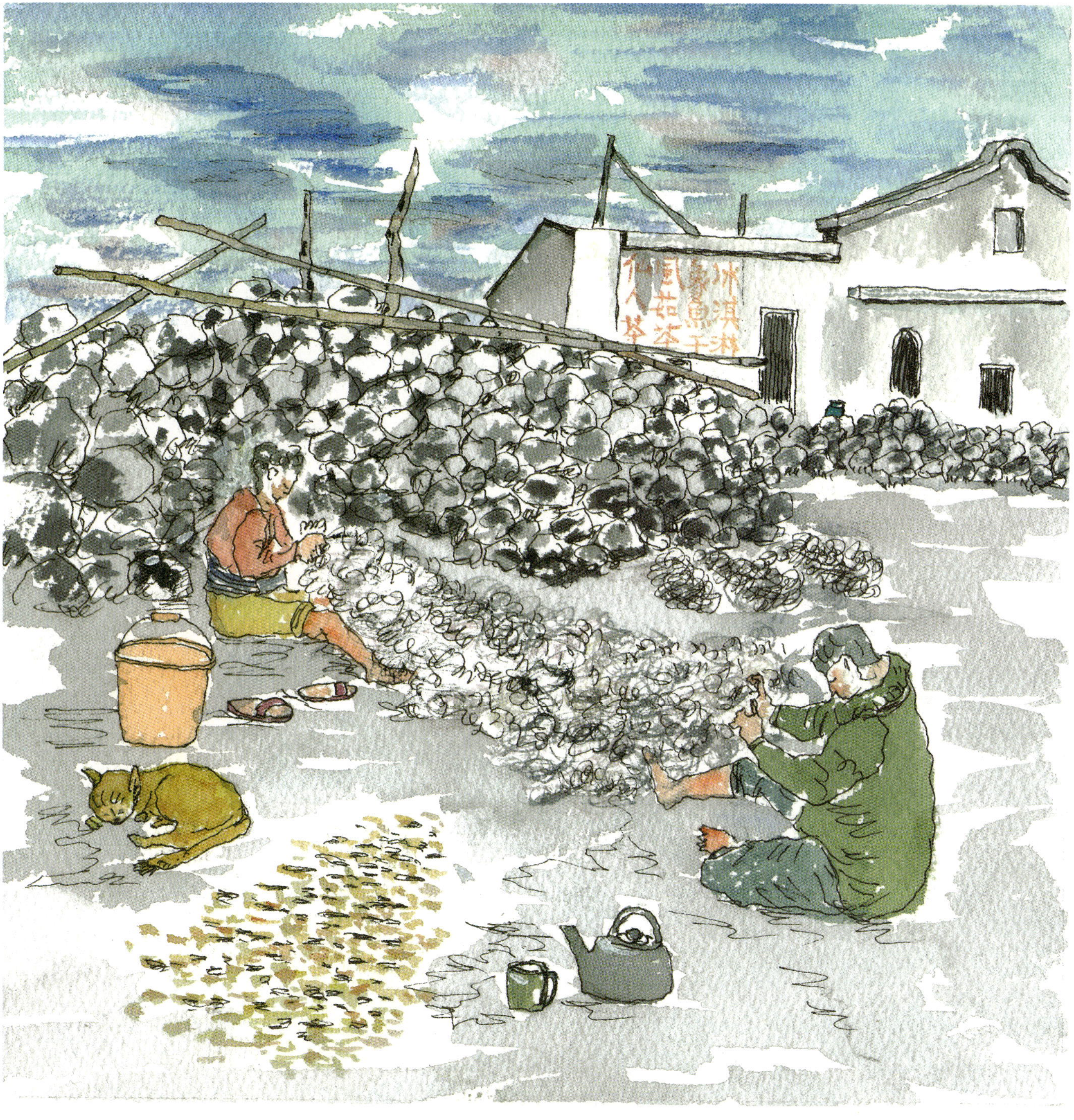

澎湖東北季風強勁，為了避免蔬果受鹽霧與鹹雨影響，島民就地取材，為辛苦耕耘的果實築起「菜宅」擋風。

The northeast wind in Penghu is strong. To protect their hard-earned fruits and vegetables from salt spray and salt rain, the islanders gather coral stones from the beach to build walls that shield them from sandstorms.

天氣不佳時，強風與大浪席捲而來，鹹水霧氣隨風而至，飛灑到島嶼的各個角落。這種鹹分使得坪頂上的青草全都枯萎，連種植的樹木也難以存活。居民們就地取材，用硓𥑮石搭建「圍仔」（uî-á）抵擋風沙，稱為「菜宅」（tshài-thèh），牆內所種的蔬菜才會有好的收成。

生活的艱辛和材料的匱乏，讓當地人養成巧妙利用資源的習慣。他們將牛屎搓成屎餅，然後貼在圍牆上曬乾，成為最優質的燃料。而豬屎則被集中存放在豬圈裡，成為最好的肥料。等到秋天的收成季節，豬被放出圈外，讓它們自由覓食，同時也能把肥料埋入田溝，為來年的耕作提供養分。

此外，雞隻在四季中也被放養，去吃蟲和啃食青草。隨著日子一天天過去，成熟的公雞便被抓來煲湯補身，而母雞則專心生蛋，為家庭提供新鮮的蛋品。這就是昔日澎湖人的生活寫照，雖然艱難，但他們用智慧與創意，成就了每一天的溫飽。

• • •

When the weather was rough, a salty mist spread across the island. This saltiness caused the grasses to wither and even the trees struggled to survive. The residents handcrafted walls from local coral limestones to shield against the wind and sand, which the locals referred to as 'tshài-thèh'. This allowed the vegetables grown within to flourish.

Because of the harsh living conditions and lack of resources in the past, locals learned to utilise available materials cleverly. For fuel, they collected cow dung, shaped it into cakes and dried it on the walls. In this way, the dried cow dung became an effective firestarter. Chickens roamed freely throughout the year, feeding on insects and grass. Villagers caught mature roosters for soup, while hens provided fresh eggs for their families. This offers a glimpse into the lives of the early Penghu inhabitants; despite the hardships, this was simply their way of life.

東　坪　的　水　鹹　佮　澀

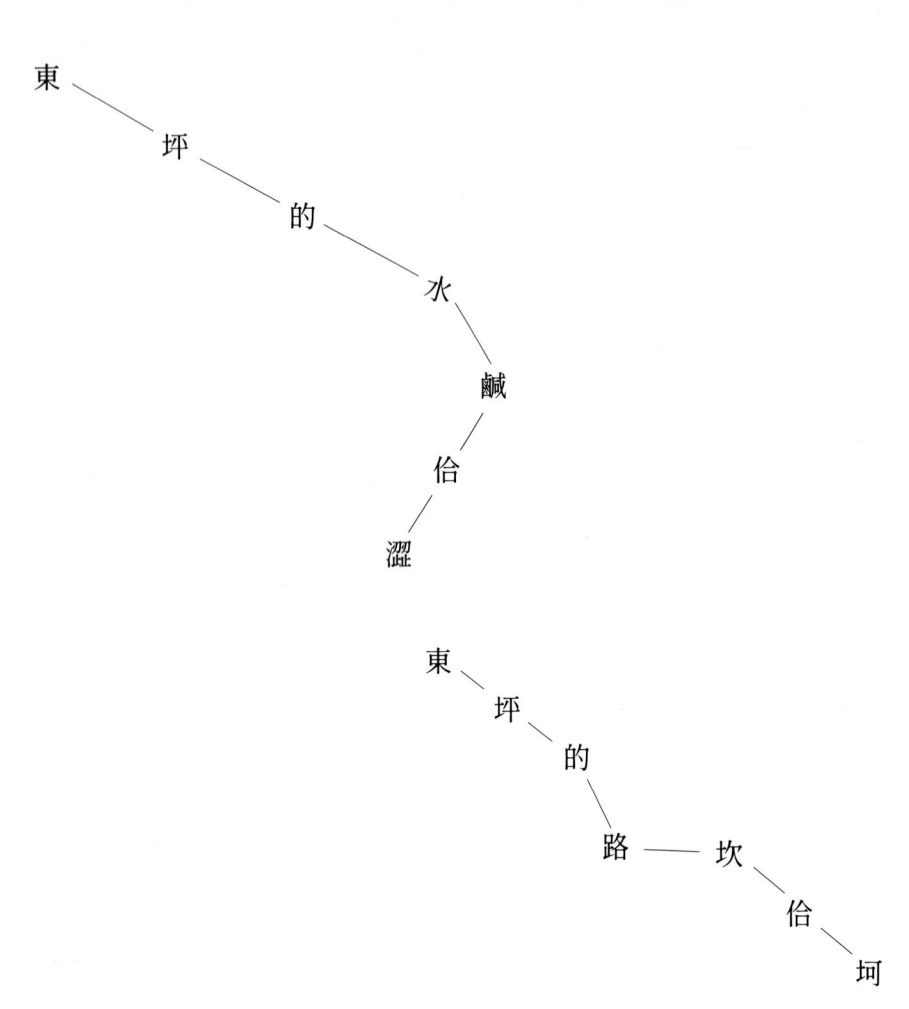

東　坪　的　路　坎　佮　坷

Í-tsá ê Tang-sū-pîng
以早的東嶼坪
The Former Tang-sū-pîng Island

無電無火無方便　　生活較實眞困難

歹天海螺搵鹹汁　　配番簽糜上紲力

Tang-pîng ê tsuí kiâm kah siap, Tang-pîng ê lōo khám kah khiat.
Bô tiān bô hé bô-hong-piān, sing-uảh khah-sit sī tsin khùn-lân.
Pháinn-thinn hái-lê-á ùn kiâm-tsap, phè han-tshiam-bê siōng suà-lát.

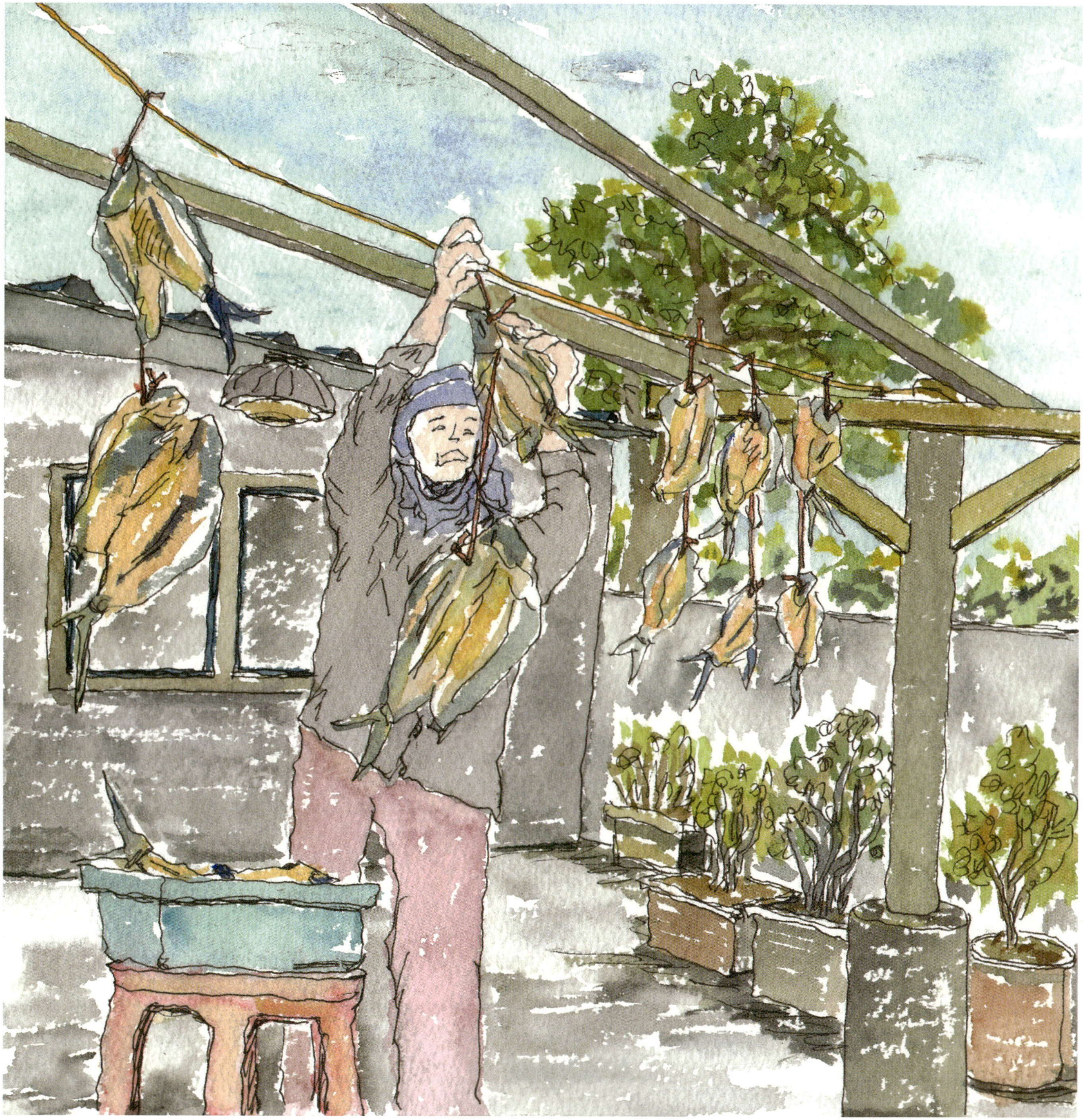

潮間帶處處可見各式螺貝、藻類為家家戶戶常備食材。

The intertidal zone is filled with a variety of shells and seaweeds, which are common ingredients in the homes of the residents.

東嶼坪四面環海,喝的水是從古井裡取來的,味道又鹹又澀。島上的路是人走出來的,崎嶇不平,「懸懸低低,坎坎坷坷,有夠歹行。」那時候沒有電話、沒有電燈、沒有冰箱,生活非常不方便。冬天來了,風大浪急,有時整整一星期都無法出海捕魚,只能去海邊撿海螺,回來沾醬油,配上蕃薯簽稀飯,生活相當艱苦。

・・・

In the early days, the people of Tang-sū-pîng (Dongyuping) Island obtained their drinking water from old wells, which tasted quite salty. There were no roads on the island; all the paths were traversed on foot and were rough and uneven. Life was very inconvenient, as there were no phones, electric lights, or refrigerators. As winter approached, strong winds and high waves prevented the residents from venturing out to sea to fish. Instead, they had to collect sea snails from the shore for food. They dipped the snails in soy sauce and ate them with porridge made from sweet potatoes, which made life quite tough.

Lȯh-hōo-thinn Pháinn Khí-hé
落雨天歹起火
It's Difficult to Light a Fire on Rainy Days

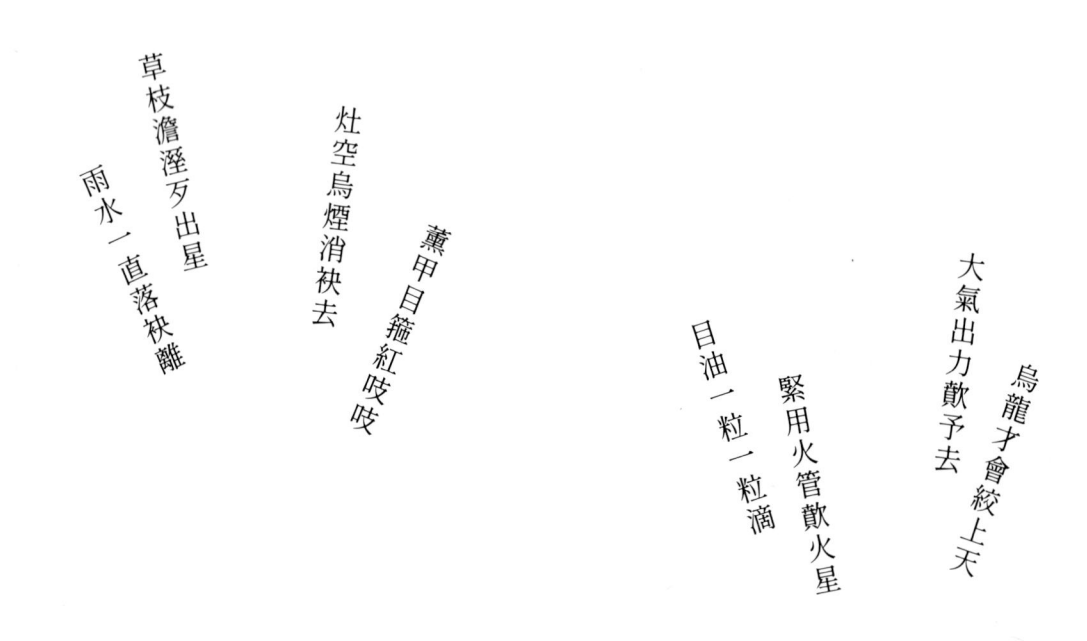

草枝澹溼歹出星
雨水一直落袂離

灶空烏煙消袂去
薰甲目箍紅吱吱

目油一粒一粒滴
緊用火管歕火星

大氣出力歕予去
烏龍才會絞上天

Hōo-tsuí it-tit lȯh buē lī, tsháu-ki tâm-sip pháinn tshut-tshinn. / Tsàu-khang ê oo-ian siau buē khì, hun kah bȧk-khoo âng-ki-ki. Bȧk-iû tsit liȧp tsit liȧp tih, kín iōng hé-kńg pûn hé-tshinn. / Tuā-khuì tshut-lȧt pûn hōo--khì, oo-liông tsiah ē ká tsiūnn-thinn.

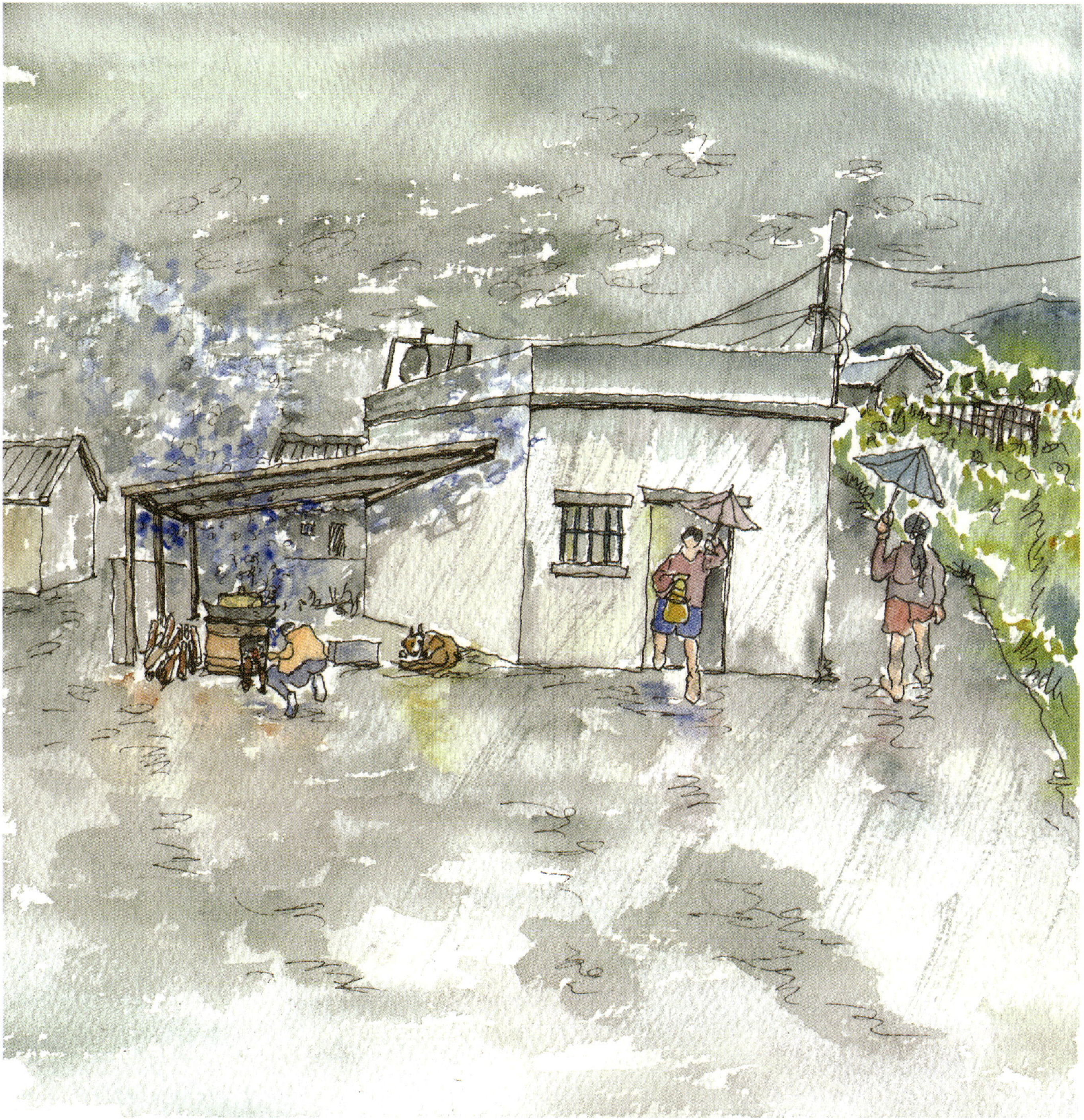

156 ｜生活 SING-UÀH

遇到下雨天，乾草濕漉漉的，生火變得特別困難。整個爐灶冒出的黑煙讓人受不了，眼睛被熏得紅紅的，忍不住眼油直流。這時，還是得趕快用火竹管用力吹氣，希望能夠點燃火星。只要出現一點火星，草就能燒起來，當烏煙就會順著煙囪飄到天空，就宣告：可以有飯吃了。

• • •

On rainy days, the dry grass used for starting a fire becomes damp, making it very difficult to light a flame. The thick smoke coming from the stove is unbearable, causing our eyes to turn red and swell, leaving us unable to help shedding tears. At this point, we have to grab a bamboo tube quickly to blow air into the fire, hoping to create a spark. As soon as a small flicker appears, the grass can catch fire and then the black smoke will rise from the chimney, curling up into the sky!

Liȧh-hû, Sinn-kiánn
掠魚、生囝
Fishing and Having Children

(女) ⌒ (男)

阿哥討海顧三頓　　　　　阿娘拚命咧生囝
五更雞啼天欲光　　　　　予阮有囝叫阿爸

小妹緊起攢早頓　　　　　手巾提來共拭汗
予哥食飽通出門　　　　　麻油雞酒攢予食

Lú Po:
A-ko--á thó-hái kòo sann-tǹg, gōo-kinn kue-thî thinn beh kng.
Sió-muē-á kín khé tshuân tsá-tǹg, hōo ko--á tsiȧh-pá thang tshut-mn̂g.

Lâm Po:
A-niû--á piànn-miā leh sinn-kiánn, hōo gún ū kiánn kiò a-pa.
Tshiú-kin-á thėh-lâi kā--tshit-kuānn, muâ-iû ke tsiú tshuân hōo--tsiȧh.

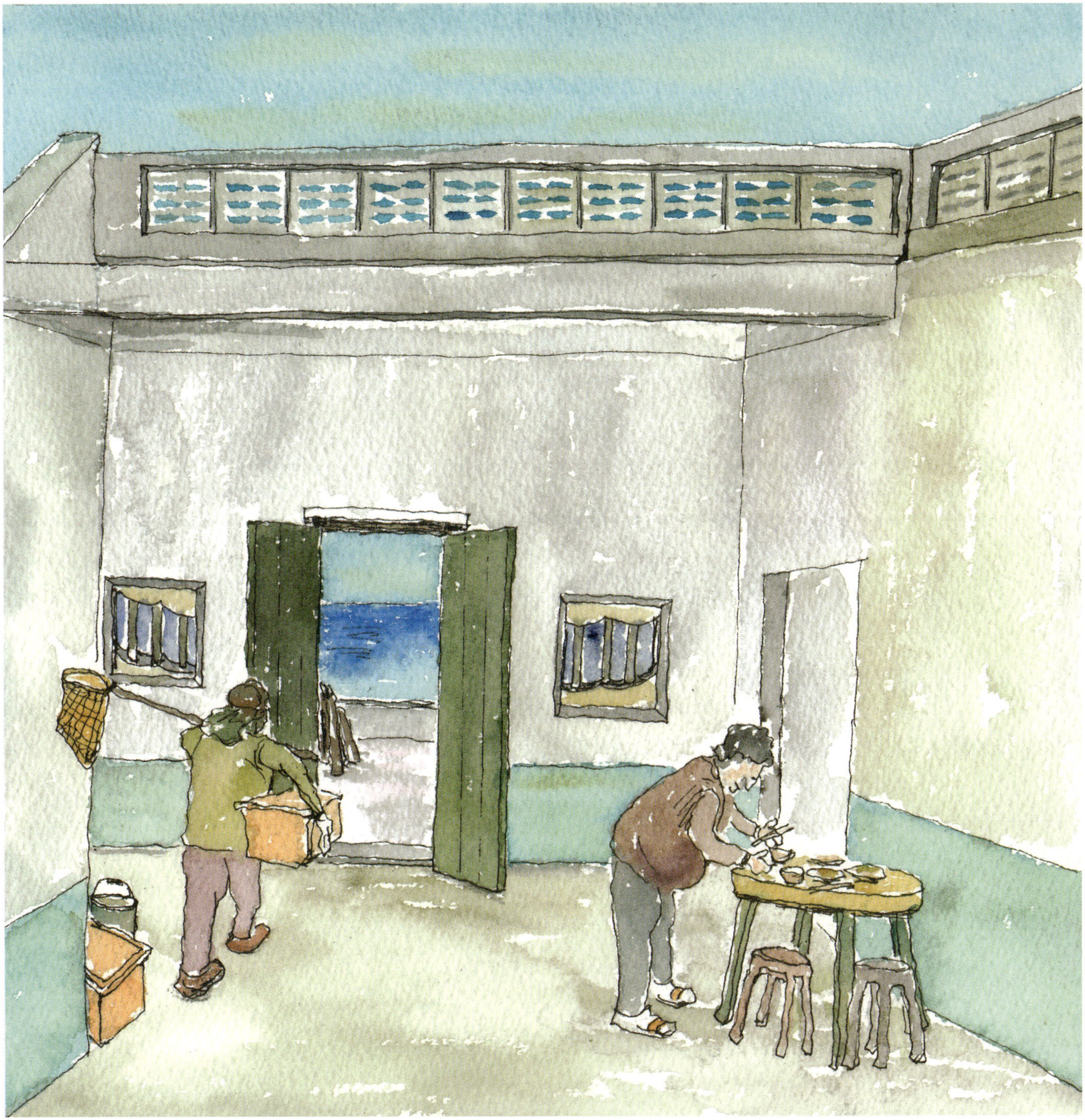

160 ｜生活 SING-UÁH

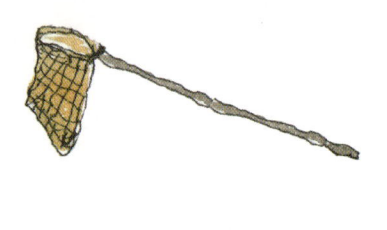

在澎湖的離島上，男人主要負責出海捕魚，而女人則在家裡照顧家庭和耕作。天氣好的時候，男人會在清晨天還未亮，悄悄起身，準備好出海的工具。這時，太太們聽到五更時的雞鳴，也會迅速起床，為丈夫準備早飯。當太太準備要生產時，丈夫知道自己即將當爸爸，會非常地高興，還會購買許多補品讓太太坐月子。在這個時候，他們的感情更加深厚，甚至比新婚時還要甜蜜。丈夫心中充滿感恩，對太太生子的辛苦更是無比珍惜。

・・・

In Penghu, men have traditionally been responsible for fishing, while women take on the responsibilities of managing the household and farming. Men often rise before dawn to prepare their fishing gear, while their wives busily prepare breakfast for them. As the time approaches for a wife to give birth, her husband feels a surge of excitement and joy at the thought of becoming a father. He makes a special effort to purchase a variety of nutritious foods to help his wife regain her strength. Their bond deepens as they await the arrival of their new baby, growing even sweeter than during their honeymoon period.

Ná Ē Án-ne

哪會按呢
How Could This Happen?

今日海面平波波

阿哥招阮去撿蚵

踏著青苔來

滑

倒　　害阮褲底澹膏膏

Kin-á-jit hái-bīn pînn-pho-pho, a-ko--á tsio gún khù tshiàm-ô.
Gún tȧh tiȯh tshinn-thî lâi kút-tó, hāi gún khòo-tué tâm-ko-ko.

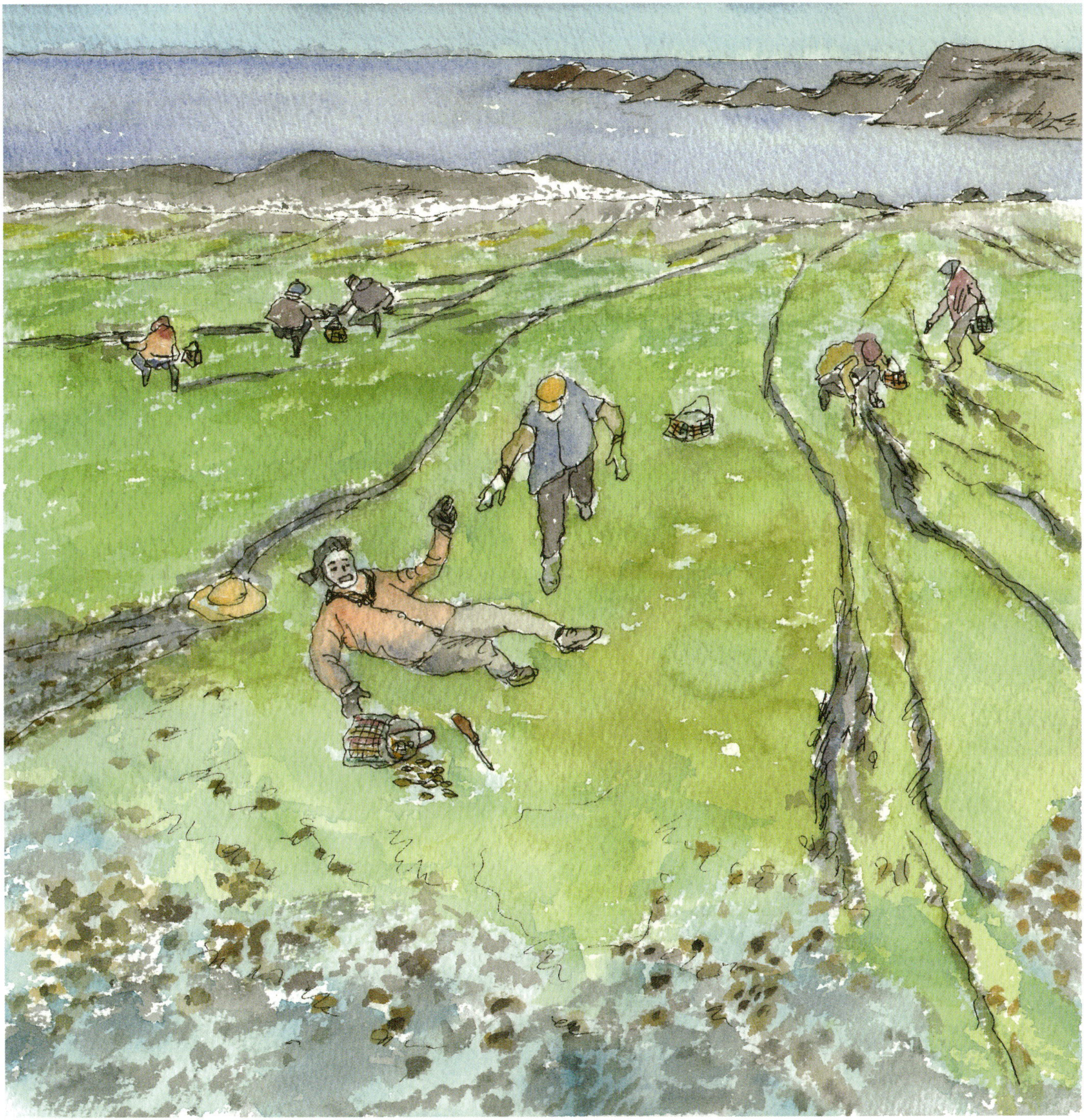

164 | 生活 SING-UÁH

今天天氣晴朗，風平浪靜。男生邀請女生一起去海邊敲牡蠣，女生高興得跟著去了，結果卻不小心踩到青苔，滑了一跤，四腳朝天，整個褲底都濕透了，感覺真見笑（kiàn-siàu）。只好趕緊回家換內褲，心裡不停擔心被人看見，恨不得找個地洞鑽進去，哪會按呢！

． ． ．

It had been a calm and lovely day. A boy invited a girl to go to the seaside to collect oysters and she happily agreed. However, she accidentally stepped on some seaweed and slipped, landing flat on her backside, completely soaking her trousers. It was incredibly embarrassing! She had to rush home to change, all the while worrying about whether anyone had seen her. She felt so shy that she wished she could just find a hole in the ground to hide in!

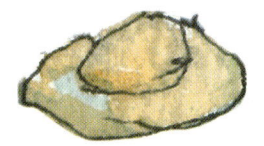

Khik-lān Ha̍k-hāu

克難學校（小學一年到六年）
Difficult Times at a Remote Primary School

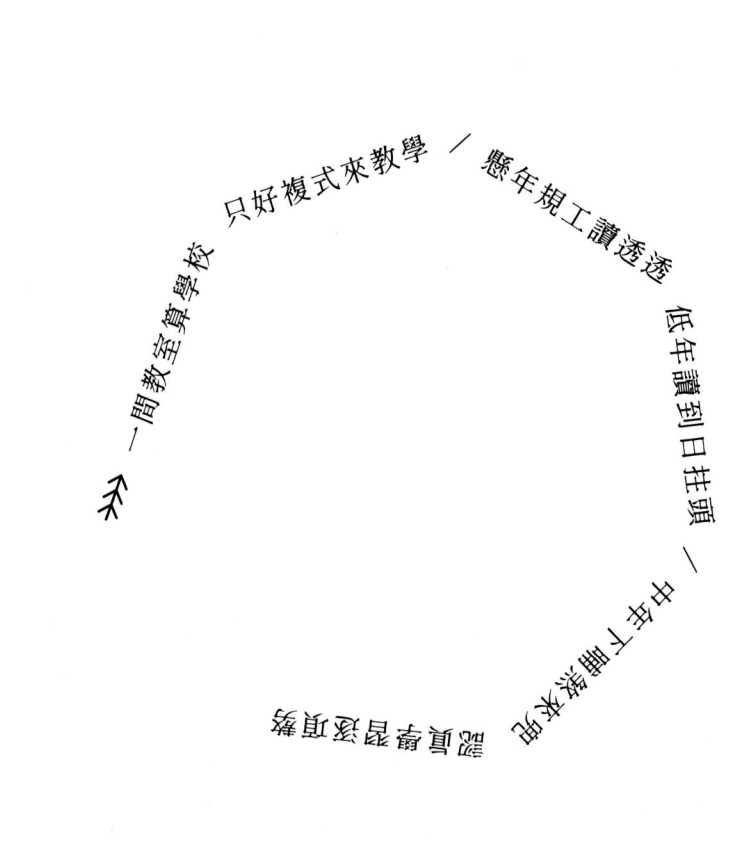

一間教室算學校　／　只好複式來教學　／　懸年規工讀透透　／　低年讀到日拄頭　／　中年下晡紲來到　／　認真學習逐項賢

Tsit king kàu-sik sǹg ha̍k-hāu, tsí-hó ho̍k-sik lâi kà-ha̍k.
Kuân-nî-ê kui kang tha̍k thàu-thàu, kē-nî-ê tha̍k kàu jit tú-thâu.
Tiong-nî-ê ē-poo suah lâi tau, jīn-tsin ha̍k-si̍p ta̍k hāng gâu.

成績欄

嶼坪國小西坪分校於 1988 年 8 月停止招生，現已廢校，位置緊鄰西坪村的發電廠房。

The Xiping Branch of the Yuping Primary School stopped enrolling pupils in August 1988 and has since been closed. It is located next to the generator room on Sai-sū-pîng (Xiyuping) Island.

在 1949 年的澎湖南方四島，由於學生人數不多，每隔一年才招生一次。在西嶼坪的小學裡，只有一間教室和一位老師。老師不得不採用複式教學，教室裡同時有兩班學生，高年級的學生整天上課，中年級的學生則在下午上課，而低年級的學生則在上午上課。例如，當老師為高年級的學生授課時，另一邊的學生則進行寫字、畫圖或安靜地閱讀，每天的課程都如此循環進行。雖然老師的教學工作很辛苦，但學生們都很認真學習，因此大家的成績也都非常好。

・・・

In 1949, the southern four islands of Penghu had a limited number of children of school age, so they only took new admissions every other year. On Sai-sū-pîng (Xiyuping) Island, there was only one primary school, which had just one classroom and one teacher. The teacher had to use a mixed-age teaching method to instruct all the pupils together. While the teacher was helping one group, the others kept themselves busy with writing, drawing, or reading on their own. This routine was carried out daily. Although the learning environment was not ideal, both the teacher and the pupils greatly valued the rare opportunity to learn on this remote island.

Khuài-lȯk ê Phînn-ôo-lâng
快樂的澎湖人
The Happy People of Penghu

澎湖攏是小所在　靠海生活通人知　/　歹天漁船無出海　招恁褒歌對遮來
阮的褒歌兼勸世　誠心娛樂恁逐家　/　有閒請來阮遮坐　互相褒歌兼話題

Phînn-ôo lóng sī sió sóo-tsāi, khò hái sing-uȧh thong-lâng tsai.
Pháinn-thinn hû-tsûn-á bô tshut-hái, tsio lín po-kua tuì tsia lâi.
Gún ê po-kua kiam khǹg-sè, sîng-sim ngôo-lȯk lín tȧk-ke.
Ū-îng tshiánn lâi gún tsia tsē, hōo-siong po-kua kiam uī-tê.

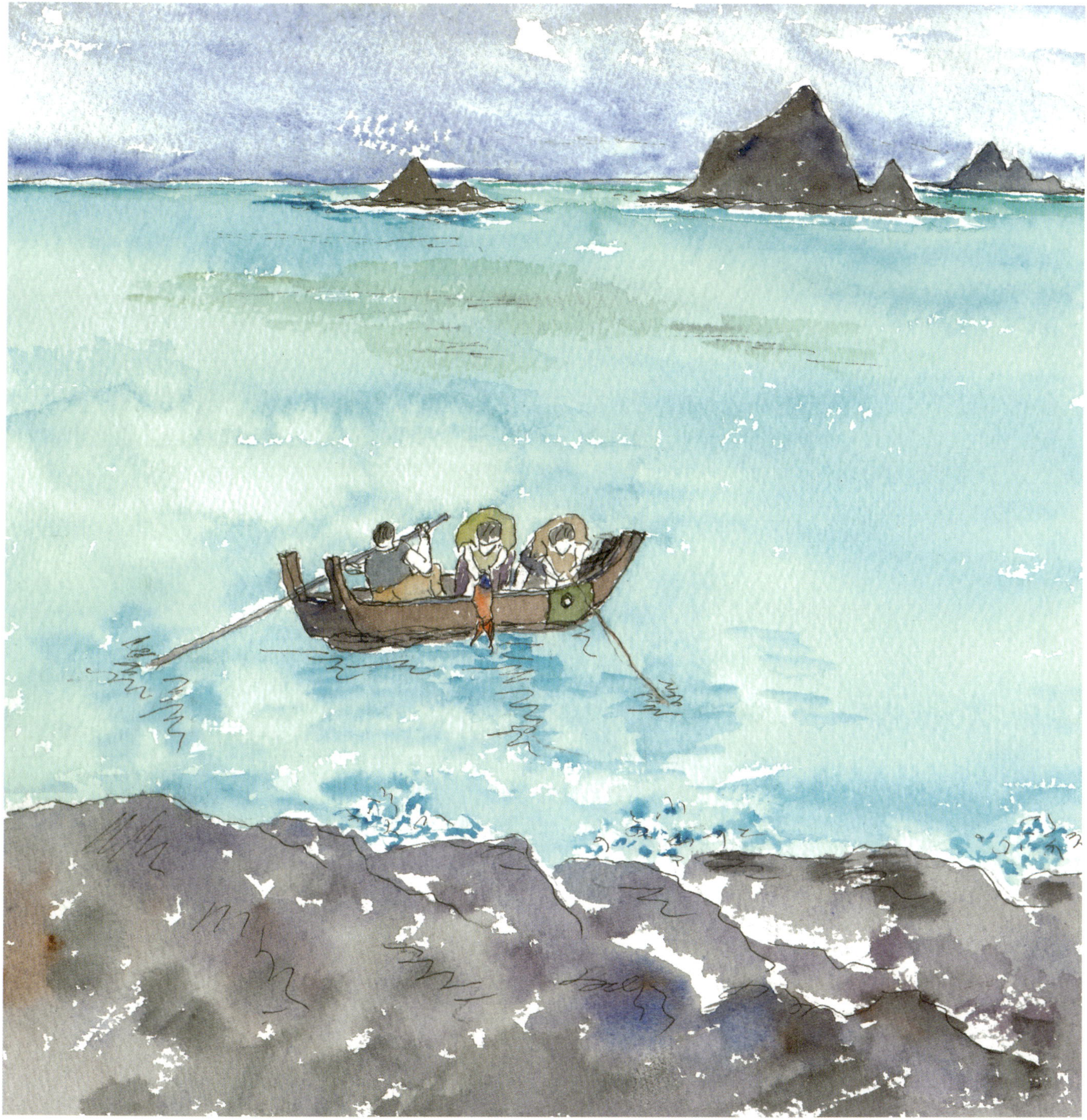

冬日陽光正暖，東嶼坪村民悠悠等船入港。

In the warm winter sunshine, villagers leisurely wait for the boats to arrive at the harbor.

澎湖是一個小地方，居民大多依賴捕魚過生活。每當遇到惡劣天氣無法出海捕魚，或在農忙結束後，大家會聚在一起，談天說地，閒話家常。其實，談論的話題多數圍繞著捕魚的經歷、農田耕作的故事、夫妻之間的趣事，甚至還有賭博打牌的點滴。不過，偶爾也會大家邀約一同來唱褒歌，無論是討海歌、種作歌、愛情歌、跋筊（puȧh-kiáu）歌、勸世歌還是剾洗（khau-sé）歌，只要能夠褒得出來，都趣味無窮。

· · ·

Penghu is a lovely little island where most residents depend on fishing for their livelihood. During stormy weather, when the sea is too rough for fishing, or after the harvest season, the locals often gather to share stories and remember their lives and work. In these moments of friendship, they occasionally join in singing ballads together—be it fishing ballads, farming ballads, love ballads, or playful teasing ballads. The air fills with laughter and music and as long as there is a song to sing, the atmosphere becomes lively and joyful.

澎湖褒歌自早有

笑詼趣味一大垺

褒歌愛有鬥四句

正剾倒削展工夫

呵咾剾洗攏嘛有

無比哪知啥贏輸

若是需要褒較濟

有彼才調無問題

八句十句隨人做　褒出趣味兼笑詼

Phînn-ôo-lâng Ài Po-kua

澎湖人愛褒歌
The People of Penghu Love to Sing Ballads

Phînn-ôo po-kua tsū-tsá ū, tshiò-khue tshù-bī tsit tuā pû.
Po-kua ài ū tàu sì kù, tsiànn-khau-tò-siah tián kang-hu.
O-ló khau-sé lóng mā ū, bô pí ná tsai siánn iânn-su.
Nā-sī su-iàu po khah tsuē, ū he tsâi-tiāu sī bô-būn-tuê.
Pueh kù tsa̍p kù suî-lâng tsuè, po tshut tshù-bī kiam tshiò-khue.

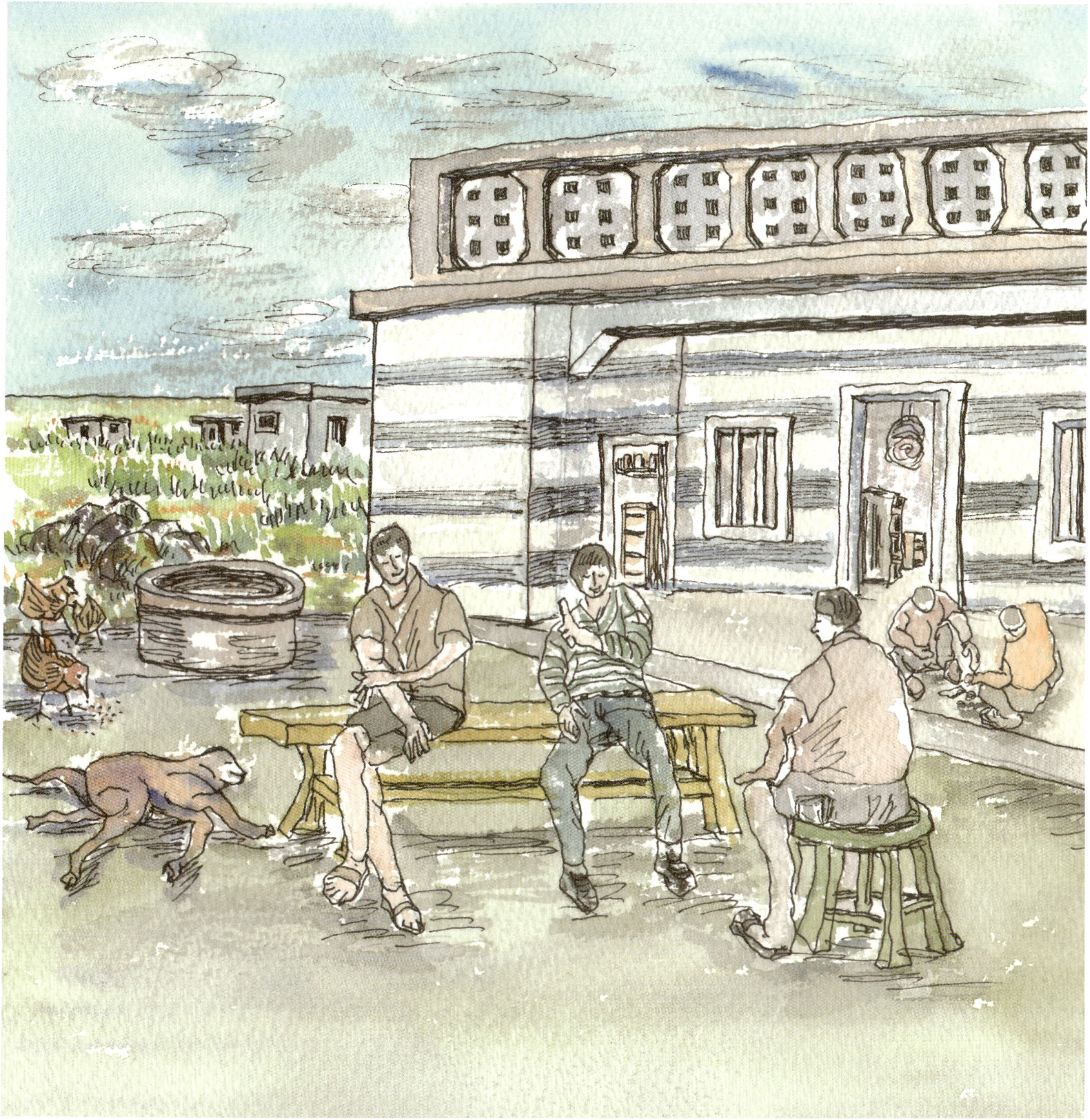

守護東吉燈塔的林阿燦，在啟明宮聽到呂坤翰老師唱褒歌時，不禁驚呼：「這正是我小時候聽大人唱的褒歌啊！」

Lin A-Tsan, who retired from his work at the Tang-kiat (Dongji) lighthouse, couldn't help but exclaim upon hearing Mr Lu Kun-Han sing Penghu ballads at the Tang-kiat Khé-bîng Temple, 'This is exactly the ballad I heard adults sing when I was a child!'

澎湖一直以來便流傳著動人的褒歌，每首褒歌通常由四句組成，且講究押韻，因而音韻優美。歌詞中既有相互自嘲的幽默，也有誇獎讚美的風度，這使得褒歌富含趣味，充滿變化。有時候若想加褒幾句，若你有本事，就儘量展（tián）出來褒，將歡樂帶給眾人！

• • •

The ballads of Penghu are incredibly melodic, with each song typically comprising four lines, featuring rhymed endings that make them particularly delightful to sing. These ballads encompass a variety of themes and are rich in interest, offering endless diversity. Occasionally, if singers wish to add a few lines, they are free to do so, provided they have the necessary skill, bringing joy and delight to all.

LÔ-TŌNG

勞

動

　台灣有一句俗話說:「上山看山勢,入門看人意」,然而對於澎湖人來說,「落海知海音」更是與海共生的必修課。在〈天照甲子佇咧行〉中,呂坤翰生動描繪早期人們在不同季節的勞動情景,與面對自然考驗的心境。〈熱天焰小管〉和〈大流去抾螺仔〉兩首作品,分別展現了漁民們如何根據季節與海象的變化捕捉小卷,和在退潮時結伴前往潮間帶,尋找各種美味的貝類、螺類和螃蟹。對許多澎湖漁民來說,土魠魚是大海的新年贈禮,也是整年收入的主要來源,因此在〈浮著塗魠好過年〉中,展現出漁民們在海上拚搏的精神中,那給家人豐足生活的自許。

　〈作田人的心聲〉描繪了因長期乾旱而耕作困難的窘境,為了滋潤土地,人們不得不挑水灌溉,努力換來豐收的希望。〈台灣牛強閣勇〉讚頌了島民的最佳夥伴——牛,表達對其默默奉獻的感謝。〈擔肥去壅田〉描述了農曆初六婦女們互相合作,將堆肥挑到田裡的辛勤過程,以及村民在農忙後,款待宴客的熱情與滿足。〈雨水來到當著時〉與〈塗豆大豐收〉慶祝了雨水充沛,農田裡的番薯和花生豐收,大家共享這份富饒與快樂之情。

　從海田到陸地,一起聽他唱出島民為生計拚搏的勞動之歌。

LABOR

In Taiwan, there is a saying that highlights the importance of being aware of one's surroundings. For the people of Penghu, however, it is vital to pay attention to ocean currents to ensure safety while fishing—an essential lesson for those who depend on the sea for their livelihood.

In 'There is a Time for Everything', the work explores the different seasons and shows how people need to adapt their lives and work to follow the natural rhythms of the world. In 'Catch Pencil Squid in Summer' and 'Collecting Shells at Low Tide', he illustrates how fishermen catch pencil squid based on sea conditions and gather shellfish during low tide. For many fishermen in Penghu, the Spanish mackerel is a key source of income throughout the year. In 'Catch Spanish Mackerel for a Prosperous Lunar New Year', the piece conveys the determination of these fishermen, who never give up.

'The Hearts of Farmers' reveals the struggles of farmers facing challenges in growing their crops due to prolonged dry spells. 'Taiwanese Cattle: Reliable Helpers for Farmers' praises the hard work and loyalty of these animals. In 'A Farmer Carrying Fertiliser to the Fields', set on the sixth day of the Lunar New Year, the story highlights women working together to carry fertiliser to the fields, along with the joyful gatherings of villagers celebrating after a busy farming season. 'Just in Time for the Rain' and 'A Bountiful Peanut Harvest' capture the happiness of farmers as they celebrate the much-needed rain that leads to an abundant harvest of sweet potatoes and peanuts. From the sea to the land, Lu Kun-Han's songs reflect the struggles and resilience of the people in Penghu as they strive for their livelihoods.

Thinn Tsiàu Kah-tsí tī leh Kiânn
天照甲子佇咧行
There is a Time for Everything

[呂坤翰採集後改編]

It-geh líng-hong kuânn-sí tu, Jī-geh sng-tàng kuânn-sí gû.
Sann-geh kuânn-sí tsa-bóo-á sin-pū, sì-geh kuânn-sí pòo-tshân hu.
Nā-sī bô tsiah gōo-geh-tsàng, phuà-hiû thǹg-tiāu ē kuânn-sí-lâng.
Lak-geh iām-jit tshit-geh hé, khuê-sìnn theh-lâi iat-hong tshe.
Pueh káu nn̄g geh thinn tńg-liâng, he-ku khàm-sàu ài thê-hông.
Tsap-geh nā lâi pak-hong tân, tshiō-tsan kuè liáu uānn phû-lân.
Tsap-it-geh siu-sîng jip kng-àng, lah-geh it-tīng ài póo-tang.
Tsit nî sù-kuì bô-kāng-khuán, thinn tsiàu kah-tsí leh sûn-khuân.

一月冷風寒死豬

二月霜凍寒死牛

三月寒死查某新婦

四月寒死佈田夫

若是無食五月粽

破裘褪掉寒死人

六月炎日七月火

葵扇提來撰風吹

八九兩月天轉涼

痎呴咳嗽愛提防

十月若來北風霆

炤罾過了換浮笭

十一月收成入缸甕

臘月一定愛補冬

一年四季無全款

天照甲子咧循環

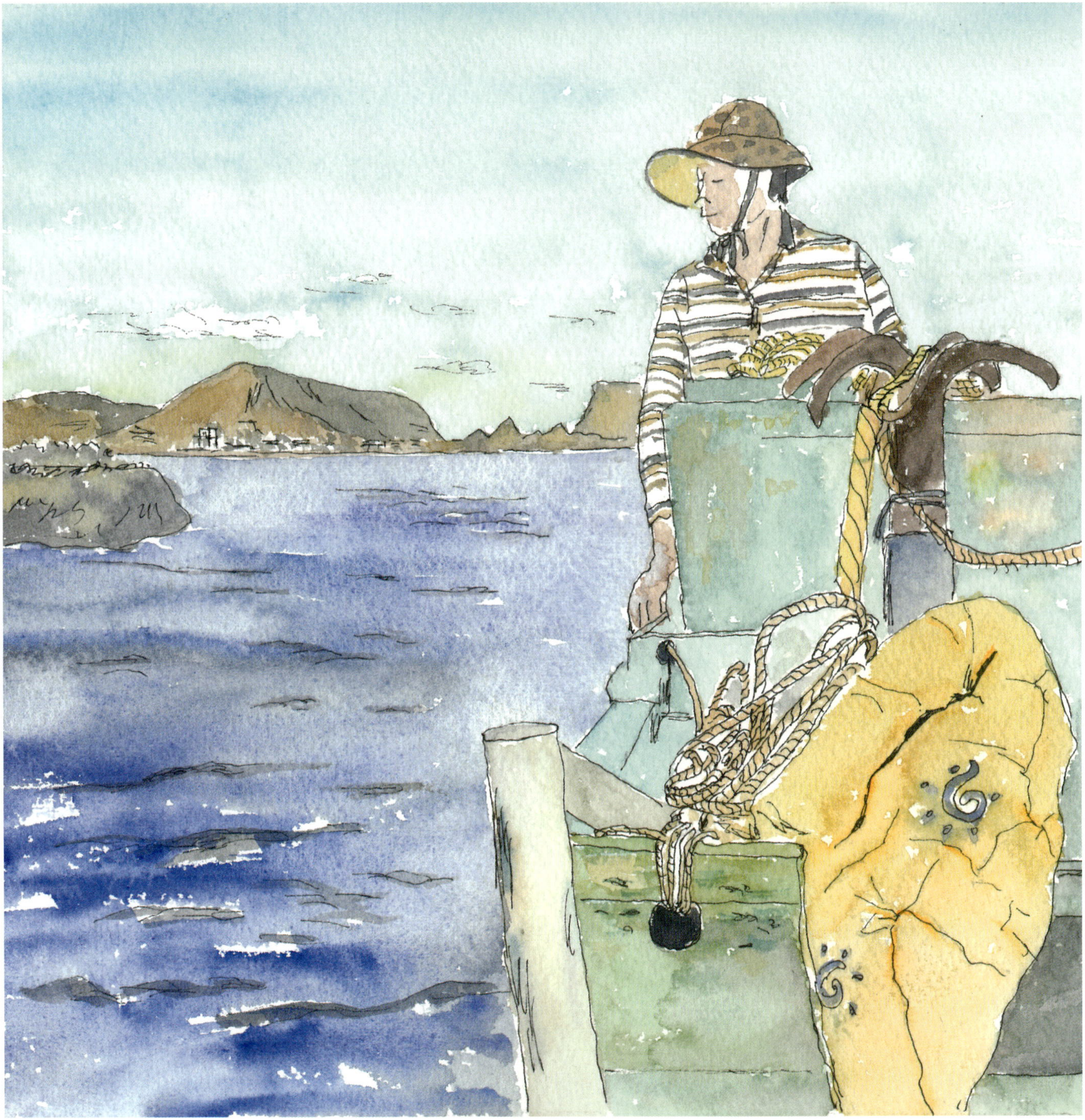

182 ｜ 勞動 LÔ-TŌNG

在以前的年代，一年四季的變化都依循著節氣的規律，天氣寒暖轉變層次分明。寒冷的冬季、炎熱的夏天、潤澤的梅雨，以及辛勤耕作的季節，這些自然的現象總是準時來臨。許多耆老深諳這些變化，將遵循自然韻律的生活智慧化作褒歌，代代相傳。呂坤翰回憶起他的童年，母親常常在家門口輕聲吟唱那首褒歌。島嶼鄉音，伴隨著眼前的日常景象，深深烙印在他的心中。直到 1964 年他考進入師範學校後，才忍不住向哥哥請教這首褒歌的全文。當他終於確定了內容，便迫不及待地將它詳盡記錄下來。這不僅是褒歌的保存，更是對隨著季節流轉運作生活的島嶼之珍貴印記。

• • •

In earlier times, the changes in the four seasons followed the patterns of the solar terms and the shifts in weather were quite clear. We experienced cold winters, hot summers, nourishing rainy seasons and periods of hard work in the fields; these natural events always arrived on time. Many elders understood these changes well and turned their knowledge of living in harmony with nature into songs, passing them down through the generations. Thinking back to my childhood, I remember my mother often singing those songs softly at the front door. It wasn't until 1964, when I began my teacher training course, that I couldn't help but ask my brother for the complete lyrics of the ballad. When I finally figured out the words, I eagerly wrote them down. This was not just about preserving a song; it was also a precious reminder of island life that changes with the seasons.

Juah-thinn Tshiō Sió-kńg
熱天炤小管
Catch Pencil Squid in Summer

今年小管順時來　　佇咱花嶼大嶼西　/　下晡船仔總出海　欲炤小管對遮來

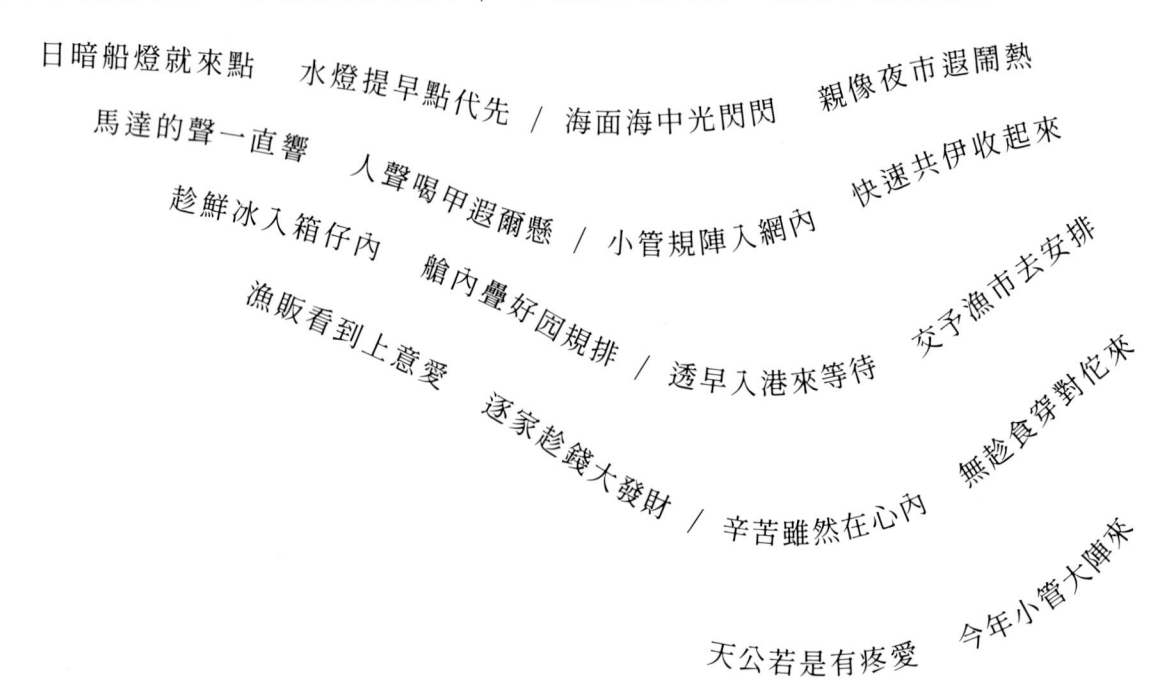

日暗船燈就來點　　水燈提早點代先　/　海面海中光閃閃　　親像夜市遐鬧熱

馬達的聲一直響　　人聲喝甲遐爾懸　/　小管規陣入網內　快速共伊收起來

趁鮮冰入箱仔內　　艙內疊好囥規排　/　透早入港來等待　交予漁市去安排

漁販看到上意愛　　逐家趁錢大發財　/　辛苦雖然在心內　無趁食穿對佗來

天公若是有疼愛　今年小管大陣來

Kin-nî sió-kńg-á sūn-sî lâi, tī lán Hue-sū Tuā-sū sai. / Ē-poo tsûn-á tsóng tshut-hái, beh tshiō sió-kńg-á tòh tuì tsia lâi.
Jit--àm tsûn-ting tō lâi tiám, tsuí-ting thê-tsá tiám tāi-sing. / Hái-bīn hái-tiong kng-siám-siám, tshin-tshiūnn iā-tshī-á hiah lāu-liàt.
Mòo-tà ê siann it-tit hiáng, lâng-siann huah kah sī hiah-nī-á kuân. / Sió-kńg-á kui tīn jip bāng lāi, khuài-sok kā i siu khí-lâi.
Thàn tshinn ping lip siunn-á lāi, tshng lāi thiàp hó khǹg kui pâi. / Thàu-tsá jip-káng lâi tán-thāi, kau hōo hû-tshī khù an-pâi.
Hû-huān-á khuànn tiòh siōng ì-ài, tàk-ke thàn-tsînn tuā huat-tsâi. / Sin-khóo sui-jiân tsāi sim-lāi, bô thàn tsiàh-tshīng tuì tó lâi.
Thinn-kong nā-sī ū thiànn-ài, kin-nî sió-kńg-á tō tuā-tīn lâi.

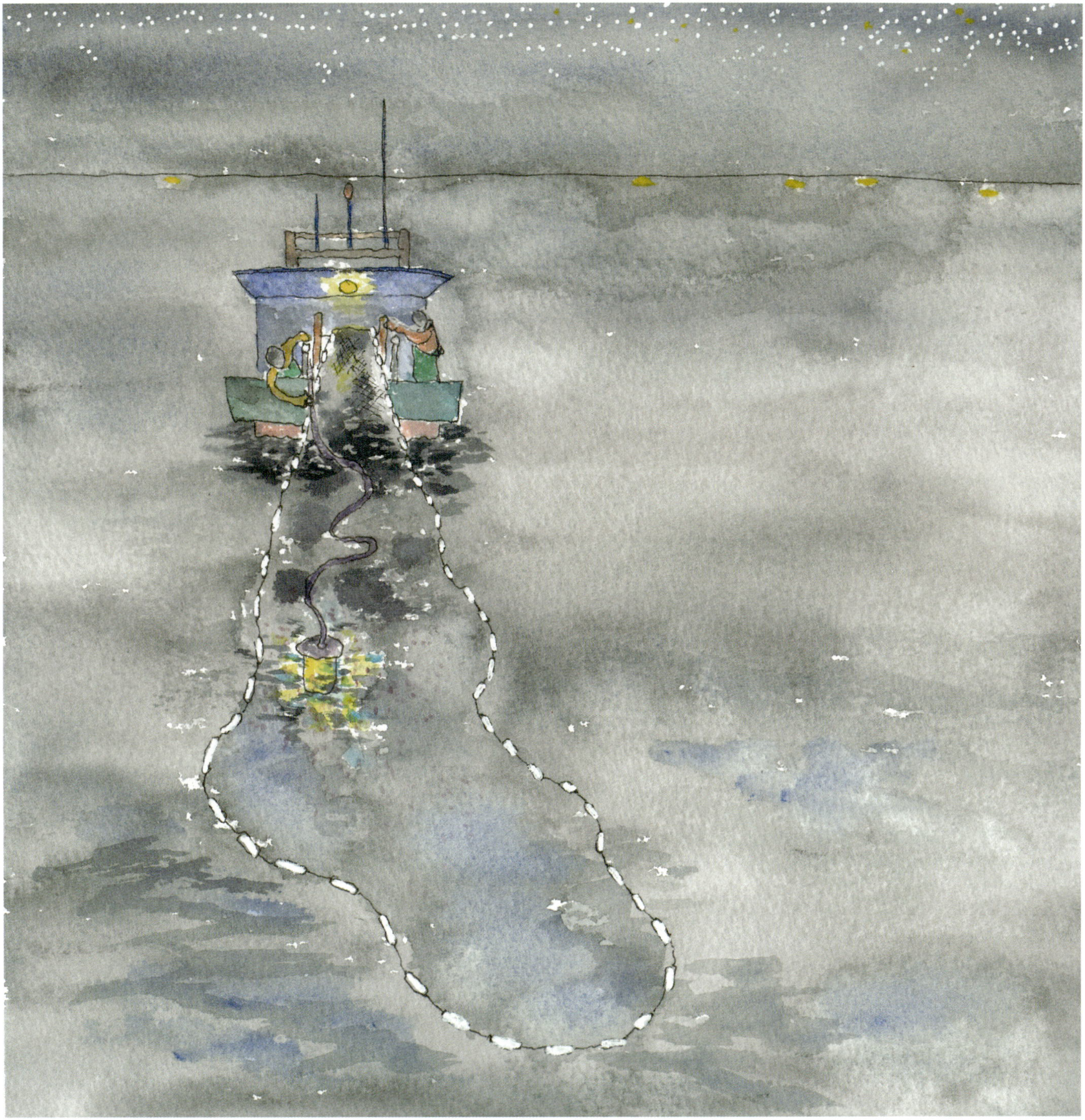

186 ｜勞動 LÔ-TŌNG

漁民在捕捉小管仔（Sió-kńg-á，小卷）之前，會先放下水燈，讓海面在夜色中閃閃發光。小管仔特別喜歡聚集在光亮的地方，漸漸地，它們便會靠近船邊。這時，漁民們小心翼翼地將漁網撒進海裡，慢慢展開。隨著船上的燈光漸漸暗下，小管仔被吸引得浮上水面。漁民們這時趕緊用網捕捉，整群小管仔瞬間落入網內。看著滿船的小管，漁民們笑逐顏開的返航。船的馬達聲轟轟作響，伴隨著漁民們的開心談笑，讓整個海面變成一座熱鬧的夜市。

• • •

Before the fishermen catch the pencil squid, they first lower the fishing lights, making the sea sparkle in the night. The pencil squid particularly like to gather in bright areas and gradually they move closer to the side of the boat. At this point, the fishermen carefully throw their nets into the water, slowly spreading them out. As the lights on the boat gradually dim, the pencil squid are drawn to the surface. The fishermen quickly use the nets to catch them and in an instant, a whole group of pencil squid falls into the nets. The sound of the boat's engine roars, while the fishermen chat happily, making the whole sea feel like a lively night market.

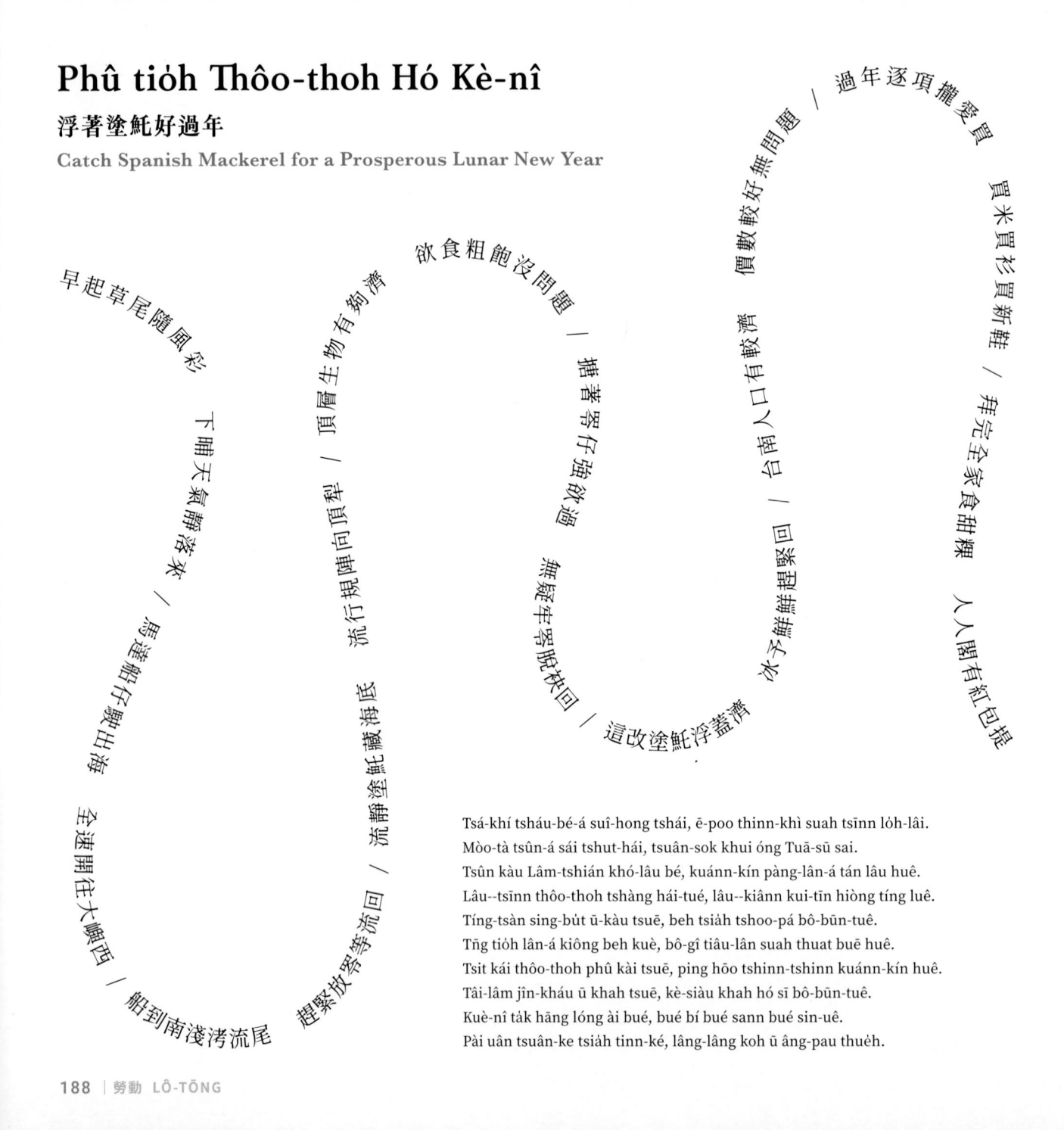

Phû tiȯh Thôo-thoh Hó Kè-nî
浮著塗魠好過年
Catch Spanish Mackerel for a Prosperous Lunar New Year

早起草尾隨風筅 / 下晡天氣煞變懸 / 船到南淺洘流尾 / 全速開往大礁西 / 流靜塗魠藏海底 / 流行規陣向頂犁 / 頂層生物有夠濟 / 欲食粗飽沒問題 / 揣著崙仔強欲過 / 無疑蹺崙煞脫梭 / 趕緊放索等流回 / 這改塗魠浮蓋濟 / 冰子鮮鮮趕緊回 / 台南人口有較濟 / 價數較好無問題 / 過年逐項攏愛買 / 買米買衫買新鞋 / 拜完全家食甜粿 / 人人閣有紅包捏

Tsá-khí tsháu-bé-á suî-hong tshái, ē-poo thinn-khì suah tsīnn lȯh-lâi.
Mòo-tà tsûn-á sái tshut-hái, tsuân-sok khui óng Tuā-sū sai.
Tsûn kàu Lâm-tshián khó-lâu bé, kuánn-kín pàng-lân-á tán lâu huê.
Lâu--tsīnn thôo-thoh tshàng hái-tué, lâu--kiânn kui-tīn hiòng tíng luê.
Tíng-tsàn sing-bu̍t ū-kàu tsuē, beh tsia̍h tshoo-pá bô-būn-tuê.
Tn̄g tio̍h lân-á kiông beh kuè, bô-gî tiâu-lân suah thuat buē huê.
Tsit kái thôo-thoh phû kài tsuē, ping hōo tshinn-tshinn kuánn-kín huê.
Tâi-lâm jîn-kháu ū khah tsuē, kè-siàu khah hó sī bô-būn-tuê.
Kuè-nî ta̍k hāng lóng ài bué, bué bí bué sann bué sin-uê.
Pài uân tsuân-ke tsia̍h tinn-ké, lâng-lâng koh ū âng-pau thue̍h.

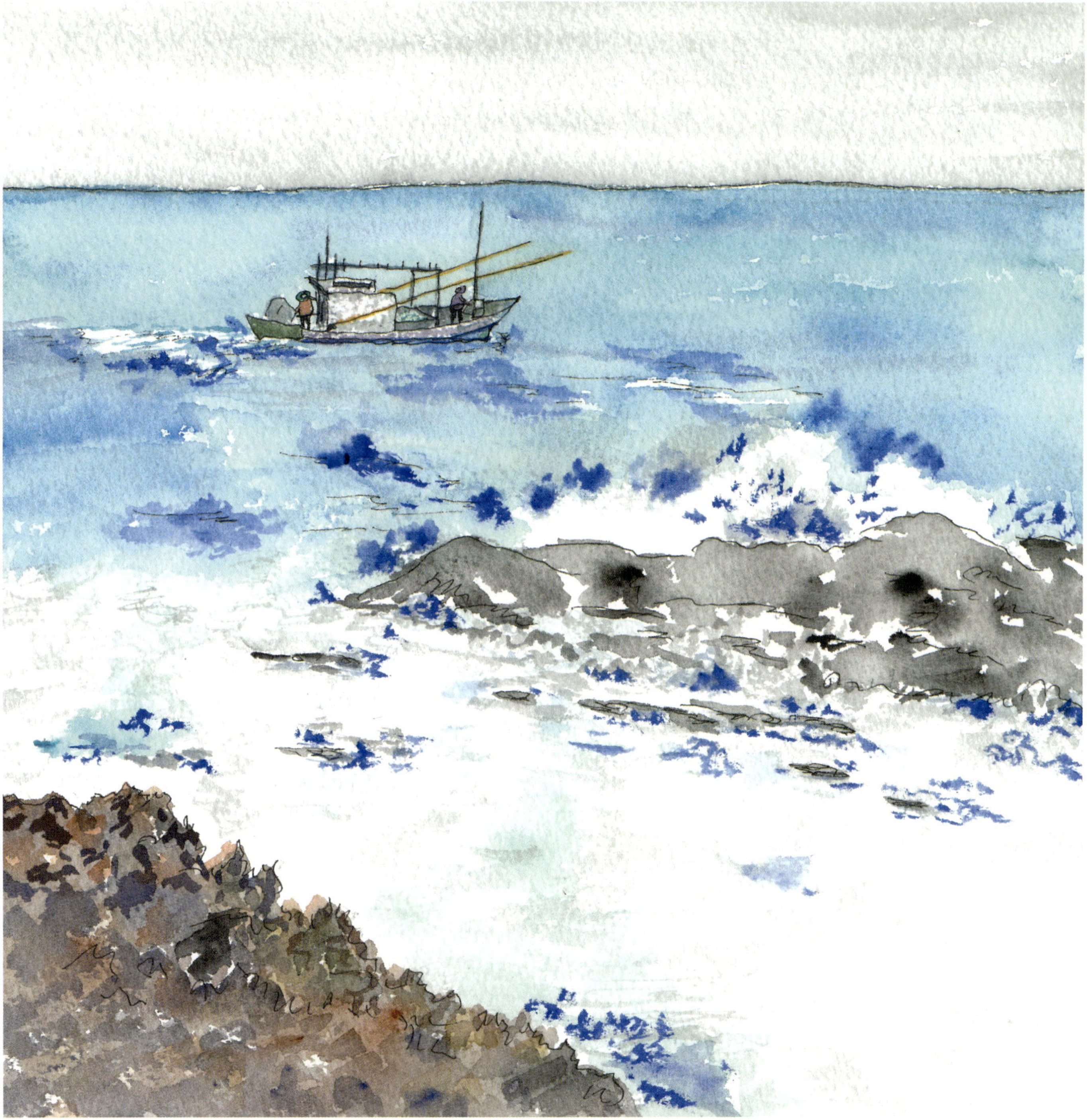

對許多澎湖漁民來說,土魠魚是大海的新年贈禮,也是整年收入的主要來源,不畏強風巨浪,清晨出港,天黑入港,展現堅毅勇健的氣魄。

For many fishermen in Penghu, the Spanish mackerel is a New Year's gift from the sea and a primary source of income throughout the year. Undeterred by strong winds and high waves, the fishermen set sail at dawn and return home after dark, showcasing their resilient spirit.

上午天空雲層密佈，伴隨狂驟的東北風，水溝邊的長尾草，草浪一波一波隨風起舞；下午，風竟平靜下來。趕緊啟動馬達船，出海駛向七美（大嶼）西南的南淺海域。在「洘流尾」（khó-lâu bé，退潮之後）水流慢慢靜止的時候，抓緊時間撒網。等到漲潮時，藏在海底的土魠魚群會衝到水面上，追著小魚群，這樣它們就被捕獲了。

澎湖的海產有很大一部分賣到台南，台南人多，地方大，魚很好賣，價格也很好，所以又可以過個歡樂無比的好年了。

• • •

In the morning, the sky was heavily overcast, with the northeast wind howling fiercely. By afternoon, the wind had calmed down. The fishermen quickly set out to sea, heading towards the southwest of Tshit-bí (Qimei) Island. When the tide went out and the water started to settle, they seized the opportunity to cast their nets. As the tide came in, the Spanish mackerel hiding on the seabed would surge to the surface, chasing small fish, making them easier to catch. Much of Penghu's seafood is sold in Tainan, where there is a large population and a bustling market. This often leads to good prices, allowing the fishermen to earn a decent income and happily welcome the arrival of the Lunar New Year.

Tuā-lâu Khù Khioh Lê-á
大流去抾螺仔
Collecting Conches at Low Tide

初一十五大洘流　阿娘提籃佮螺鉤　/　有的用行佮用走　來到海墘反石頭

大石細石反透透　螺仔落落水底溝　/　大粒抾起細放走　抾抾規籃提咱兜

囥入鼎鍋來起灶　煠熟用針撠螺頭

青胭的尾像仙草　就水的尾白泡泡　/　食著苦疕苦袂了　食著甜螺好落喉

海墘好耍講袂了　　　　　　　　　　　　　　　阿娘抾螺第一勢

Tshue-it tsa̍p-gōo tuā khó-lâu, a-niû-á the̍h nâ-á kah lê-kau. / Ū-ê iōng kiânn kah iōng tsáu ê, lâi-kàu hái-kînn-á píng tsio̍h-thâu.
Tuā-tsio̍h suè-tsio̍h píng thàu-thàu, lê-á lak lo̍h tsuí-té-kau. / Tuā-lia̍p-ê khioh khí suè-ê pàng tsáu, khioh-khioh kui nâ-á the̍h lán-tau.
Khǹg jip tiánn-ue-á lâi khí tsàu, sa̍h-sik iōng tsiam kiah lê-á-thâu.
Tshinn-ian ê bé tshiūnn sian-tsháu, tsiūnn-tsuí-á ê bé pe̍h-phau-phau. / Tsia̍h tio̍h khóo-phí-á khóo buē liáu, tsia̍h tio̍h tinn-lê-á hó lo̍h-âu.
Hái-kînn-á hó-sńg kóng buē liáu, a-niû-á khioh lê-á sī tē-it gâu.

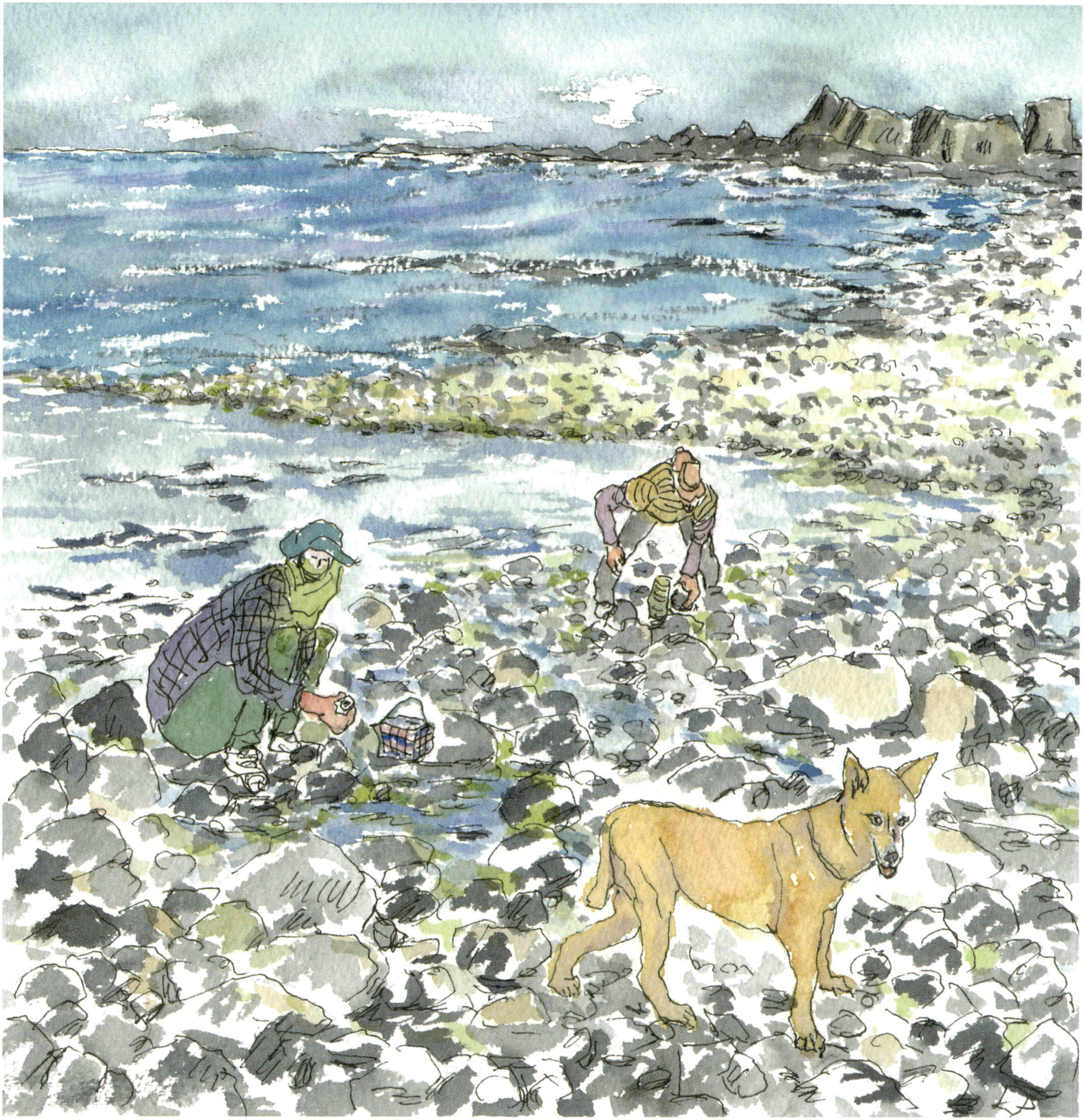

勞動 LÔ-TŌNG

澎湖的居民世代討海爲生，每當農曆初一和十五的大洘流（退潮），婦女們便迫不及待前往海岸撿螺仔。她們俐落地翻動岸邊的大小石頭尋找，大的螺仔一一拾起，小的則放回海中，讓它們有機會長大。

婦女們會將螺仔以滾水中煮熟，用針把螺肉挑出來。青胭（tshinn-ian，黑鐘螺）和就水仔（tsiūnn-tsuí-á，臍孔黑鐘螺）前半段的肉甜又飪（khiū）；青胭尾是仙草的顏色，就水仔尾則是白泡泡，沾上點醬油，更是讓人垂涎。偶爾吃到苦疕仔（khóo-phí-á，漁舟蜑螺），先苦後甘，相對地甜螺仔（tinn-lê-á，粗紋蜑螺）則味道甘甜。海邊的東西多到說不完，不過，若提到撿螺仔，婦女們就是真正的高手。

• • •

For generations, many residents of Penghu have made their living from the sea. Every lunar month, on the first and 15th days during low tide, the women go to the seaside to collect conch shells. They skillfully turn over various sizes of stones along the shore, picking up the larger shells while returning the smaller ones to the sea to give them a chance to grow. The women cook the shells in boiling water and then use a needle to extract the meat, dipping it in a little soy sauce, which makes it very tempting. There are countless treasures to be found by the seaside but when it comes to collecting shells, the women are true experts.

Tsoh-tshân-lâng ê Sim-siann
作田人的心聲
The Hearts of Farmers

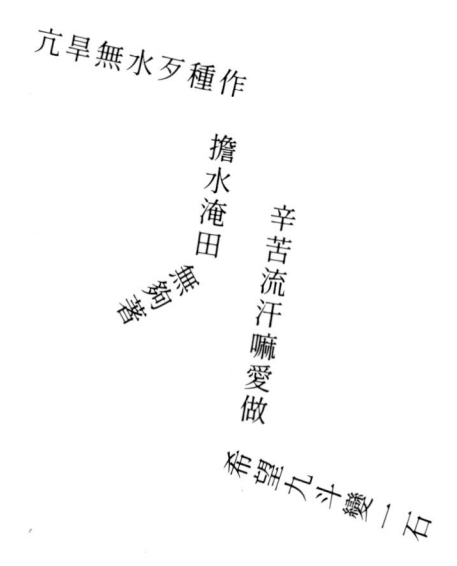

亢旱無水歹種作

擔水淹田濺菊莘

辛苦流汗嘛愛做

希望九斗變一石

Khòng-hān bô tsuí pháinn tsìng-tsoh, tann-tsuí im-tshân bô-kàu tiȯh.
Sin-khóo lâu-kuānn mā ài tsò, hi-bāng káu táu piàn tsit tsiȯh.

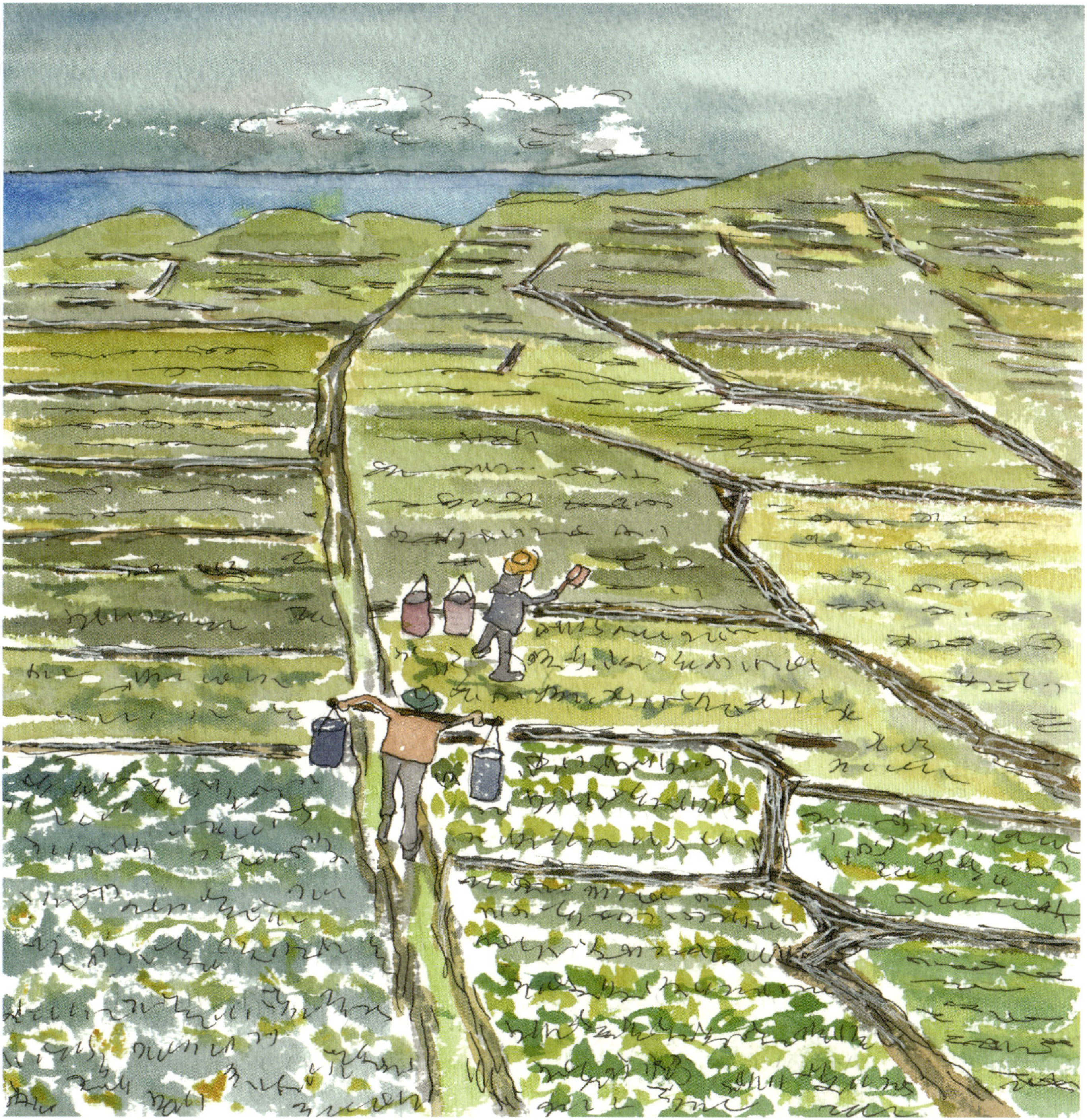

澎湖秋冬季節幾乎沒有雨水，加上強勁的東北季風，讓東嶼坪的大地顯得格外蕭瑟。

In Penghu, the autumn and winter months are nearly devoid of rain and with the fierce northeast wind, the landscape takes on a desolate appearance.

已經很久沒有下雨，田土變得乾硬，耕作變得十分困難。為了滋潤土壤，賣力挑水澆灌田地。這雖然讓人流了很多汗水、也非常疲累，但大家都知道，還是要「骨力」（kut-la̍t）去做，才能獲得好收成。

・ ・ ・

It had been a long time since it last rained, and the fields had become dry, making farming quite difficult. To moisten the soil, the villagers had no choice but to fetch water from a nearby well and carry it to the fields. Although this left them sweating a lot and feeling extremely tired, everyone knew that only by putting in the hard work could they hope for a good harvest.

Tâi-uân-gû Kiông koh Ióng

台灣牛強閣勇
Taiwanese Cattle: Reliable Helpers for Farmers

主人褒阮牛狀元　名聲迵到全台灣／阮袂喝苦袂怨嘆　一心一意為主人

阮是一隻大牛犅　專為主人咧犁田／每工犁甲日落暗　工課較實無輕鬆

春雷連聲來報喜　春雨繼落規暝／主人早就有準備　等待雨停佈種時

Tshun-luî liân-siann lâi pò-hí, tshun-hōo liân-suà lỏh kui mî.
Tsú-lâng tsá--tō ū tsún-pī, tán-thāi hōo thîng pòo-tsíng sî.
Gún sī tsit tsiah tuā-gû-káng, tsuan uī tsú-lâng leh luê-tshân.
Muí kang luê kah jit--lỏh àm, khang-khè khah-sit sī bô khin-sang.
Tsú-lâng po gún gû-tsiōng-guân, miâ-siann thàng kàu tsuân Tâi-uân.
Gún buē huah khóo buē uàn-thàn, it-sim it-ì uī tsú-lâng.

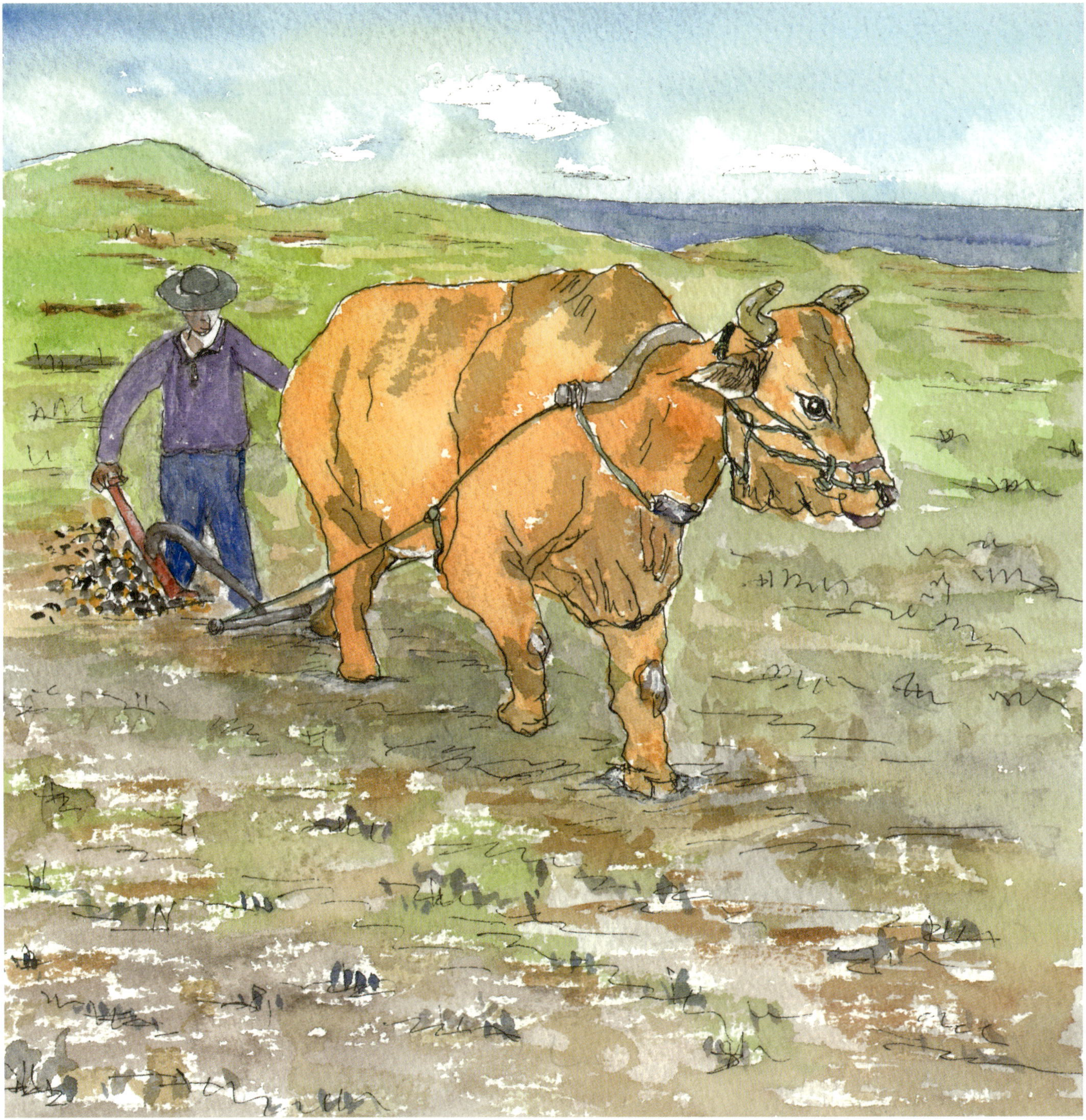

202 ｜勞動 LÔ-TŌNG

春天來了，天空開始打雷閃電，連續下了好幾天的雨，田地濕潤潤的。農田的主人早早就準備好種子，等著雨停就能下田播種忙活。我是一頭負責拉犁的大公牛，這次的工作還真不輕鬆，每天都要忙碌到太陽下山才能休息。主人常常稱讚我是「牛狀元」，耐勞又聰明，從來不抱怨！

. . .

Spring has arrived, bringing thunder and lightning, along with several days of continuous rain that have left the fields damp. The owner of the farmland has prepared the seeds in advance, eagerly waiting for the rain to stop so that he can rush out to sow them. I am a large bull responsible for pulling the plough and this task is no easy feat; I have to toil until the sun sets before I can rest. My owner often praises me as the 'top bull', recognising my hard work, diligence and intelligence as his most reliable helper!

Tann-puî Khù Ìng-tshân
擔肥去壅田
A Farmer Carrying Fertiliser to the Fields

出年初五是隔開　初六準備欲壅肥

小姐太太總來去　互相支援去擔肥

肥料攏愛擔誠遠　搖搖擺擺行到園

主人趕緊去煮飯　順紲炒菜佮煮湯

為著擔肥食好頓　䛴甲頷頸伸長長

Tshut nî tshue-gōo sī keh-khui, tshue-la̍k tsún-pī beh ìng-puî.
Sió-tsiá thài-thài tsóng lâi-khì, hōo-siong tsi-uân khù tann-puî.
Puî-liāu lóng ài tann tsiânn hn̄g, iô-iô-pái-pái kiânn kàu hn̂g.
Tsú-lâng kuánn-kín khù tsú-pn̄g, sūn-suà tshá-tshài kah tsú-thng.
Uī tio̍h tann-puî tsia̍h hó-tǹg, teh kah ām-kún-á tshun tn̂g-tn̂g.

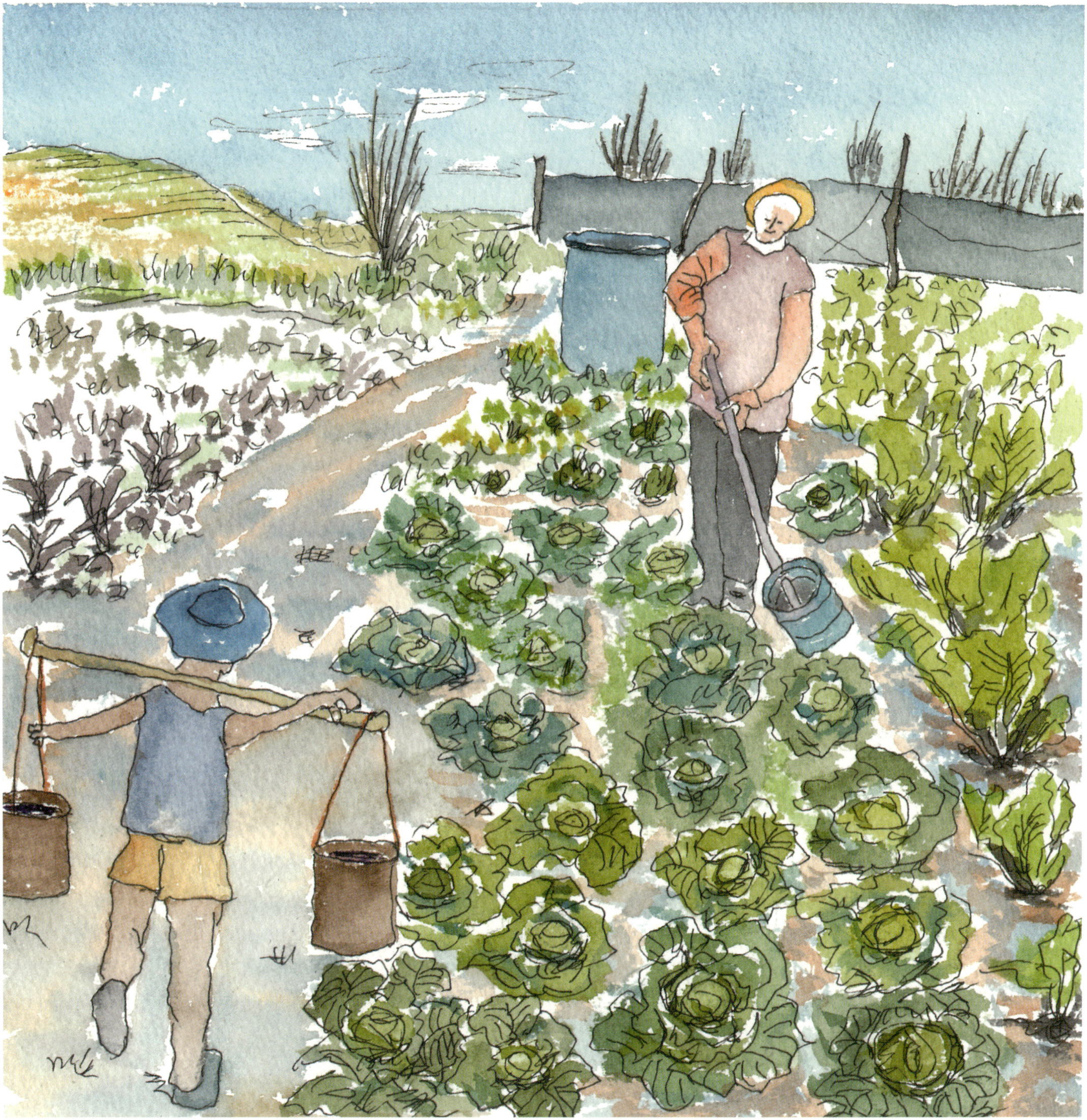

206 | 勞動 LÔ-TŌNG

農曆初六，對生活在都市的人來說，是開工上班的日子。但在農村，這一天是把一年堆積的肥料挑去「掖」（iā）到田裡的時候。村裡的婦女們會互相幫忙，大家協力合作。主人家會準備一頓豐盛的飯菜來款待大家。雖然挑肥料的路途很遠，也很辛苦，但主人的熱情和大家的團結，讓彼此都覺得心滿意足，即使身體疲累，內心卻充實快樂。

· · ·

On the sixth day of the Lunar New Year, urban residents typically returned to work, while villagers in the countryside dedicated the day to transporting nearly a year's worth of fertiliser to the fields using shoulder poles. The women came together, supporting one another as they worked. The host prepared a hearty meal for everyone, creating a sense of community. Although the journey to carry the fertiliser was long and tiring, the host's warmth and the villagers' friendship brought them great satisfaction. Despite their exhaustion, their spirits remained joyful.

Hōo-tsuí Lâi kah Tng-tio̍h-sî
雨水來到當著時
Just in Time for the Rain

今年雨水順時到　番薯生甲攀過溝

藤頭大粒閣袂臭　溝邊單稱百百條

Kin-nî hōo-tsuí sūn-sî kàu, han-tsû sinn kah phuànn kuè kau.
Tîn-thâu tuā-lia̍p koh buē tshàu, kau pinn ê tàn-tshìng-á pah-pah tiâu.

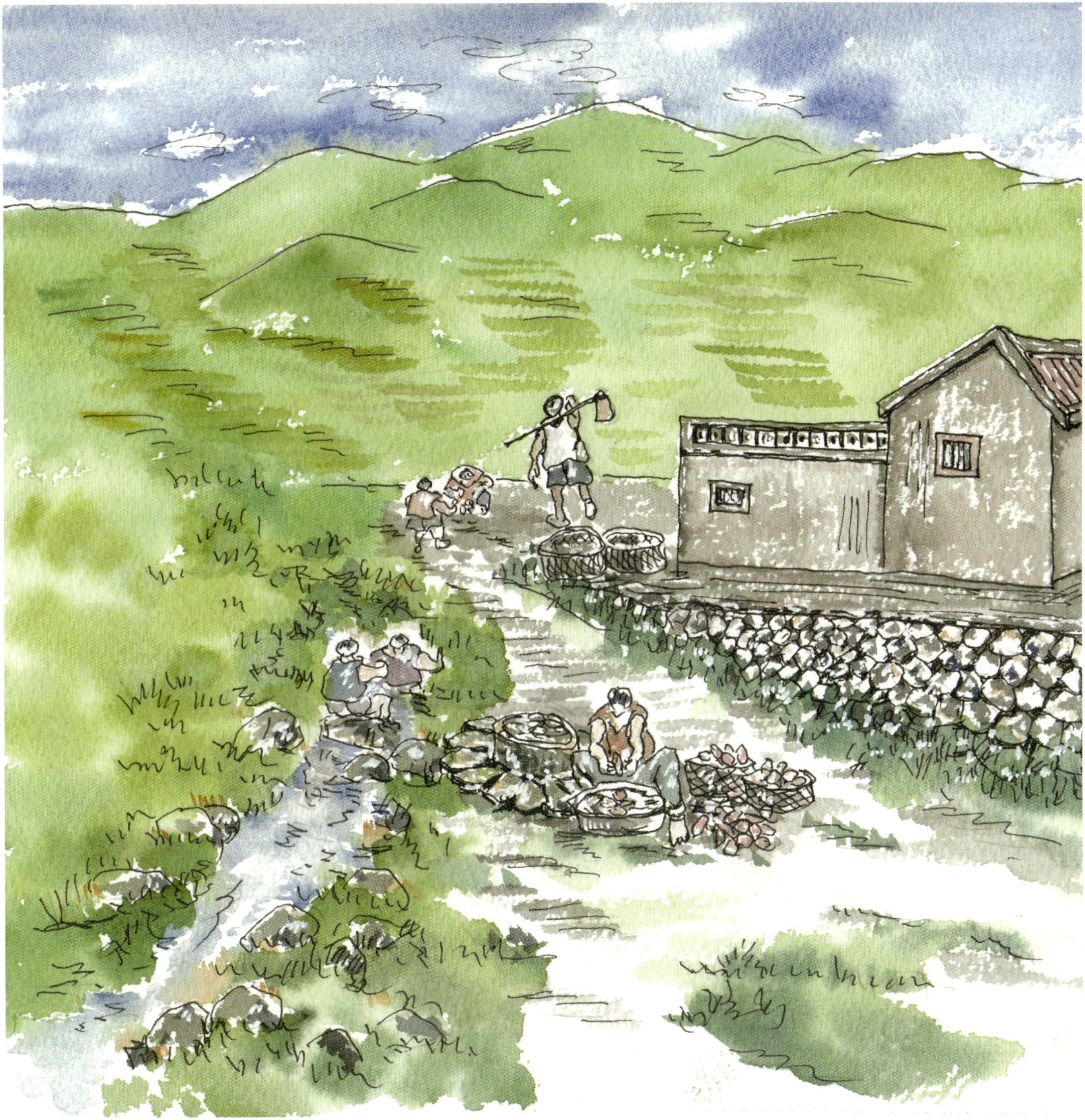

勞動 LÔ-TŌNG

今年的耕作季節之前,雨水特別充足,番薯藤茂密到攀過別條的甘薯溝。 壟上藤頭,生出的甘藷又粗又壯又香。溝邊和溝底的單稱仔(tàn-tshìng-á,小蕃薯)隨處可見。

• • •

As this year's farming season approached, the plentiful rainfall was causing the sweet potato vines to grow exceptionally lush, even reaching over the nearby ditch. The sweet potatoes emerging from the mounds were thick and robust, exuding an enticing aroma. Meanwhile, smaller sweet potatoes could be found scattered around the edges and bases of the ditches.

Thôo-tāu Tuā-hong-siu

塗豆大豐收
A Bountiful Peanut Harvest

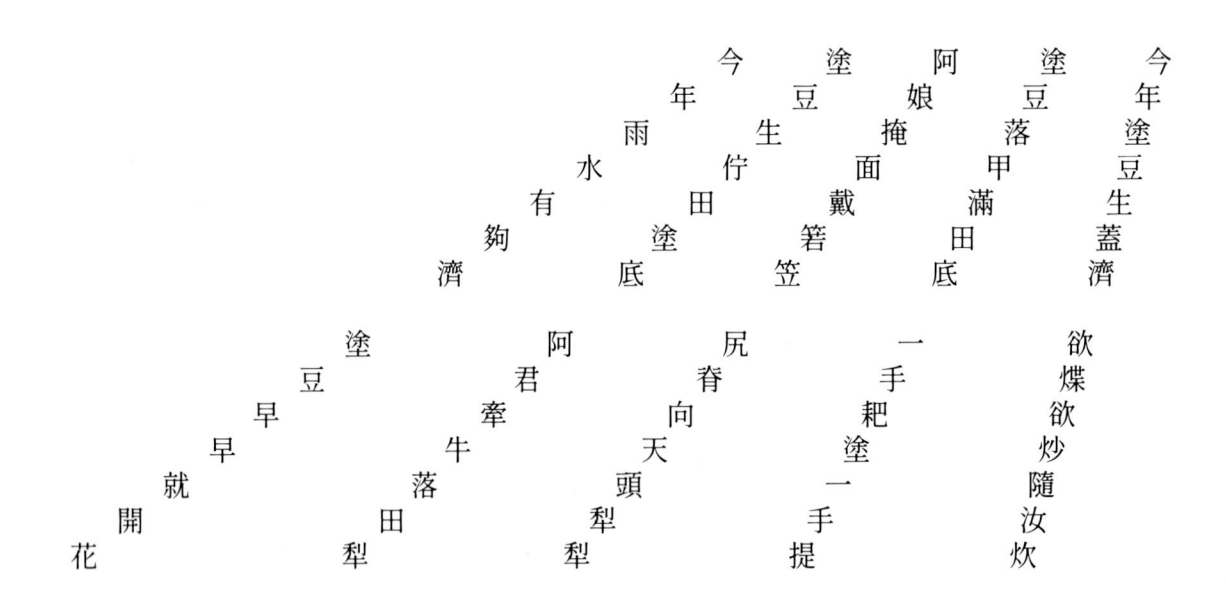

今年塗豆生蓋濟
塗豆落甲滿田底
阿娘掩面戴箬笠
塗豆生佇田底
今年雨水有夠濟

塗豆早早就開花
阿君牽牛落田犁
尻脊向天頭犁犁
一手耙塗一手提
欲煠欲炒隨汝炊

Kin-nî hōo-tsuí ū-kàu tsuē, thôo-tāu tsá-tsá tiō khui-hue.
Thôo-tāu sinn tī tshân thôo tué, a-ko--á khan gû lȯh tshân luê.
A-niû-á ng-bīn tì ha̍h-lue̍h, ka-tsiah hiòng thinn thâu luê-luê.
Thôo-tāu lak kah muá tshân tué, tsit tshiú pê-thôo tsit tshiú the̍h.
Kin-nî thôo-tāu sinn kài tsuē, beh sa̍h beh tshá suî lú tshue.

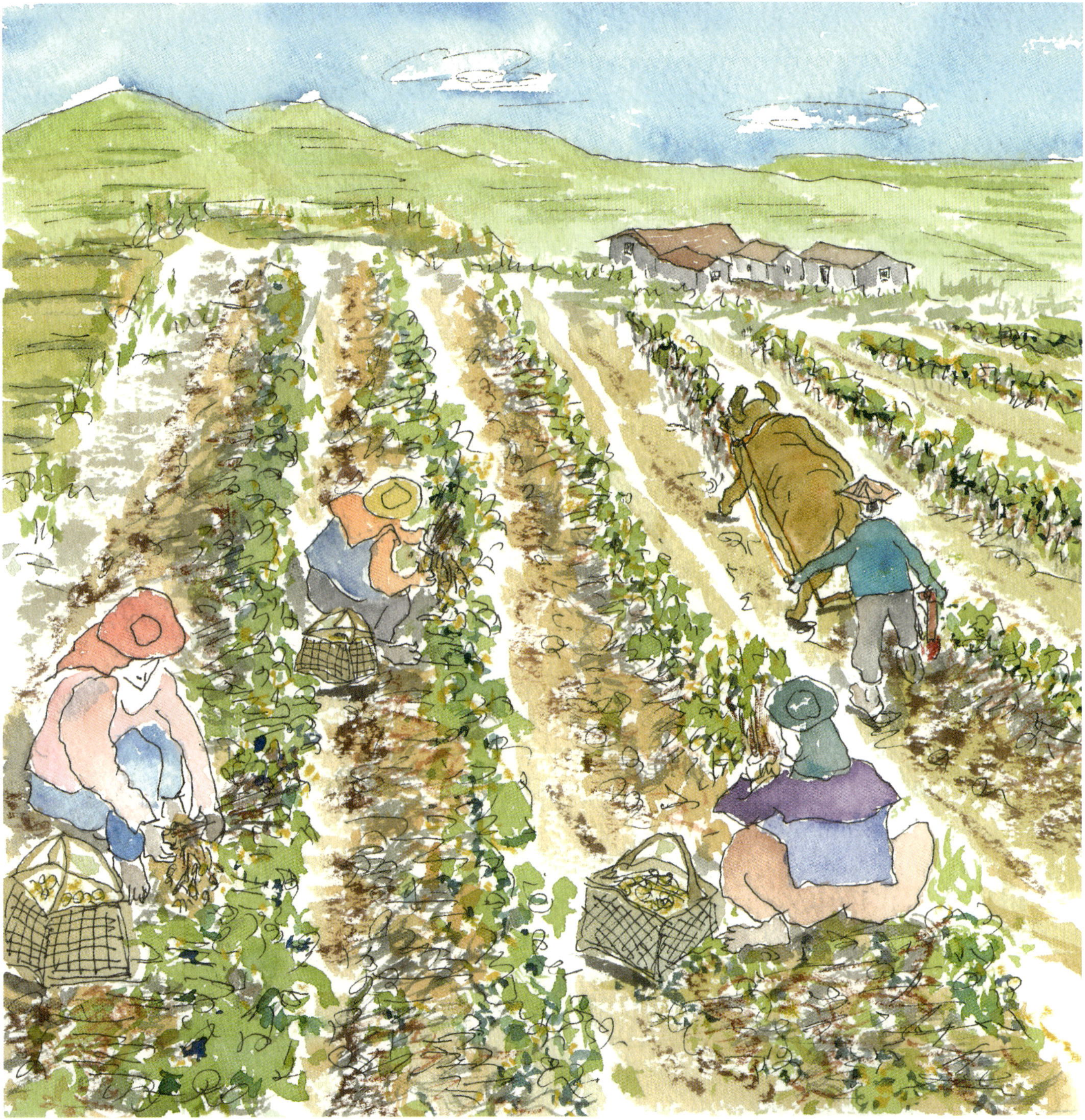

214 | 勞動 LÔ-TŌNG

今年雨水充沛，花生的收成特別好。平常忙於出海捕魚的男人也趕來幫忙犁田。婦女們爲了怕曬太陽，裝扮成了標準的澎湖蒙面女郎，戴上草笠，低著頭，彎著腰，專心挖著花生。右手不停地扒土，左手小心翼翼地將花生一一撿起，靈巧的動作令人讚賞！大家都說：今年花生產量多、品質優，可以煮、可以炒，各種巧妙做法任君選擇，一定可以吃得痛快！

• • •

This year, the rainfall has been abundant, resulting in a splendid peanut harvest. Consequently, the men—who usually spend their time fishing—have come to help with the farming. To avoid sunburn, the women have donned straw hats, transforming into masked figures as they lower their heads and bend down to dig diligently for peanuts. You can see them busy scraping the soil with their right hands while carefully picking up the peanuts one by one with their left; their deft movements are quite entertaining! Everyone agrees that this year's peanut yield is plentiful, allowing for various cooking methods—whether boiled or fried, you can choose how to prepare them and enjoy every delicious bite!

鄉 HIONG-TSHIÛ 愁

　　隨著年歲漸長，黑水溝那一頭，成了呂坤翰心中遙遠的鄉愁。親情、人情和愛情化作娓娓道來的褒歌，訴說著生命中那刻骨銘心的點滴。

　　在〈讀書才會出頭天〉和〈菩薩老師〉中，他回憶起那段艱辛的求學之路，老師的鼓勵與激勵是他心靈的燈塔。〈西坪哥、東坪妹〉、〈嶼坪鉸刀師〉則描繪了他與妻子從最初的邂逅、相識到相伴，對妻子無私奉獻的感念，深情在字句中。

　　在昔日當兵就是離鄉的年代，〈衛國做兵上光榮〉描繪出他搭船準備當兵時，學生依依惜別的場景。成家立業後的他，在〈食穿全靠君一人〉、〈思君情深深〉唱出夫妻間的角色與相處之道。而〈阿公勇壯、阿媽活潑〉則用幽默的口吻，唱出長輩們樂觀面對生活的態度。

　　在〈鄉愁〉這首作品中，他描繪了在生活與交通極為不便的1960年代，岸邊時常上映著「鄉村往大都市移民」的戲碼。而那一艘艘看似不起眼的小漁船，不僅是討生活的工具，當居民生病需要就醫時，也義務擔任起「海上救護車」的角色。短短幾句話，卻道盡了生活在三級離島曾經的辛酸、無奈與堅強。

　　時光荏苒，曾經的舢舨船早已被馬達漁船和更大的交通船所取代，返回故鄉已不再是那遙不可及的夢。如今，搭上返鄉的船，透過那扇正方形的船窗望出，熟悉的海岸線逐漸浮現，讓他想起了年少的回憶，也連結著家的溫暖與熟悉的土壤。

　　在海風的撫慰下，這些作品被重新醞釀，回首來時路的重重波濤，情意悠長而餘韻無窮。

NOSTALGIA

As the years passed, the hometown across the Penghu Channel became Lu Kun-Han's deepest longing. In the ballads he composed, he expressed unforgettable memories and stories from his life.

In 'Only by Studying Can One Have a Future' and 'A Primary School Teacher with a Bodhisattva's Heart', he recalled the challenging journey of learning during his childhood and the inspiration he received from Mr Hsu. 'When a Gentleman of Tang-sū-pîng Island Met a Lady of Sai-sū-pîng Island' and 'A Barber in Sū-pîng Islands' depicted his encounters with his wife, tracing their relationship from their initial meeting through to their shared life together, expressing his profound gratitude for her. In 'Serving the Country is the Greatest Honor', he recounted the bittersweet farewells with his students as he departed by boat to join the army.

In the final piece, 'Nostalgia', he reflected on the small fishing boats of the challenging 1960s, which served not only as tools for making a living but also as 'sea ambulances' for residents in need of medical assistance. In just a few poignant lines, he conveyed the helplessness of life on a remote island. Nowadays, those small fishing boats have been replaced by larger ferries and the prospect of returning to his hometown no longer felt like an unattainable dream.

As he boarded the boat home, he gazed through the square porthole and saw familiar islands emerging before him, evoking memories of his youth and deepening his yearning for his hometown.

Tha̍k-tsir tsiah Ē Tshut-thâu-thinn
讀書才會出頭天
Only by Studying Can One Have a Future

細漢父母離世間　予阮變成孤兒人　/　佳哉兄哥有疼痛

共阮晟甲轉大人　/　離島生活有夠慘　逐家攏是散赤人

/　小學畢業無向望　只好做个討海人　/

細漢阮就無仝款　毋驚食苦毋驚難　/　認真讀冊就有望

拍死毋做討海人　/　搪著恩師許明鑑　教育局長洪玉山　/

兩人用心栽培阮　三年公費讀初中

/　師範又閣免費用　予阮專心一直衝　/　認真學習有增長

畢業派阮回家鄉　/　阮將智識全部放　專心來教小孩童　/

學生受教有進展　頭腦思考億萬千　/　智識提高會改變　大漢攏變巧巧人

Sè-hàn pē-bú lī sè-kan, hōo gún piàn-sîng koo-jî-lâng. / Ka-tsài hiann-ko ū thiànn-thàng,
kā gún tshiânn kah tńg-tuā-lâng. / Lī-tó sing-ua̍h ū-kàu tshám, ta̍k-ke lóng sī sàn-tshiah lâng.
/ Sió-ha̍k pit-gia̍p bô ǹg-bāng, tsí-hó tsò tsit ê thó-hái-lâng. /
Suè-hàn gún tiō bô-kāng-khuán, m̄-kiann tsia̍h-khóo m̄-kiann lân. / Jīn-tsin tha̍k-tsheh tō ū-bāng,
phah-sí m̄-tsò thó-hái-lâng. / Tn̄g to̍h un-sir Khóo Bîng-kàm, kàu-io̍k kio̍k-tiúnn Âng Gio̍k-san. /
Nn̄g lâng iōng-sim tsai-puê gún, sann nî kong-huì tha̍k tshoo-tiong.
/ Su-huān iū-koh bián huì-iōng, hōo gún tsuan-sim it-ti̍t tshiong. / Jīn-tsin ha̍k-si̍p ū tsing-tióng,
pit-gia̍p phài gún huê ka-hiong. / Gún tsiong tì-sik tsuân-pōo pàng, tsuan-sim lâi kà sió hâi-tâng. /
Ha̍k-sing siū-kà ū tsìn-tián, thâu-náu su-khó ik-bān-tshian. / Tì-sik thê-ko ē kái-piàn, tuā-hàn lóng piàn khiáu-khiáu-á lâng.

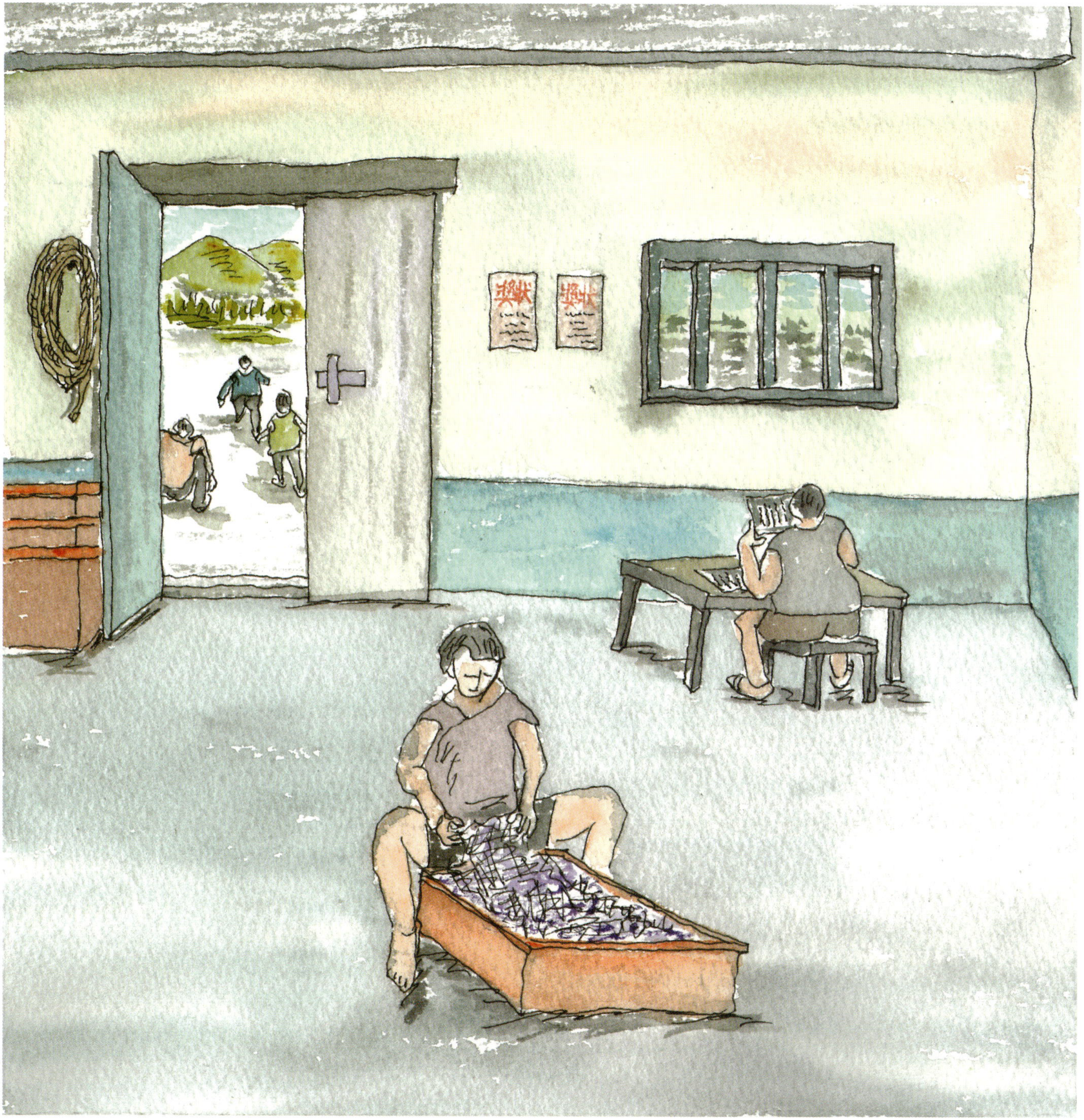

220 ｜鄉愁 HIONG-TSHIÛ

這個故事發生在 1952 至 1964 年，這段時光對呂坤翰的一生有深遠影響。呂坤翰本名叫呂通要，在民國一百年改名。在未上小學與剛上初中時，父母親不幸相繼過世，幸虧哥哥呂在悉心照顧與撫養，且鼓勵努力讀書，15 歲小學畢業時成為嶼坪第一位考上省立馬公中學初中部的學生。

小學老師許明鑑和教育局長洪玉山一直關心呂坤翰的學業，他們特地向省立馬公中學及教育局申請清寒獎學金，有了這份支持，他順利完成三年的初中學業後，又考上台南師範學校。由於獲得全額獎學金，因此能夠全心投入學習。21 歲順利畢業成為一名教師，澎湖縣政府將呂坤翰派回故鄉的嶼坪國小任教，從那時起，他全心全意教導每一位學生，希望能把曾經受到的愛與支持回饋給他們。

• • •

This story took place between 1952 and 1964, a period that had a profound impact on Lu Kun-Han's life. Lu Kun-Han (Taiwanese: Lū Khun-hān) was originally named Lu Tung-Yao (Taiwanese: Lū Thong-iàu) and changed his name in 2011. When Tung-Yao was six years old, his father sadly passed away but fortunately, his brother, Lū Tsāi, took good care of him and encouraged him to study hard. When he graduated from primary school at the age of 15, he became the first pupil from Sai-sū-pîng (Xiyuping) Island to gain admission to the Magong Secondary School.

During that time, his primary school teacher, Hsu Ming-Chien, and the Director of Education, Hung Yu-Shan, both made special requests to the Magong Secondary School and the education authority for a scholarship for him. With this support, Lu Kun-Han was able to continue his studies and later gained entry to the National Tainan Teachers College. After he graduated at the age of 21 and obtained his teaching qualification, the Penghu County Government sent him back to his hometown to teach at the Yuping Primary School. He devoted himself wholeheartedly to teaching every pupil, working hard to pass on the love and support he had once received to the next generation.

Phôo-sat Lāu-sir

菩薩老師
A Primary School Teacher with a Bodhisattva's Heart

恩師正名許明鑑 ● 人攏叫伊是先的 ／
　　　　　　　　　伊的教學有夠讚
認眞教好每一人 ／ 學生受教有進展

　　　● 智識提高日日強 ／ 恩師鼓勵的力量　逐家勇敢向前衝

　　　　　● 大漢出外去發展

發揮士農佮工商 ／
恩師正確的觀念　庇蔭學生每一人

　　　感謝恩師菩薩願 ● 恩情像天遐爾懸

Un-sir tsiànn-miâ Khóo Bîng-kàm, lâng lóng kiò i sī sian--ê.
I ê kà-hȧk ū-kàu tsán, jīn-tsin kà hó muí tsit lâng.
Hȧk-sing siū-kà ū tsìn-tián, tì-sik thê-ko jit-jit kiông.
Un-sir kóo-lē ê lȧk-liōng, tȧk-ke ióng-kám hiòng-tsiân tshiong.
Tuā-hàn tshut-guā khù huat-tián, huat-hui sū-lông kah kong-siong.
Un-sir tsìng-khak ê kuan-liām, pì-ìm hȧk-sing muí tsit lâng.
Kám-siā ūn-sir phôo-sat guān, un-tsîng tshiūnn thinn hiah-nī-á kuân.

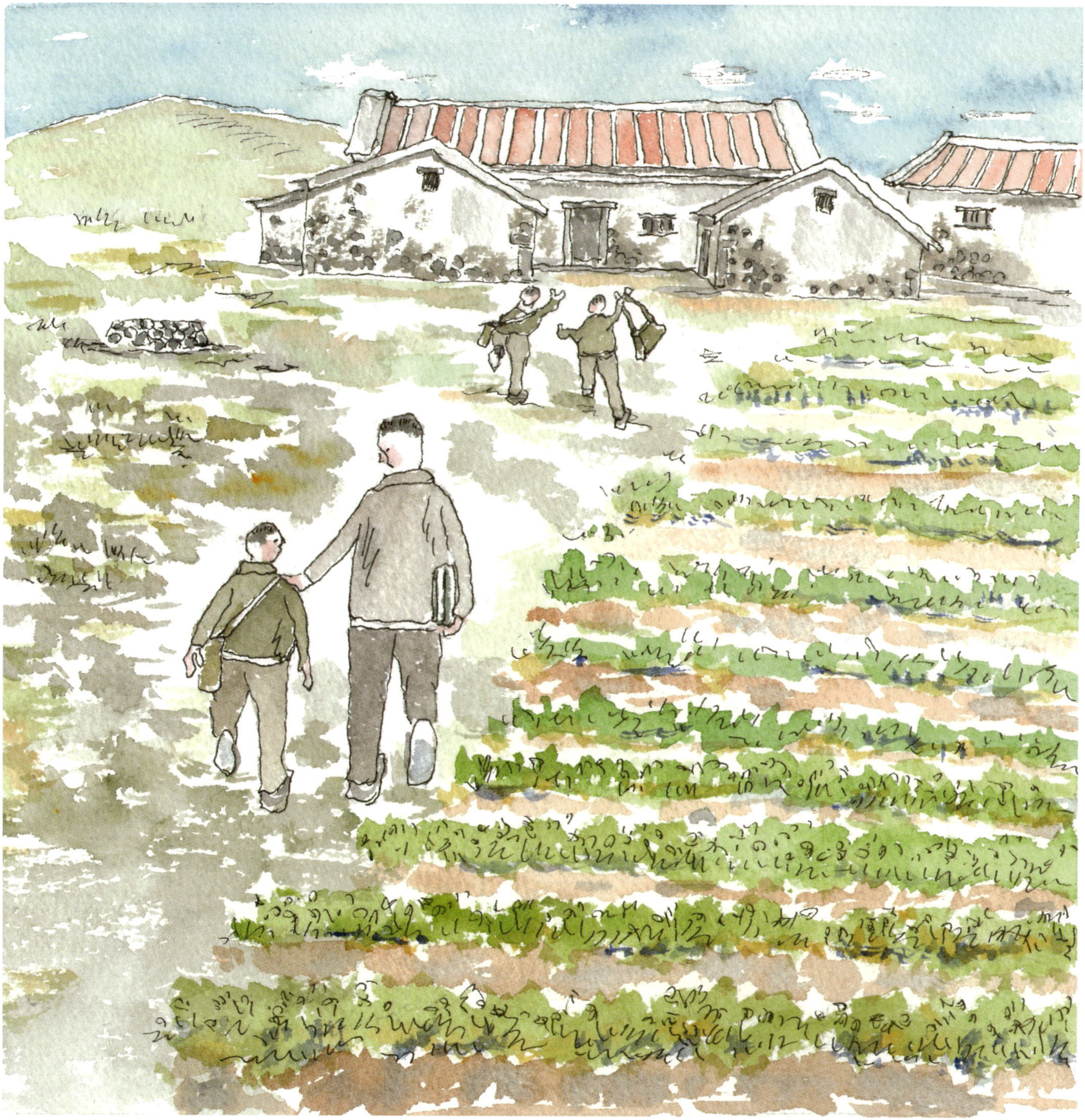

這張照片中,後排右起第一位站立者是許明鑑老師。他是應呂坤翰老師的邀請出席婚禮,這張合影展現了師生間深厚情誼。

In this photograph, the first person standing from the right in the back row is Mr Hsu Ming-Chien. He attended the wedding at the invitation of Mr Lu Kun-Han and this group photo reflects the deep bond between teacher and student.

呂坤翰回憶，恩師許明鑑是一位令人尊敬的好老師，他總是請求調派到偏僻的小島任教，比如西嶼鄉小門國小、望安鄉的西吉國小，以及西嶼坪國小。除了認真負責，他還經常分享當時台灣一些大都市的進步情況，激勵同學要努力讀書，期望在未來出社會能有更好的成就。許老師不僅學識淵博，還具有遠見卓識，用心去培育每一位學生，真是一位菩薩老師，被他教過的學生都很感念許老師。

・・・

Lu Kun-Han's primary school teacher, Mr Hsu Ming-Chien, is a respected and exceptional educator. He always requested assignments in remote islands, such as the Xiaomen Primary School in Sai-sū (Xiyu) Township, the Xiji Primary School in Bāng-uann (Wang'an) Township and the Xiyuping Primary School. Mr Hsu shared stories about the progress being made in some of Taiwan's major cities, encouraging his pupils to study diligently, with the hope that they would all achieve greater success after graduation. Not only was Mr Hsu knowledgeable but he also possessed great vision and dedicated himself to nurturing every pupil. He truly was a teacher with a bodhisattva's heart and all of his former pupils remember him fondly.

Sai-pîng Ko, Tang-pîng Muē

西坪哥、東坪妹

When a Gentleman of Tang-sū-pîng Island
Met a Lady of Sai-sū-pîng Island

（男）日夜思妹心袂靜　規氣划船過東坪　小妹見阮笑咳咳　抾掉相思談愛情

（女）小妹徛佇下厝岸　阿哥蹛佇西坪山　頷頸伸長金金看　阿哥何時欲來遮

Lú Po:
Sió-muē--á khiā tī Ē-tshù-á huānn, a-ko--á tuà tī Sai-pîng suann.
Ām-kún-á tshun-tn̂g kim-kim-khuànn, a-ko--á hô-sî beh lâi tsia.

Lâm Po:
Jit-iā su muē sī sim buē tsīng, kui-khì kò-tsûn-á kè Tang-pîng.
Sió-muē--á kìnn gún tshiò-bún-bún, hiat tiāu siunn-si tâm ài-tsîng.

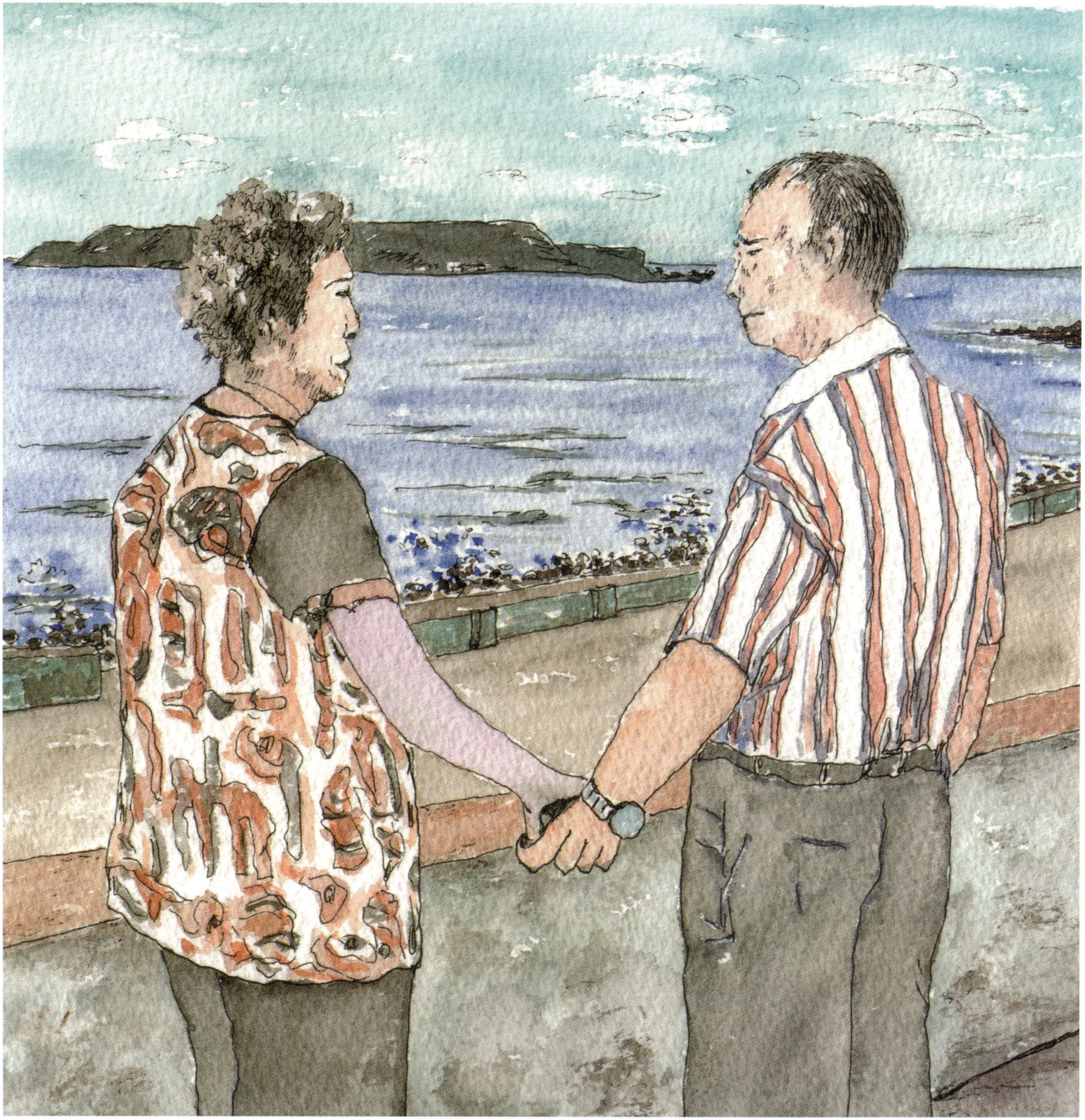

呂坤翰老師和妻子陳渼樺,在 2022 年夏天,再次回到當年常常散步的東嶼坪海邊河堤,回憶他們的戀愛時光。

In the summer of 2022, Mr Lu Kun-Han and his wife, Ms Chen Mei-Hua, returned to the embankment of Tang-sū-pîng Island, where they often strolled during their courting days, reminiscing about their romantic past.

有一位住在東嶼坪下厝仔的美麗姑娘，她和住在西嶼坪山頂的老師正在展開一段甜蜜的戀情。姑娘每天望眼欲穿，翹首期待著老師什麼時候會來找她。而那位老師心中也時刻念著這位姑娘，渴望能早日見到她。反正是暑假嘛！他果斷決定划一艘小舢舨，直奔東嶼坪去見她。當姑娘看到老師來的時候，臉上立刻「笑微微」（tshiò-bi-bi）。兩人手牽手，漫步在島嶼的每個角落，沉浸在兩人世界。這首褒歌，就是呂坤翰和他的「牽手」（khan-tshiú）阿玉當年青澀戀愛故事的實景。那一年是 1965 年。

• • •

On Tang-sū-pîng (Dongyuping) Island, there lived a beautiful lady who was in love with a teacher from Sai-sū-pîng (Xiyuping) Island. Each day, she eagerly awaited the moment when the teacher would come to see her. Likewise, the teacher constantly thought of her, yearning for the day they could be together again. Taking advantage of the summer holiday, he decided to row his small boat across to Tang-sū-pîng to visit her. When she saw him approaching, a joyful smile spread across her face. Hand in hand, they strolled through every corner of the island, enveloped in their own little world. This enchanting tale is the true love story of Lu Kun-Han and his wife, Chen Mei-Hua, from 1965.

Sū-pîng Ka-to-sai
嶼坪鉸刀師
A Barber in Sū-pîng Islands

阿玉是个鉸刀仙
專做衫褲佮頭鬃
做衫做褲免拍版　車線注重袂跳針
嶼坪人人阿咾讚　逐家穿甲婧噹噹
予伊做頭上方便　誠懇服務排代先
手攑鉸刀一直剪　頭毛形體隨『變天』
用心詳細共汝電
阿婆較穗變少年

A-gio̍k-á sī tsit ê ka-to-sian, tsuan tsò sann-khòo tiān thâu-tsang.
Tsò sann tsò khòo bián phah-pán, tshia-suànn tsù-tiōng buē thiàu-tsiam.
Sū-pîng lâng-lâng o-ló tsán, ta̍k-ke mā tshīng kah suí-tang-tang.
Hōo i tsò thâu siōng hong-piān, sîng-khún ho̍k-bū pâi tāi-sian.
Tshiú gia̍h ka-to it-ti̍t tsián, thâu-mn̂g hîng-thé suî "piàn-thian".
Iōng-sim siông-sè kā lú tiān, a-pô-á khah bái mā piàn siàu-liân.

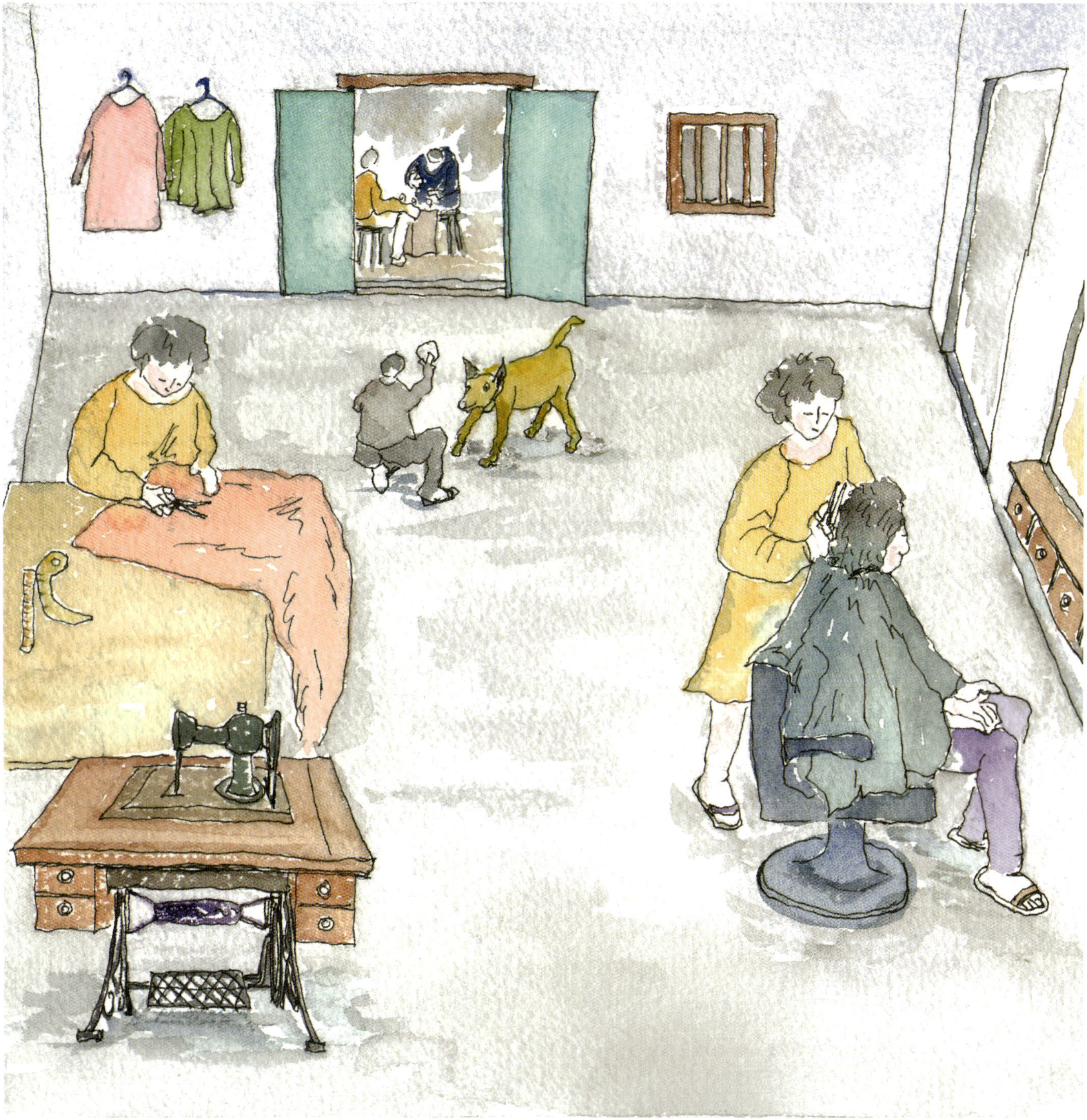

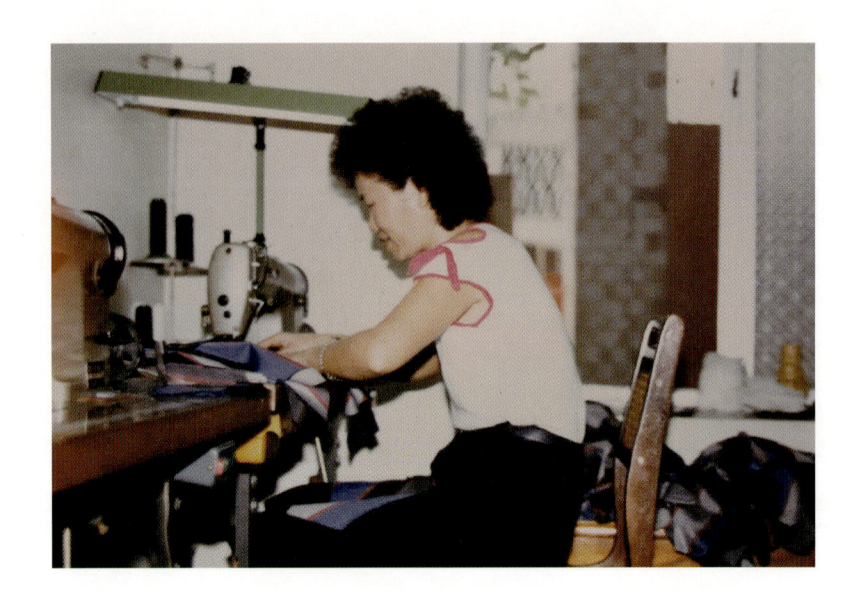

陳渼樺的手藝很精湛，即使搬到台南之後，還是經常忙著為人們造衫。

Ms Chen Mei-Hua is a skilled craftswoman and even after moving to Tainan, she frequently busies herself making clothes for others.

阿玉是呂坤翰的「牽手」，民國一百年時改了名字叫渼樺。回想 1964 到 1971 年，那時候做一件衣服或一條褲子，工資只要 10 元，「電」(tiān) 一次頭髮 18 元。阿玉做的襯衫和褲子合身，無論是東嶼坪還是西嶼坪的居民，大家都喜歡穿她做的衣服，既體面又舒適。另外，她的另一項手藝就是燙頭髮，造型多樣，東、西嶼坪村人人誇讚。阿玉每個月的收入，常常比小學老師每月 700 多元的薪水還要多。

• • •

Chen Jin-Yu (Tân Kim-gio̍k) is the wife of Lu Kun-Han, and she changed her name to Chen Mei-Hua in 2011. Between 1964 and 1971, she handcrafted pairs of trousers or other pieces of clothing for just NT$10 each. The local residents loved to wear the clothes she made because they were both well-fitting and comfortable. Additionally, she was skilled at perming hair, charging only NT$18 for her services, which were widely recognised. Jin-Yu's monthly income often exceeded Lu Kun-Han's salary of over NT$700 as a primary school teacher.

Uī-kok Tsò-ping Siōng Kong-îng

衛國做兵上光榮（1967 年 11 月）

Serving the Country is the Greatest Honor

十月接著做兵單　十一月欲入兵營

望安接兵的船隻　拋佇海墘接阮行

阮掛紅綾五彩帶　若像上任欲做官

全校學生圍來看　大聲唱出愛國歌

山頭綴船趈海岸　攑旗目送隨船行

場面親像搬電影　一幕一幕放咧行

師生目屎拼袂煞　聲聲感動佇心肝

學生掌旗迒上山

村民規陣出來看　呵咾師生好名聲

山頭旗仔隨仔退

等到船煙看無影　學生收旗才回家

師生兩冬袂當看　思念永遠囥心肝

接兵船隻欲離岸

船仔離遠愈細隻

Tsa̍p-gue̍h tsiap tio̍h tsò-ping-tuann, tsa̍p-it-ge̍h berh jip ping-iânn. / Bāng-uann tsiap ping ê tsûn-tsiah, pha tī hái-kînn-á tsiap gún kiânn.
Gún kuà âng-lîng ngóo-tshái tuà, ná-tshiūnn tsiūnn-jīm beh tsò-kuann. / Tsuân hāu ha̍k-sing uî lâi khuànn, tuā-siann tshiùnn tshut ài-kok kua.
Su-sing ba̍k-sái pué buē suah, siann-siann kám-tōng tī sim-kuann. / Tsiap ping tsûn-tsiah beh lī huānn, ha̍k-sing tsiáng kî tsáu tsiūnn-suann.
Suann-thâu tè tsûn-á se̍h hái-huānn, ia̍t kî ba̍k-sàng suî tsûn kiânn. / Tiûnn-bīn tshin-tshiūnn puann tiān-iánn, tsit bōo tsit bōo pàng teh kiânn.
Tshun-bîn kui-tīn tshut-lâi khuànn, o-ló su-sing hó miâ-siann. / Tsûn-á lī hn̄g lú suè-tsiah, suann-thâu kî-á iá tī hia.
Tán kàu tsûn-ian lóng khuànn-bô iánn, ha̍k-sing siu kî tsiah huê ka. / Su-sing nn̄g tang bē-tàng khuànn, su-liām íng-uán khǹg sim-kuann.

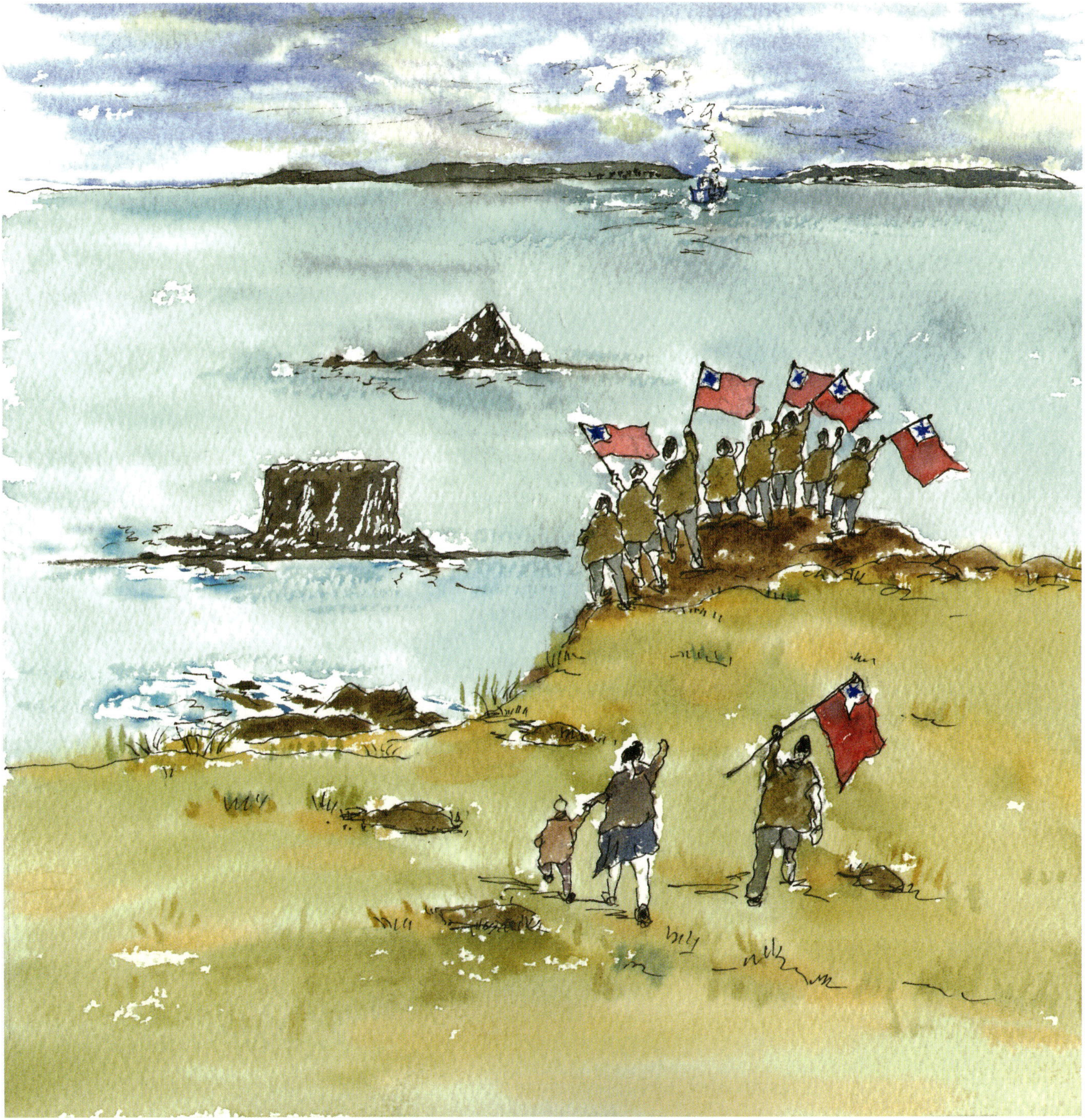

西嶼坪的西馬山,是學生們目送他們最敬愛的呂坤翰老師搭船遠行、服兵役的地方。

The Hill Sai-bé-suann of Sai-sū-pîng Island is where the pupils bid farewell to their beloved teacher, Mr Lu Kun-Han, as he departed by boat for military service.

1964 年呂坤翰回到故鄉西嶼坪任教，學生們非常用心地學習，師生之間感情格外深厚。1967 年 11 月，呂坤翰即將去當兵時，學生們決定做一件特別的事情。那天，國旗和廟旗一一被拿出，愛國歌曲在海風中響起，學生拚命高歌。當接兵船即將駛向望安鄉本島，學生們急忙舉起旗子，奔向西馬山，一邊唱著歌、一邊揮舞著旗幟，跟著船隻行駛的方向繞著，希望能多留住一分鐘與我的身影。村莊裡的人們也全都跑出來看，簡直像在演電影，這個前所未見，深刻動人的景象，真是讓人深深感動。

• • •

In 1964, Lu Kun-Han returned to his hometown of Sai-sū-pîng (Xiyuping) to teach. His three years of dedicated instruction earned him the trust and respect of his pupils. In November 1967, just as Lu Kun-Han was about to begin his military service, the pupils decided to organise a special surprise for him. On that day, the pupils took the national flag and temple flags from the island. When the troop transport vessel was approaching the main island of Bāng-uann (Wang'an), the pupils hurriedly raised the flags and ran towards Hill Sai-bé-suann, the highest point in the northwestern part of the island, which offers a clear view of Bāng-uann Island. They sang songs and waved the flags as they ran in the direction of the ship, hoping to keep the image of their teacher, Mr. Lu, deeply in their hearts. Villagers also came out to watch and the scene felt like a film, evoking deep emotions in everyone, as they had never witnessed anything quite like it before.

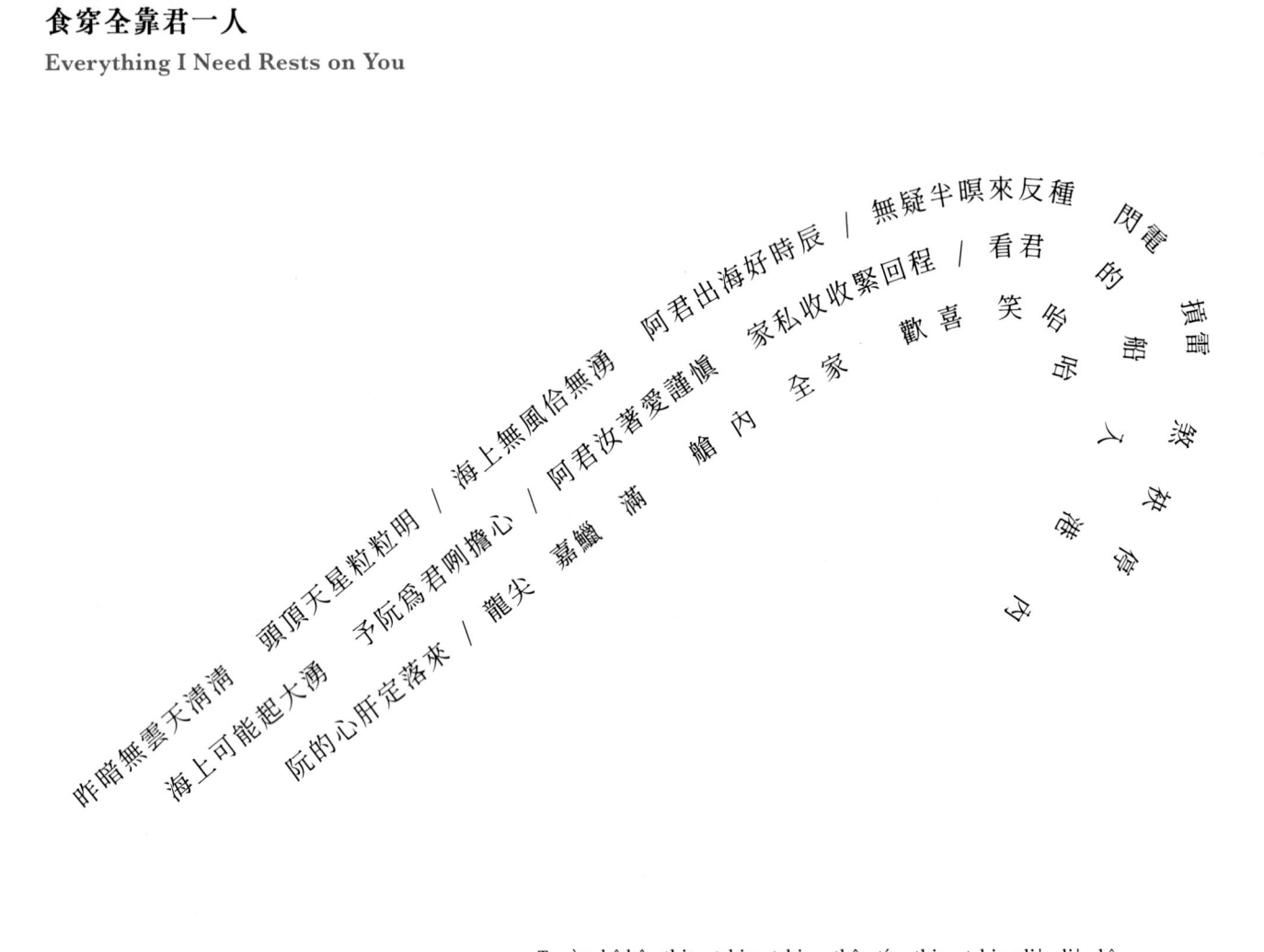

Tsia̍h-tshīng Tsuân Khò Kun Tsi̍t Lâng
食穿全靠君一人
Everything I Need Rests on You

昨暗無雲天清清　頭頂天星粒粒明　／　海上無風佮無湧　阿君出海好時辰　／　無疑半暝來反種　閃電摃雷摵船人　／　海上可能起大湧　予阮為君咧擔心　／　阿君汝著愛謹慎　家私收收緊回程　／　看君的船入港內　阮的心肝定落來　／　龍尖嘉鱲滿艙內　全家歡喜笑咍咍

Tsa-àm bô hûn thinn tshing-tshing, thâu-tíng thinn-tshinn lia̍p-lia̍p bîng.
Hái-siōng bô hong kah bô íng, a-kun-á tshut-hái hó sî-sîn.
bô-gî puànn-mî lâi huán-tsíng, siám-tiān kòng-luî suah buē thîng.
Hái-siōng khó-lîng khí tuā-íng, hōo gún uī kun-á leh tam-sim.
A-kun-á lú tio̍h ài kín-sīn, ke-si siu-siu kín huê-tîng.
Khuànn kun-á ê tsûn ji̍p káng lāi, gún ê sim-kuann tsiah tīng lo̍h-lâi.
Lîng-tsiam ka-la̍h muá tshng lāi, tsuân-ke huann-hí tshiò-hai-hai.

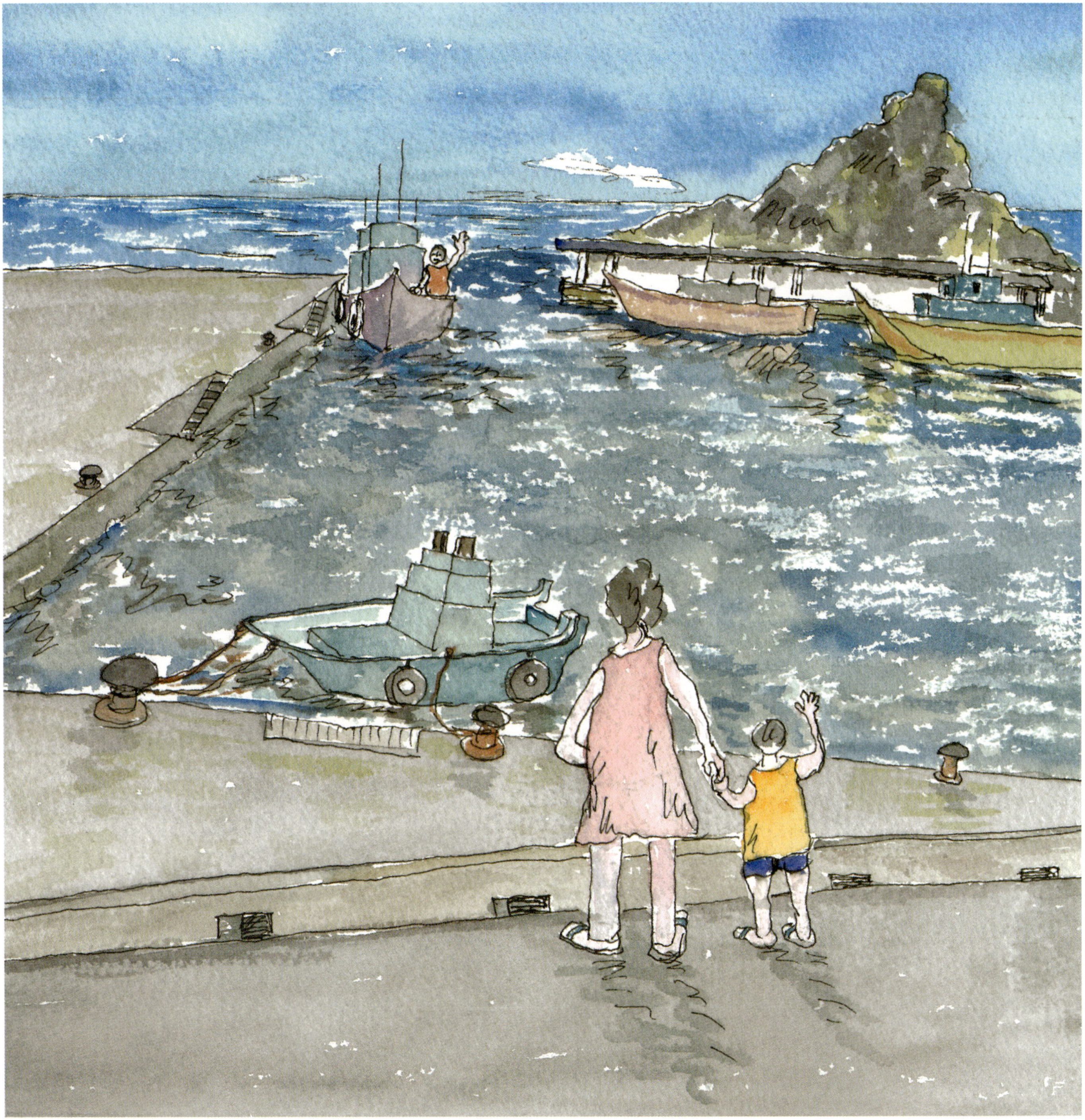

240 | 鄉愁 HIONG-TSHIÛ

天氣好的晚上，天空就會繁星閃爍，這也意味著海上風平浪靜。這樣的好天氣，漁船都會出海捕魚。但天氣變化無常，一旦突然打雷閃電，海上就會掀起大風，海浪也隨之翻湧。這時，妻子的心裡就會感到非常焦急，擔心丈夫的安全，希望他能儘快將漁船駛回港內。直到丈夫的漁船安全進港，緊繃的心情才會稍微放鬆。再看到滿艙的龍尖（lîng-tsiam，龍占魚屬泛稱）和嘉鱲（ka-la̍h，真鯛），全家人都高興得「笑哈哈」（tshiò-hai-hai）了。

・ ・ ・

On a clear night, when the sky was dotted with stars, it usually meant the sea was calm. During such good weather, the men would take their boats out to fish. However, the weather could change unexpectedly and when a thunderstorm hit, the winds and waves could suddenly become rough. At that time, the wife at home felt very anxious, worrying about her husband's safety and hoping he could return to harbor quickly. Only when her husband's boat safely arrived back in the harbor did her worried heart start to relax a little.

Su Kun Tsîng Tshim-tshim

思君情深深
Deep Longing for You

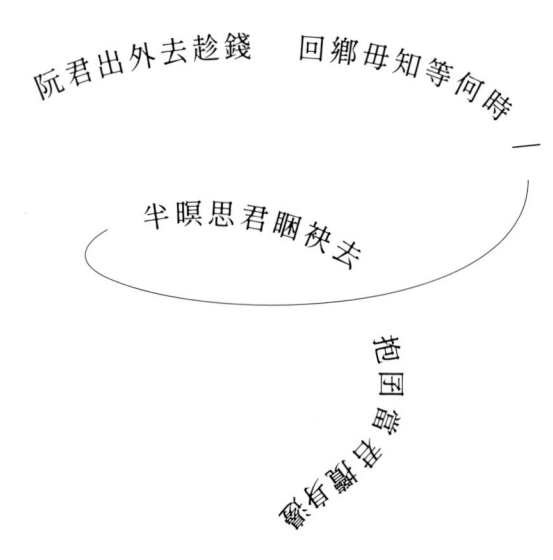

阮君出外去趁錢　回鄉毋知等何時

半暝思君睏抹去

抱囝當君攬身邊

Gún kun-á tshut-guā khù thàn-tsînn, huê-hiong m̄-tsai tán hô-sî.
Puànn-mî-á su kun khùn-buē-khì, phō kiánn tòng kun-á lám sin-pinn.

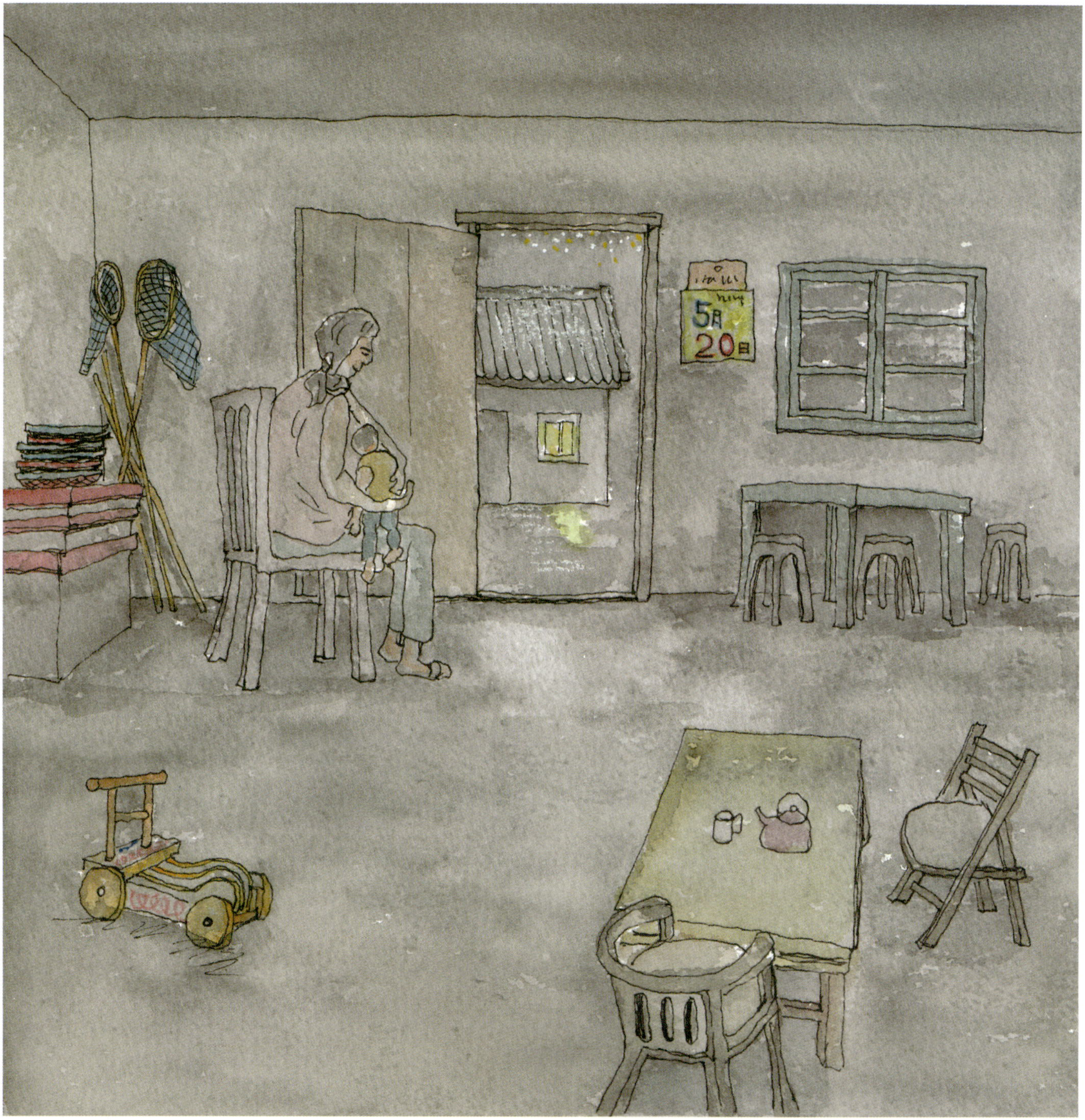
5月
20日

244 ｜鄉愁 HIONG-TSHIÛ

討海的人一生都以海為家，一旦探聽（thàm-thiann）哪裡有魚可以補，便會燃起一股立刻出發的動力。譬如，聽說宜蘭南方澳的青花魚大豐收，這裡的漁船便會馬上啟程，前往南方澳。然而，出海之後卻不知道何時才能重返故鄉，每當妻子想到丈夫在外的各種不確定，夜裡常常輾轉難眠，只能將兒子緊抱，舒緩對丈夫的思念。

• • •

The fisherman spent his life considering the sea his home, sailing wherever there were fish to be caught. For instance, upon hearing that there were abundant mackerel near Lâm-hong-ò (Nanfang'ao) in Yilan County, the fishing boats from Penghu would set off immediately to Lâm-hong-ò. However, once at sea, they had no idea when they would be able to return home. Whenever his wife thought about the uncertainties her husband faced out there, a deep sense of anxiety washed over her. She often found herself tossing and turning at night, unable to sleep, and could only hold her son tightly, seeking comfort in her longing for her husband.

A-kong-á Ióng-tsòng, A-má Uáh-phuat
阿公勇壯、阿媽活潑
Vigorous Grandpa, Lively Grandma

(女)

阮君今年七十外　身體親像虎豹爺

港墘擔魚兼跙崎　大步袂喘擔上山

孫仔規陣圍來看　呵咾阿公第一名

Lú Po:
Gún kun-á kin-nî tshit-tsáp guā, sin-thé tshin-tshiūnn hóo-pà-iâ.
Káng-kînn-á tann hû kiam peh kiā, tuā-pōo buē tshuán tann tsiūnn-suann.
Sun-á kui-tīn uî lâi khuànn, o-ló a-kong tē-it-miâ.

(男)

牽手今年七十捅　厝邊頭尾四界從

講伊佮阮全款勇　若做代誌一直衝

平時骨力愛活動　面皮光絲倒少年

Lâm Po:
Khan-tshiú--ê kin-nî tshit-tsáp thóng, tshù-pinn thâu-bé sì-kuè tsông.
Kóng i kah gún kāng-khuán ióng, nā tsò tāi-tsì it-tit tshiong.
Pîng-sî kut-lát ài uáh-tāng, bīn-phê kng-si tò siàu-liân.

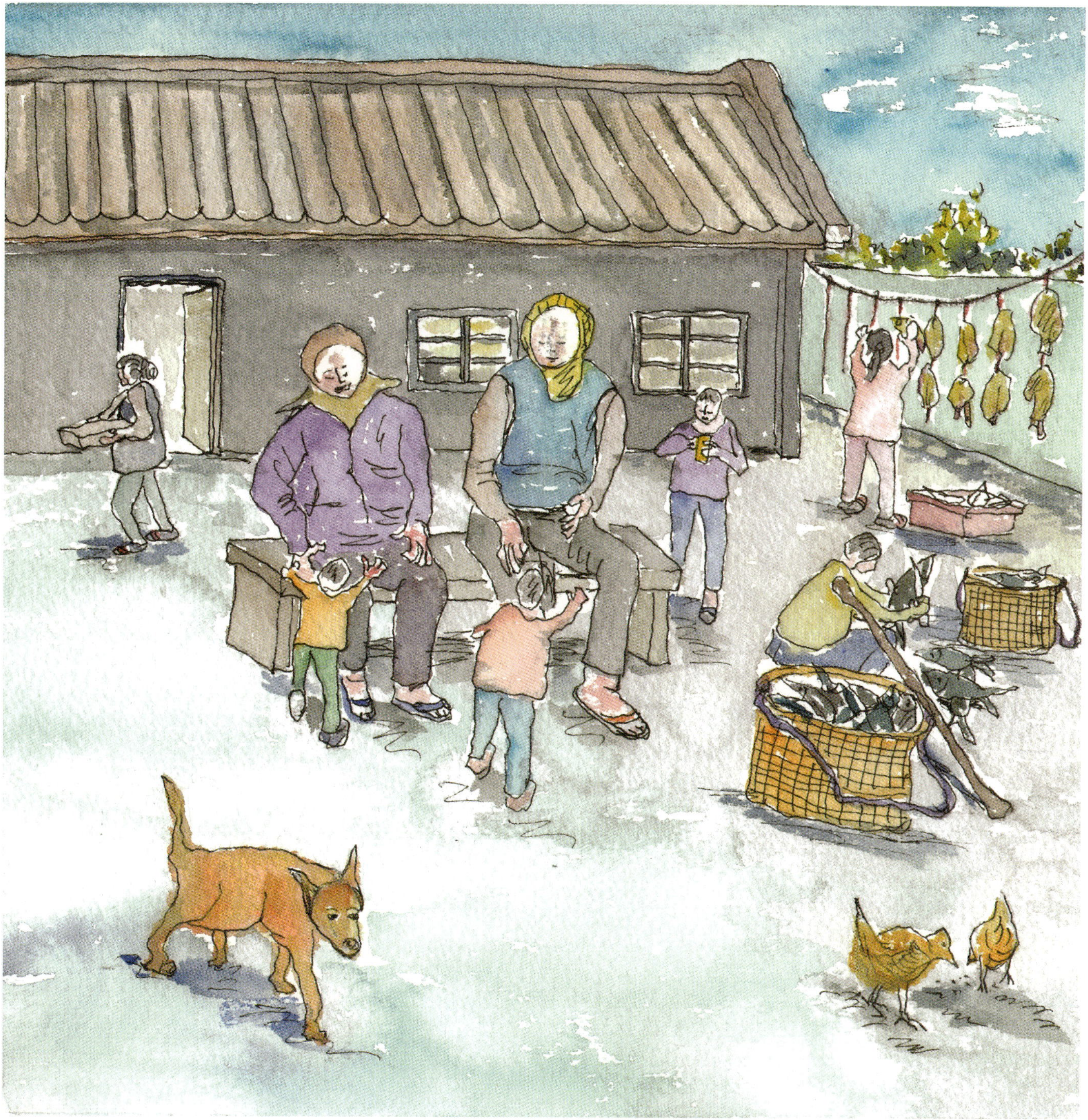

248 | 鄉愁 HIONG-TSHIÛ

西坪村的民家都在山坡頂，從碼頭到山頂有一段相當陡峭的「好漢坡」。男性村民卽使七十多歲，還能輕鬆挑魚上山。孫子們看到阿公挑著漁獲回來，紛紛鼓掌爲他喝采，稱讚阿公是最棒的男子漢！同樣七十多歲的老伴，身體依然硬朗。在家裡忙完所有的家務後，總會抽空去探望鄰居，熱心地幫助大家。因爲平時運動量充足，村裡的人都讚美她是一位充滿愛心、活力十足的阿媽！

• • •

On Sai-sū-pîng (Xiyuping) Island, the villagers lived at the top of a hill. There was a steep path from the harbor to the summit, which everyone called 'Hó-hàn-pho'. Even men in their seventies could still carry fish back up the hill with ease. When the grandchildren saw their grandfather coming home with his catch, they cheered for him and said he was the greatest man! His wife, who was also in her seventies, remained strong and healthy. After finishing all her housework, she always made time to visit the neighbors and offered her help with enthusiasm. Because she stayed active, everyone in the village praised her as a caring and lively grandmother!

Hiong-tshiû

鄉愁
Nostalgia

離島出外全靠船　船仔就是救命根　/　破病生囝俗討海　全部攏著揣船來
有船無港大不便　鬧風搰湧有困難　/　出入舢舨來接送　大湧舂岸拆船枋　/　這種生活真無奈　村民只好遷出來
外地比較有錢趁　生活嘛快遮困難　/　包袱款款離家鄉　離開嘛是姑不將
時間過了數十冬　阮嘛已經變老人　/　回鄉探親揣向望　心情較實『好緊張』
這馬交通大改變　好天日日有船班　/　船內看出窗外口　每島有港有碼頭
回鄉有船才會到　予阮歡喜目屎流

Lī-tó tshut-guā tsuân khò tsûn, tsûn-á tiō-sī kiù-miā kun. / Phuà-pīnn sinn-kiánn kah thó-hái, tsuân-pōo lóng tiȯh tshē tsûn-á lâi.
Ū tsûn bô káng tuā put-piān, tsȧh hong bih íng ū khùn-lân. / Tshut-jip san-pán lâi tsiap-sàng, tuā-íng tsinn huānn thiah tsûn-pang. Tsit tsióng sing-uȧh sī tsin bô-nāi, tshun-bîn tsí-hó thian tshut--lâi. / Guā-tē pí-kàu ū tsînn thàn, sing-uȧh mā buē tsiah khùn-lân.
Pau-hȯk-á khuán-khuán lī ka-hiong, lî-khui mā sī koo-put-tsiong. / Sî-kan kè liáu sòo-tsȧp tang, gún mā í-king piàn lāu-lâng.
Huê-hiong thàm-tshin tshē ǹg-bāng, sim-tsîng khah-sȧt "hâu--tsīn-tsang". / Tsit-má kau-thong tuā kái-piàn, hó-thinn jȧt-jȧt ū tsûn-pan.
Tsûn lāi khuànn tshut thang guā-kháu, muí tó ū káng koh ū bé-thâu. / Huê-hiong ū tsûn tsiah ē kàu, hōo gún huann-hí kah bȧk-sái lâu.

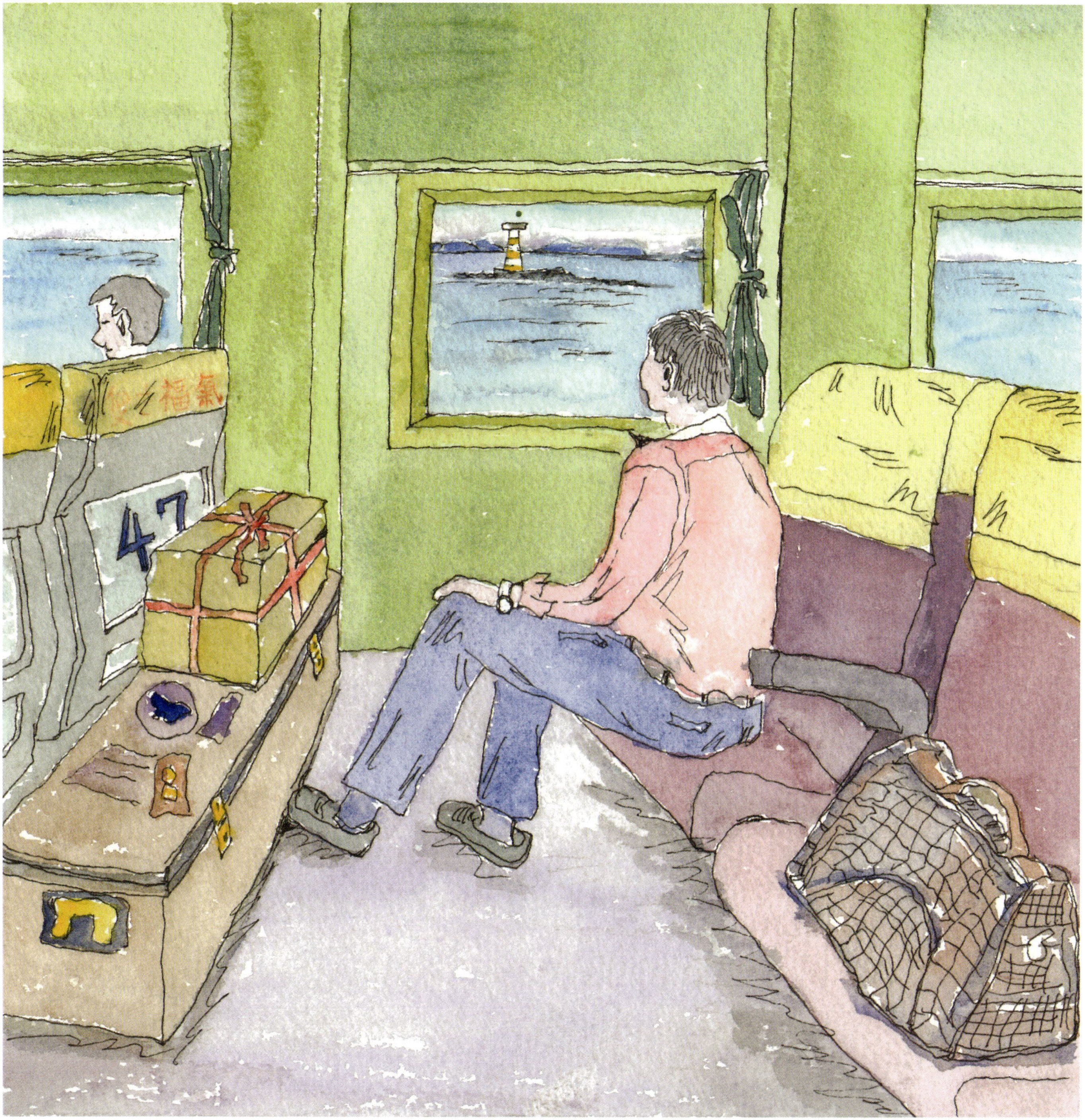
福氣
47

在離島的生活中，船隻是不可或缺的工具。無論是討海，還是有人生病、要生小孩，或是需要到外地賣魚和補貨，都需要船。它無形中就像離島人的雙腳，唯有它才能承載大家解決生活中的種種難題。以前，島上沒有港口碼頭，更別提直升機停機坪。人們只能倚賴舢舨船，克難地搖到泊岸外的馬達船去接送人或運送貨物。每當風浪興起，舢舨船隨時可能被打向岸邊的岩石，撞得粉碎。

呂坤翰回憶，曾經有位老人突發重病，村民們齊心協力輪流把人背下好漢坡，港邊的漁夫也毫不猶豫地伸出援手，準備開漁船送往馬公治療。然而，當時的海面波濤洶湧，旁邊的人忍不住感嘆：「湧遐爾大，就算有船通坐，無死也半條命！」生活在這艱難環境中，天天都得看老天的臉色，逼得人們無奈選擇遷居外地。時光荏苒，幾十年一晃而過，少年遊子們也都滿髮風霜。然而，思鄉之情始終纏繞在心頭，心中常揪著那股想返鄉探親的渴望。

回鄉的路上怎能不坐船？以往的小船，不但速度慢，還飄散著柴油的味道，上船後很容易暈船，狼狽不堪。如今，時代進步了，只要天氣好，每天都有船班。大型的交通船速度快，且沒有油煙味，船艙內更是配有冷氣，讓整個旅程變得舒適愉快。

坐在船艙內，透過方格的船窗望向外面，故鄉的景色依然如故，而海岸邊卻多了港口碼頭。頓時，一股喜悅帶著一絲酸楚湧上心頭，久久無法平靜。呂坤翰心中呼叫著：「故鄉，我轉來（tńg--lâi）矣！」

船不僅承載著居民生活物品的運送，更扮演著捕魚、觀光與醫生巡迴看診等多重角色。對呂坤翰老師而言，船更是他與故鄉深厚情感與記憶的連結。

Boats not only facilitate the transport of everyday goods for the residents but also serve multiple purposes, such as fishing, tourism and medical visits by doctors. For Mr Lu Kun-Han, boats represent a profound connection to his hometown and evoke cherished memories.

On a remote island, boats are the most important means of transport. Whether for fishing, rushing a sick person to hospital, or transporting supplies for daily living, boats are essential.

Lu Kun-Han recalls an incident that occurred on the island: "There was once an old man who suddenly fell seriously ill. The villagers worked together, taking turns to carry him down Hó-hàn-pho, the only steep path connecting the harbor to the hill top. Fishermen by the harbour immediately offered their help, launching their boats to take the old man to Má-king (Magong) for treatment." However, at that time, the sea was very rough and people nearby couldn't help but exclaim, "With waves this big, even if a boat takes him to hospital, who can guarantee what will happen on the way?"

As time has passed, nowadays, as long as the weather is good, there are ferries travelling back and forth between the islands every day. The journeys are no longer fraught with the dangers that once characterised them.

Sitting in the cabin, Lu Kun-Han looked out through the square porthole. He saw that his hometown still looked the same but the coastline now boasted busy port facilities. Suddenly, a wave of joy filled his heart and he found it hard to calm down. He silently shouted, "Hometown, I'm back!"

鄉愁 Hiong-tshiû | 253

後記 | EPILOGUE
遇見用褒歌說故事的人
作者 ——— 吳明翰

Meeting the Storyteller of Penghu Ballads (Po-kua)
Wu Ming-Han

　　我在澎湖南方四島國家公園工作時，其中一個業務，就是每週撰寫兩則中英雙語圖文，介紹島嶼人文風貌。坦白說這樣的分享，並未引起太多關注，直到2020年11月25日一則有關東、西嶼坪的貼文下面，出現一位署名「呂坤翰」的先生留言表示，東嶼坪是他太太出生的地方，而前方的西嶼坪則是他自己出生的地方，還風趣地說「我們天天吃魚配飯」。從那之後，每當我介紹東、西嶼坪的故事時，總能收到這位呂坤翰先生給予的鼓勵。

　　2021年的夏天，為了記錄東嶼坪手作步道第二年的歷程，我時常攜帶相機，捕捉志工們從清晨到日落投入的身影。不僅如此，為了鼓勵在地民眾參與「家鄉路」的修築活動，我也經常在聚落之間走動，向村民介紹，現在回想起來，還真有些「村里幹事」的樣子。

　　有一天，我在派出所旁的古厝拍攝，突然一對手牽手的老夫妻問我：「汝好？汝咧翕（hip）啥物？」經過交談，得知這棟古厝竟然就是老太太娘家，太巧了，而老先生也在本地當老師，當他說起「我就出生在對面那座島上」的瞬間，我立刻明白，他們正是我的「忠實讀者」——呂坤翰老師與他的妻子陳湙樺。

　　我們一見如故，交談愉快，我便藉此機會向他們介紹屋後志工們的活動。驚喜的是，老師對此表現出濃厚的興趣，還分享說那裡以前是通往坪頂停機坪的路，很陡不好走，每次聽到有人要後送，都會替他們擔心。之後，他便對我說，「汝炁我去看覓。」

　　於是，我帶著呂老師走在步道上，向他說明志工如何疊石鋪路。沒想到，他對眼前的情景感到十分感動，立刻捲起袖子，加入志工行列。休息期間，他主動詢問大家的來歷與當志工的心情。有這樣一位和藹可親的在地阿公，關心著晚輩的事務，為大家帶來莫大的鼓勵。

　　隔天再次相遇時，他與我分享了一首名為〈鋪路做義工〉的褒歌，以我從未聽過的台語小調，將他昨日的經歷與志工的心聲傳達出來，每一句都深切動人，當下我被他「圈粉」了。

　　之後，老師用手指輕滑他的iPad，逐一展示他創作的作品。我驚訝地發現，來自西嶼坪的呂坤翰老師對島嶼、地景、生活與家庭有著深刻的觀察，這些作品並不是憑空想像的創作，而且他能在四句話裡精準抓住重點，傳遞故事的精髓，唱出最質樸、最直接的生命之歌。

　　那時，我剛完成《他鄉、故鄉：澎湖南方四島紀行》一書，心中萌生一個念頭：邀請呂老師與我共同運用這本書及他的褒歌來介紹澎湖故事。老師不僅立刻答應，還針對不同鄉市、島嶼創作了新的褒歌。於是，我們自2021年12月展開了一系列的分享，足跡遍及澎湖、高雄、台南、台中，以及我的故鄉嘉義。有時車程很遠，聽眾也不一定很多，但這絲毫不減我們分享的熱情。

　　有一次，我們受邀在高雄的「旗津thàk冊」書店分享。來自屏東的聽眾林芸姿說道：「聽到正港的澎湖腔，講澎湖故事，搭配這些照片，真合味！」那一刻，我們由衷感到欣慰。漸漸地，我們的心中浮現出一個聲音：或許，我們可以寫一本用褒歌講述澎湖故事的書。

呂坤翰

澎湖南方四島國家公園，其中的東嶼坪島，是我太太陳渼樺（金玉）出生的地方。前方西嶼坪島是我呂坤翰（通要）出生的地方。兩島四周靠海，熱帶魚多又漂亮。海珊瑚美得讓人讚嘆！我們可是天天吃魚配飯菜，因為海產新鮮，百吃不厭。夏天歡迎大家僱遊艇去狂歡一趟，保證此生難忘。

經過1125個日子，我們用褒歌與繪畫譜寫出澎湖生活之歌。

回首在踏查旅程中，幫助我們的人其實很多。首先，我要特別感謝東華商號的許朝德與朱美華夫婦，在我們前往東嶼坪期間，為我們準備道地的家鄉菜，並提供舒適住宿，使我們在四島間穿梭能無後顧之憂。公共電視的蔡明孝攝影師，用他的鏡頭捕捉我們重返島嶼的尋根與探索歷程。陳福慶先生則為我們登上西嶼坪提供完善的寶貴協助，讓我們的返鄉之路得以順利完成。而我們特別要感謝東吉的許光輝理事長，他帶領我們登上西吉，並慷慨分享他多年來調研的豐富資訊，讓我們對西吉的過去和現在有了更深入的了解。

同時，我們也感謝海洋國家公園管理處與台灣千里步道協會在東嶼坪舉辦的手作步道活動，讓我們得以相遇與交流。感謝曾經邀請我們的所有學校、圖書館與書店，以及所有聆聽的聽眾。因為有你們的支持與鼓勵，我們才燃起創作的勇氣。期盼透過這本書，帶領大家認識褒歌、親近海洋，一起走讀澎湖島嶼。

吳明翰

While working at the South Penghu Marine National Park, one of my tasks was to write two weekly stories introducing the island's cultural features in both Chinese and English. Initially, there wasn't much attention from readers until a special comment appeared on 25th November 2020. I had written a post about Tang-sū-pîng (Dongyuping) Island and Sai-sū-pîng (Xiyuping) Island and a comment from someone named 'Lu Kun-Han' mentioned that Tang-sū-pîng Island was where his wife was born, while Sai-sū-pîng Island was his birthplace. Since then, whenever I shared stories about these two small islands, I would always receive encouragement from him.

In the summer of 2021, to document the second year of the Eco-Friendly Trail on Tang-sū-pîng Island, I often carried my camera to capture the volunteers' efforts from dawn until sunset. Furthermore, to encourage local participation, I frequently communicated with the villagers to gain their support and involvement.

One day, while photographing a historic house next to the police station, an elderly couple holding hands approached me and asked, 'Hello? What are you photographing?' After chatting, I learned that this historic house was the elderly lady's family home. Coincidentally, the elderly gentleman was a local teacher. When he mentioned, 'I was born on the island across', I realised they were my 'loyal readers'—Mr Lu and his wife, Chen Mei-hua.

We hit it off immediately, enjoying our conversation and I took the chance to introduce them to the volunteers' activities behind the house. To my surprise, the teacher showed great interest and shared that the area used to be a steep path to a helipad on the mountain. He then said to me,"Take me to see it".

So, I walked the trail with Mr Lu, explaining how the volunteers were stacking stones to pave the way. To my astonishment, he felt very touched by what he saw and immediately rolled up his sleeves to join in. During breaks, he actively inquired about everyone's backgrounds and the volunteers' feelings. With such a kind elderly gentleman caring for younger generations, he brought immense encouragement to all involved.

The next day, he shared a ballad titled 'Tales of Eco-Friendly Trail Volunteers on Tang-sū-pîng Island'. He sang about his experiences and the volunteers' sentiments in a Taiwanese tune I had never heard before. Each line was so moving that I instantly became his fan.

Afterward, he gently swiped through his iPad, introducing various works he had created over the years. I was amazed to discover his deep observations of the island, landscape, life and family. Not only could he succinctly capture the essence of a story in four lines but he also sang the most sincere and straightforward songs of life.

At that time, I had just completed a book titled *Ranger Diaries: Work and Life in the South Penghu Marine National Park* and the idea struck me: to invite Mr Lu to co-utilise this book and his ballads to introduce Penghu stories. He readily agreed. Thus, starting in December 2021, we embarked on a series of presentations across Penghu, Kaohsiung, Tainan, Taichung and my hometown Chaiyi. Sometimes the travel was far and the audience small but it never diminished our enthusiasm for sharing.

Once, we were invited to share at an independent bookshop in Kaohsiung. A listener from Pingtung, Lin Yun-Zi, remarked, "Hearing the authentic Penghu dialect tell Penghu stories, along with these photos, couldn't be more harmonious!" In that moment, our inner fatigue was soothed and we felt gratified. Gradually, a voice emerged in our hearts: perhaps we could write a book about Penghu stories using songs from Song of Life in Penghu.

After 1125 days, we completed this book, *Framed by the Sea: Through a Square Window onto the Island - Penghu Ballads: A Selection by Lu Kun-Han*.

During our research journey, many people assisted us. First, I want to thank especially Khóo Tiâu-tik and Tsu Bí-huâ from the Donghua Store, who prepared delicious and authentic hometown dishes and provided comfortable and clean accommodation during our time on Tang-sū-pîng Island. Mr. Tsai Ming-Hsiao, a photographer at Public Television, visited Mr Lu's home to record each piece, allowing readers to scan QR codes to listen to the beautiful songs. I'd also like to thank Mr. Tân Hok-khìng for providing invaluable assistance during our visit to Sai-sū-pîng Island, ensuring our journey home was smooth and safe. We are especially grateful to Chairman Khóo Kong-hui from Tang-kiat (Dongji) Island, who led us to Sai-kiat (Xiji) Island and shared his extensive knowledge and research from years of exploration, giving us a deeper understanding of Sai-kiat Island's past and present.

At the same time, we are thankful to the Marine National Park Headquarters and the Taiwan Thousand Miles Trail Association for organising the eco-friendly trail construction activities on Tang-sū-pîng Island, which allowed me to meet Mr Lu. Thank you to all the schools, libraries and bookshops that have invited us and to all the listeners who supported us. Your encouragement ignited our courage to create. We hope this book will help everyone connect with Penghu Ballads, get closer to the ocean and explore Penghu's islands together.

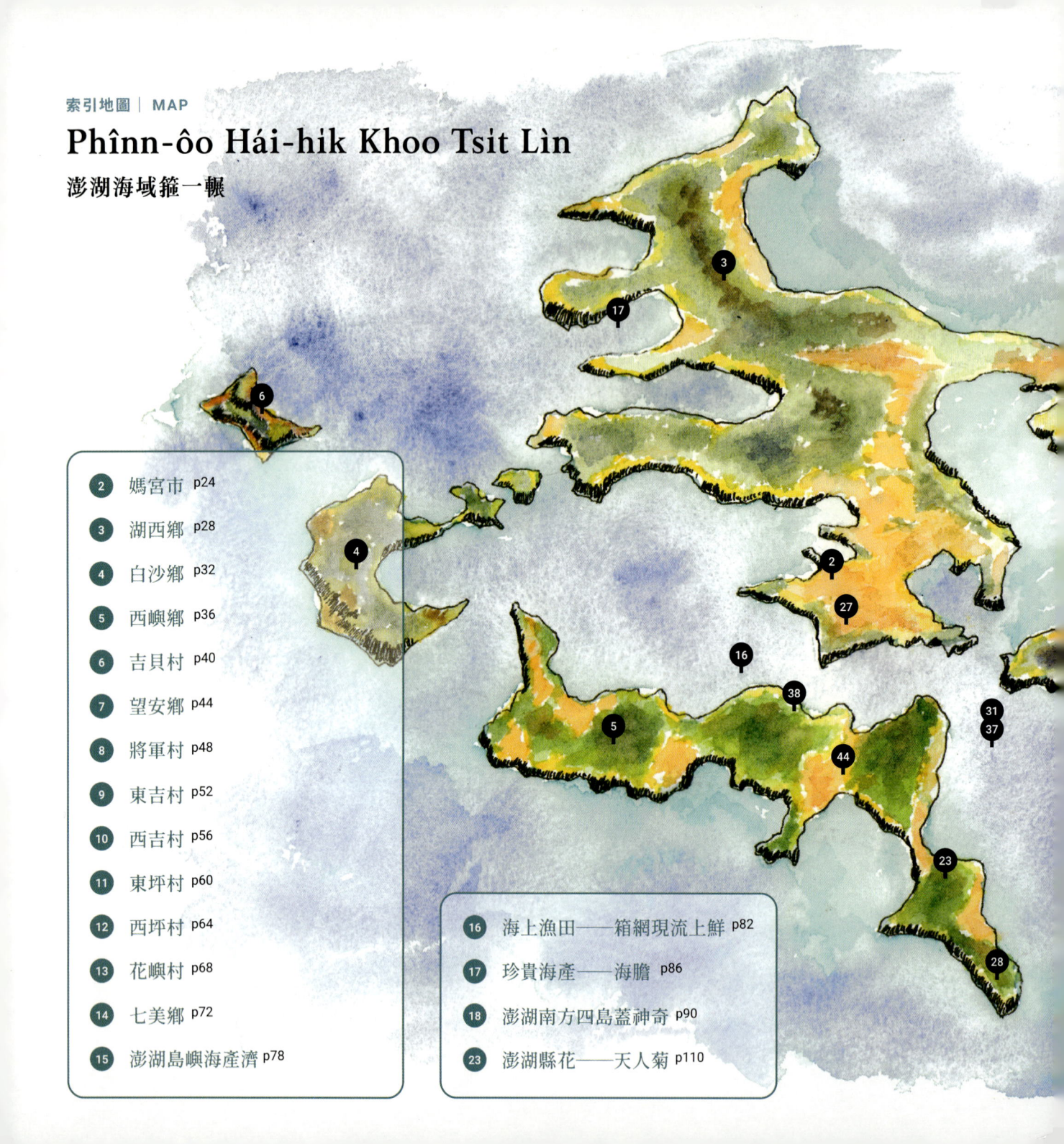

索引地圖 | MAP

Phînn-ôo Hái-hik Khoo Tsit Lìn
澎湖海域箍一輾

2	媽宮市	p24
3	湖西鄉	p28
4	白沙鄉	p32
5	西嶼鄉	p36
6	吉貝村	p40
7	望安鄉	p44
8	將軍村	p48
9	東吉村	p52
10	西吉村	p56
11	東坪村	p60
12	西坪村	p64
13	花嶼村	p68
14	七美鄉	p72
15	澎湖島嶼海產濟	p78

16	海上漁田──箱網現流上鮮	p82
17	珍貴海產──海膽	p86
18	澎湖南方四島蓋神奇	p90
23	澎湖縣花──天人菊	p110

24	澎湖茗茶──風茹草 p114
27	澎湖天后宮 p128
28	澎湖上元節 p132
30	東吉村中元普渡 p140
31	澎湖較早的生活情 p146
37	快樂的澎湖人 p170
38	澎湖人愛褒歌 p174
40	熱天焰小管 p184
41	浮著塗魠好過年 p188
44	台灣牛強閣勇 p200

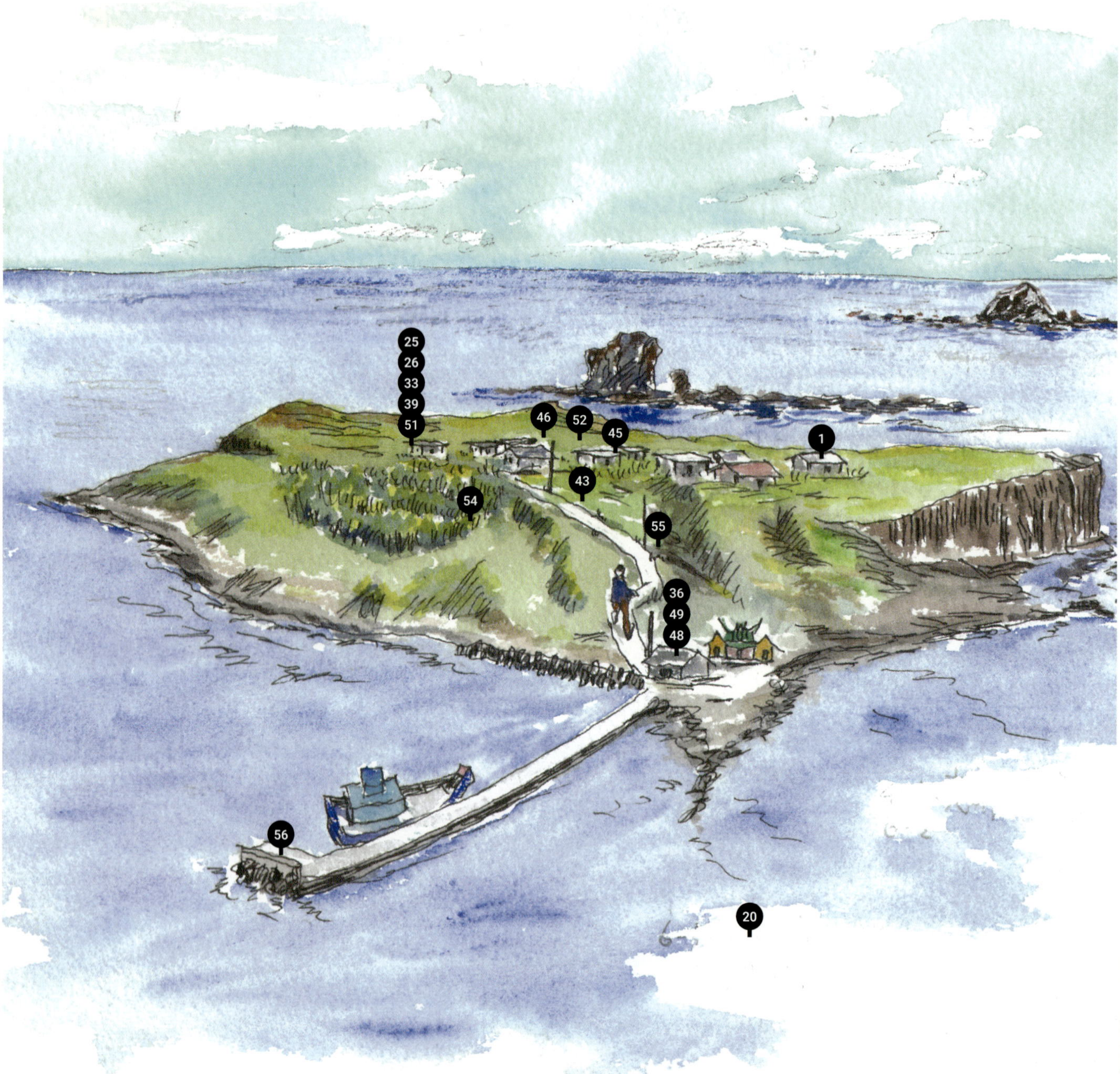
25
26
33
39
51
46
52
45
1
43
54
55
36
49
48
56
20

索引地圖 | MAP
Sai-sū-pîng
西嶼坪

- ① 一心想做文明人 p18
- ⑳ 嶼坪好山景 p98
- ㉕ 阮兜 p118
- ㉖ 三口井的故事 p122
- ㉝ 落雨天歹起火 p154
- ㊱ 克難學校 p166
- ㊴ 天照甲子佇咧行 p180
- ㊸ 作田人的心聲 p196
- ㊺ 擔肥去壅田 p204
- ㊻ 雨水來到當著時 p208
- ㊽ 讀書才會出頭天 p218
- ㊾ 菩薩老師 p222
- ㊿ 嶼坪鉸刀師 p230
- 52 衛國做兵上光榮 p234
- 54 思君情深深 p242
- 55 阿公勇壯、阿媽活潑 p246
- 56 鄉愁 p250

索引地圖 | MAP
Tang-sū-pîng
東嶼坪

- ⑲ 東坪山勢第一奇 p94
- ㉑ 鋪路做義工 p102
- ㉒ 小王子平台 p106
- ㉙ 東嶼坪池府王爺生日 p136
- ㉜ 以早的東嶼坪 p150
- ㉞ 掠魚、生囝 p158
- ㉟ 哪會按呢 p162
- ㊷ 大流去抾螺仔 p192
- ㊼ 塗豆大豐收 p212
- ㊿ 西坪哥、東坪妹 p226
- ㊾ 食穿全靠君一人 p238

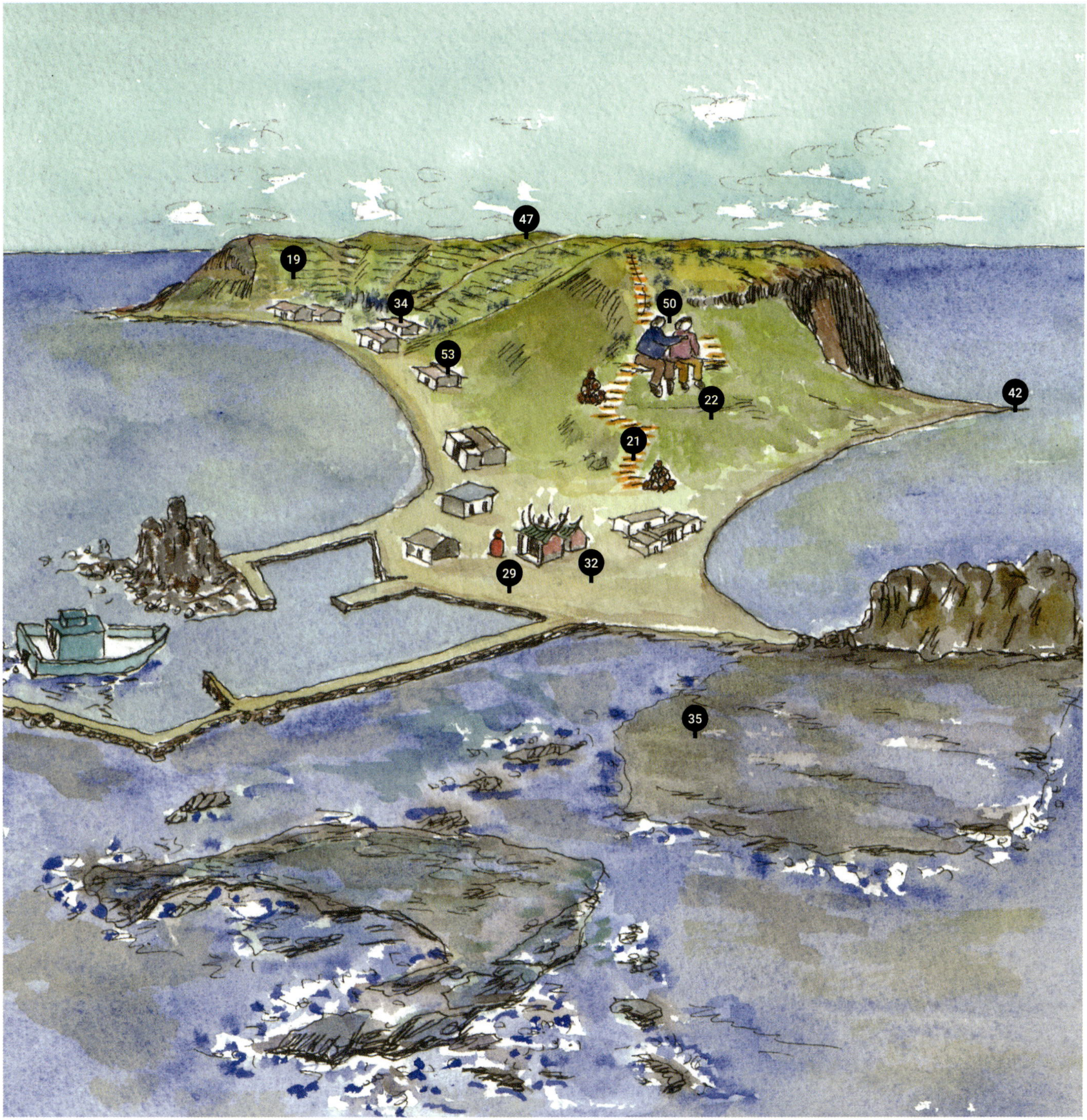
47
19
34
50
53
42
22
21
32
29
35

Iōng Po-kua Kóng Kòo-sū ê Lâng: Lū Khun-hān Phînn-ôo Po-kua Suán-tsip
用褒歌說故事的人：呂坤翰澎湖褒歌選集
Framed by the Sea: Through a Square Window onto the Island
Penghu Ballads: A Selection by Lu Kun-Han

作　　者	呂坤翰、吳明翰
插　　畫	陳春星
攝　　影	吳明翰
主　　編	吳明翰
編　　輯	古庭維
文字編輯	陳亮均
台文翻譯	陳亮均
英文翻譯	吳明翰
美術設計	王藝臻
褒歌吟唱	呂坤翰
褒歌錄製	蔡明孝
校　　對	潘燕玉（中文）、Hugo van den Berghe（英文）
發 行 人	林佳誼
出 版 者	小野心文化事業有限公司
	地址：114 台北市內湖區內湖路1段66號3樓
	電話：02-2642-8196
	Email：yethings@gmail.com
	網址：https://www.yethings.com/
贊助單位	NCAF 國｜藝｜會
印　　刷	世和印製企業有限公司
總 經 銷	大和書報圖書股份有限公司
	電話：02-8990-2588
初版一刷	2025年6月
定　　價	600元
I S B N	978-626-99250-1-8

版權所有・翻印必究

國家圖書館出版品預行編目(CIP)資料

用褒歌說故事的人：呂坤翰澎湖褒歌選集 = Framed by the sea : through a square window onto the island : Penghu ballads : a selection by Lu Kun-Han/ 呂坤翰, 吳明翰作. -- 初版. -- 臺北市：小野心文化事業有限公司, 2025.06
　　面；　公分
ISBN 978-626-99250-1-8(平裝)
1.CST: 民謠 2.CST: 澎湖縣
539.133/141　　　　　　　　　114006105